THE
CLOSET

THE CLOSET

A coming-of-age story of the clothes that made me

Teo van den Broeke

ONE PLACE. MANY STORIES

HQ
An imprint of HarperCollins*Publishers* Ltd
1 London Bridge Street
London SE1 9GF

www.harpercollins.co.uk

Harper Ireland
Macken House, 39/40 Mayor Street Upper,
Dublin 1 D01 C9W8

This edition 2023

1
First published in Great Britain by
HQ, an imprint of HarperCollins*Publishers* Ltd 2023

For Mum and Dad.

For Amy, from your werewolf.

And for my Grandma, Anne. I miss you all the time.

CHAPTER I

The Blue Princess Dress

'Teo, hold that still, please!' Mum snapped as she walked out of the front door of the house towards the car, where I was sat waiting patiently on the back seat.

I always knew she meant business when The Claw came out. A tortoiseshell contraption that looked like the mouth of a Venus flytrap, The Claw's primary use was to hold Mum's hair away from her face, but its appearance was a sure-fire indicator that an explosion was imminent. In mellower times, she wore her hair long, but The Claw had been flashing away all morning, in and out of Mum's mane, as she repeatedly fixed and rearranged it.

I shifted nervously in my seat, adjusting the glossy beige stoneware bowl that sat in my lap, full to the brim with raspberries, M&S custard and over-whipped cream. I was wearing my favourite pair of blue and white striped dungarees, finished with shiny brass fasteners on the bib, which Mum said made me look like Andy Pandy, and I had jammed my fingers between my legs and the slippery bowl to stop it from spilling. Raspberry trifle had become Mum's signature dish that year, and, as a consequence, it had quickly become my favourite too, so it was in my best interest to do exactly as she asked.

'And stop fussing, Romy, or you're going to make us later than we already are!'

My sister, whose mop of off-auburn hair had been cut at the fringe in the shape of the bowl perched on my thighs, was wearing a black frock that finished at the knee and was covered in a purple and green floral pattern. It was my favourite of Romy's many party dresses. I'm pretty sure it was Mum's too because she made her wear it a lot.

Romy was sitting next to me in the back of Mum's midnight-blue Volkswagen Jetta. Her feet were shod in a pair of patent Mary Janes and frilly white socks to match the detailing on the dress, with the frills positioned so they jutted out over the edge of the shoes just so. Romy was using one of her jammed-up fists to rub her left eye. The other was holding on fiercely to her new doll.

'Teo said he was going to cut her haaaiiiir,' Romy whined, glancing anxiously at Tiny Tears, which, a touch eerily, could cry on demand.

It was true; I had said that.

'No, I didn't, Romy, be quiet.' I gave her a sly pinch, a trick

I'd learned from Mum, who had much sharper nails than me. Both of Romy's little fists met her eyes. Tiny Tears was left dangerously exposed.

'DAO!'

Dad's ultra-Dutch pronunciation of my name made it sound like the opening refrain from the Harry Belafonte song, only in this case much less friendly.

'What did you BLAAHDY well do to your sister now?!'

Dad had appeared at the front door of the house, filling the frame. Hands on his hips, his already quite cavernous brow was furrowed extra deep. He'd returned from a trip to Zimbabwe the night before, bringing with him the good – six beautifully painted, wooden animal toys to match the six years I'd spent on earth – and the bad – the considerably-less-than eight hours of sleep that always accompanied his jetlag, an occupational hazard in the world of a commercial pilot. Couple the latter with our fast-approaching mass-family gathering, and we all had a strong sense of impending danger.

'It's all right, Jan. We just need to go,' Mum muttered, used to his post-flight flare-ups. She was busy strapping a sizeable mushroom tart into the foot cavity of the passenger seat, on top of three chilled bottles of Wolf Blass Creek. Smoothing down the front of her rust-brown dress, which was finished with oversized white polka dots, she manoeuvred herself backwards out of the car.

Choosing to ignore her, Dad stormed out from the shadow of the big wooden door – which was finished with incongruously large wrought-iron rivets that made it look like something that belonged at Hampton Court Palace – and pulled up to my side of the car, eyeing me like a pissed-off Tyrannosaurus rex.

He was wearing a pair of paint-splattered navy-blue tracksuit bottoms with a capacious Fruit of the Loom T-shirt – fraying at the collar – and a pair of white tube socks on his feet with no shoes. 'You two behave for your Mu-tha, you hear me?' The Dutch-ness in his accent was all the more pronounced when he hadn't had enough sleep. I know I was meant to be scared; however, I couldn't help but think of how much trouble I would get in if I wore my socks outside without any shoes on like he was.

'I'll see you there later, Jane,' he said, turning back towards the house, his anger and words muffled somewhat by the wall created by his enormous shoulders. Dad always preferred to drive his own car to Grandma's, which, in his current state, was a blessing. Mum got into the front seat of the Jetta and turned back to Romy and me, giving me a knowing look and my sister a squeeze on the ankle as she reversed out of the drive.

I should probably have been more upset that Dad wasn't coming with us – I hadn't seen him for a week and it was my sixth birthday – but secretly I was a little bit relieved. I had a mission to complete that day and I didn't want anything, or anyone, getting in the way.

One of the best things about visiting my grandparents' house was that we got to rummage through the giant dressing-up box, filled bountifully by my mother's flamboyant family over the years. Fit to bursting with my grandpa's old naval uniforms, obis and saris from their various travels around the world, and odds and ends, which my mum and her five sisters had worn growing up, it was a veritable treasure trove of sartorial opportunity.

But the star of the dressing-up box was, without question, a cornflower-blue princess dress. Crafted from voluminous layers of taffeta and tulle, the gown featured a satin skirt, puffed out over multiple petticoats, finished on top with two large swathes of voile and chiffon, which were crossed over one another to create a kind of loose bustier. The surface of the dress was densely embroidered with lilac and cornflower beads, the kind that made your teeth squeak when you rubbed them against them (which I had done on many occasions), and I loved it. Whenever I had the opportunity, I would sneak up the stairs of my grandparents' house to look at it, stroking the fabric against my skin, fondling the shards of shaped plastic and glass, but I'd never been brave enough to actually wear it.

In the weeks leading up to my birthday, which landed in the middle of June, I had been quietly hatching a plan to ensure that I got to wear the dress at the party.

I took a great deal of pride in the fact that, if I had been able to drive, I would have very easily been able to figure out the way to my grandparents' house at 91 Ember Lane without the use of a map. We did the journey there and back most Sundays, and I had measured the route out in a series of ten perfectly spaced foot taps, which only I knew.

The rhythm went something like this: one tap for when we drove past Contact, the best sweet shop in Fetcham, despite the fact that it smelled of old nicotine; one tap when we went past the petrol station that wouldn't let you fill the car up yourself; a tap for when we passed Fetcham Tandoori and a series of three taps for when we drove past the various entrances to the woods that connected Fetcham with Stoke D'Abernon. There was one tap for Cobham and Stoke D'Abernon Station, one for when we went past Mum's friend Jill's house and another for when we eventually got to Sandown racecourse in Esher, a leafy suburb on the outskirts of Greater London. The final tap came at Café Rouge, which marked the turning on to my grandparents' road.

When we eventually made it to the house that day, ten-tap quota filled, the soft orange of the digital clock on Mum's dashboard read 14:32, though I knew that it was an hour fast because Mum didn't know how to change the time after daylight savings. So it in fact meant that we were two minutes late. Grandma's Sunday lunch buffets started at 13:30 sharp and, if you didn't get there on time, it meant that you a) wouldn't find a space on the driveway and b) would miss all the food.

'I told you two we wouldn't get a space,' Mum muttered under her breath as she turned down Robson & Jerome, who were crooning their version of 'Unchained Melody' on the radio.

We pulled into the road opposite the house, parked next to the pavement and Mum brought the car to a standstill. Romy was fully engrossed with her doll, as Mum and I pumped the handles to do up our windows. Mum took her lipstick out of her bag – never red, always plum – and gently pulled The Claw from her hair, transforming herself from Road Runner into Lois Lane with the sweep of a manicured hand.

'Ready, kinders?' She smiled at us in the rear-view mirror, all earlier stresses evaporating out through the sunroof, like the condensation lifting from the wine warming in the front.

We loaded ourselves up with the many party accoutrements we had packed into the car before crossing the road to the house. Romy took Mum's hand in one of hers, Tiny Tears in the other. I held on to the trifle for dear life, trotting carefully behind their dresses as they swished in succession.

'Yoohoo!' came a familiar cry from the open bay window, which looked out over the driveway from my grandparents' smarter living room. 'The PARTAY PEOPLE HAVE ARRIVED!'

It was always possible to tell how much wine Aunty Rozy, the youngest of Mum's five sisters, had drunk by how high her ponytail was sitting on her head. The Karl Lagerfeld = little to no wine. The Andre Agassi = a good half bottle. The Blond Ambition-era Madonna = all bets were off. As we got closer to the house, I could see her bouncing around the room to the strains of 'Cotton Eye Joe' blasting at full volume from the sound system with what looked like a pineapple frond protruding out from the top of her head and a flash of her trademark red lippy scratched across her mouth. Grandma opened the glossy royal-blue front door as we arrived, stroking down her silky indigo blouse and rearranging the long silver chains around her neck, an outfit that gave her the look of a kindly wizard.

'Hello, darlings!' Her voice was both high-pitched and mellifluous, accompanied by the soft under-crackle of her advancing age.

'Hello, Mummy.' Mum placed the tart on the ample mahogany sideboard that ran the length of the hall, ending at the old grandfather clock, which had long ceased telling the time, now storing the walking sticks that neither grandparent conceded to use.

'No Jan?' asked Grandma as she returned my mum's embrace with the swift love that comes with long practice.

'Later,' she responded with a tight smile.

Grandma held Romy and me close as Mum bustled the wine into the kitchen, pausing here and there to bump faces with a sister, brother-in-law or skirt-grabbing niece.

A softer version of Mum, loosened with age, Grandma had brown curls that tickled our noses as she kissed our cheeks, her gold peep-toe shoes – the ones she kept for parties – sneaking out from beneath the hem of her skirt.

My sister ran ahead into the living room to join the throng, leaving Tiny Tears face down at the foot of the clock, while Grandma – who had the same aristocratic nose and softly hooded eyes as Mum – gave me an extra squeeze, her scent of cooking, clean skin and long-since-sprayed Elnett embedding into my clothes. Everything smelled like Grandma's after having been at Grandma's.

'Happy birthday, darling,' she said. 'You'd better go and get some food before it's all gone.' Though all I could really think about was the princess dress, I was hungry, so I jostled into the back living room where the television set was kept. The queue for the buffet had died down a bit and a platter of freshly cooked chipolatas was glistening seductively on the table.

'Hello Teolini!' Aunty Rozy pulled me into an embrace from behind, the sweet sourness of her wine-breath warming my neck. 'Happy birthday, beautiful boy!'

Behind her trotted my cousins Daisy and Beatrice. 'I'm wearing the princess dress, I'm wearing the princess dress, I'm wearing the princess dress!' chanted Daisy to no one in particular. Her bright blonde ringlets were caught in the gluey primary-hued remains of the recently devoured gummy bears surrounding her mouth. Over her white OshKosh B'gosh T-shirt, Daisy was indeed wearing the princess dress. I felt my stomach drop. Suddenly I wasn't hungry anymore. I willed myself not to cry.

'That used to be my dress!' shouted Rozy, spinning across the room, tripping over Daisy's train.

'No, it didn't!' piped both Daisy and Beatrice. The latter cousin, who was the same age yet diametric opposite of the former – all moody Pre-Raphaelite curls and alabaster skin – had clearly drawn the short straw in the dressing-up box raid, as she was wearing a stained air stewardess uniform from the seventies. She had a thick pair of pink Totes toasties on her feet, and her toes were wedged into a pair of towering okobo shoes, which my grandpa had picked up on a trip to Japan.

9

'It was her dress, Daisy,' said Aunty Catherine (another of my mother's raven-haired sisters) from across the room, drily.

'Told you!' Rozy slurred, laughing. 'Can you believe I wore that to the prom?'

'I'm going to wear it to my prom!' shouted Daisy.

'So am I!' said Beatrice.

'Me too!' My voice cracked slightly as I realised what I'd said, hoping that no one had heard.

As if noticing me for the first time, Catherine pulled me in for a hug as she held her plate of food above me, balancing her glass of wine dextrously on the ball of her hand.

'I think you'd look gorgeous in that dress,' she whispered into my ear, as she kissed me on the cheek. I thought Aunty Catherine looked a bit like a model. She was wearing a forest-green crushed velvet skirt with a gauzy black blouse and her hip jutted in a way that was rare in my family.

'Why don't you all go into the other room and play?' she suggested, suddenly bored.

'Yes, that's a very good idea,' said Mum, tottering into the living room with her own plate of food piled high, eyeing her sister's to see how much avocado she'd managed to fish out of the salad. Mum was the only other vegetarian in the family and the competition for healthy fats was fierce.

'No, Jane,' said Catherine. 'Stop it, I'm vegan.'

'Catherine, you've got ALL the avocado!'

'I'm VEGAN!'

'Since when?!'

Happy to avoid the scuffle, Daisy, Beatrice, Romy and

I went to find the dressing-up box. Knowing that the one thing I wanted to wear had been taken, I sat on the bed and flicked through the well-thumbed house copy of *Where the Wild Things Are* instead. Romy, who was happy to wear whatever she was given, plunged headfirst into the dressing-up box like a seal fishing under ice, before coming up for air wearing a yellow A-line dress finished with a sixties-style floral motif on her head.

'Why don't you put this on, Teo?' asked Daisy, smiling as she held out an enormous black and red obi belt on the end of a magic wand, as one would a wet wipe on a toilet brush. I ignored her, feigning disinterest, and turned back to the book. *'And Max, the king of all wild things, was lonely and wanted to be where someone loved him best of all'* read the words on the page.

'I think Teo wants the princess dress,' said Daisy, slyly.

'No, I don't,' I responded, a little too forcefully.

Daisy and Beatrice continued goading me for a little while as I worked hard to ignore them, hoping that no one downstairs could hear. I held my breath, hunched my shoulders and delved further into the book. As quickly as they'd become animated, they grew bored, pushing past me to return to the easier audience of the adults, wafts of taffeta and cheap white satin rippling in their wake.

Disheartened, I stalked out of the room and sat at the top of the stairs. The walls were lined with memorabilia from my grandpa's time as a surgeon commander in the navy, including plaques from the various ships he had worked and lived on. My eye was always drawn to the many caricatures of him cutting off patients' legs, which had been given to him as retirement presents. Next to these, in pride of place was a drawing of him dressed up as a Wren, a female orderly. Apparently, he had, on more than one occasion, conducted his entire set of daily rounds on the HMS *Invincible*, dressed up in a black and white nurse's uniform and a brown wig, cut into an angular bob. He'd also been known to spend entire family parties wearing a plunger as a hat.

'He's an odd man, your grandpa,' my dad would say. 'A good man but an odd man.'

'Is that you, Teo?' I heard Grandpa ask. I looked up to see him padding out of his study, where he had a tendency to hide watching old episodes of *Mr Bean*. The room was off limits to grandchildren unless we were explicitly invited in. Today, he was wearing a mustard cable knit jumper, a white button-down Oxford shirt, a pair of grey slacks and, rather than the traditional plunger, a bathroom tap attached to his perfectly bald head.

'Everything OK?' he asked breezily. 'Why don't we go and see what everyone else is up to?' Tap protruding proudly from his forehead, Grandpa held my hand as we walked downstairs, where it was strangely quiet.

'Happy birthday to you, happy birthday to you, happy birthday dear TEOOOOOO, happy birthday to you!' Rozy, who had recently qualified as a music teacher, liked to finish the last two syllables of the birthday song with an uplift-ing harmony, which became particularly raucous for this rendition. Mum had made one of her more ambitious cakes for the occasion: a chocolate sponge covered in its entirety with a jungle scene made of royal icing, complete with a lake made of jelly and plastic animals peeking out from behind marzipan palm trees. She must have hidden it in the boot of the car as Romy and I were squabbling.

As the cake was slowly divided up and shared out between clamouring hands, Daisy smirked at me from behind her heavily laden paper plate, spilling crumbs as she flapped the fabric of the dress with her fingers. She spun around twice before running out into the garden through the French doors, twirling as she went.

'Daisy, we've got to go in five minutes so you'd need to go and get changed now!'

Aunty Catherine lived in Brighton, which was a not insignificant drive from Grandma's house, and it wasn't unusual for her to peel away from the family parties earlier than everyone else. Furious with sugar, Daisy pulled the dress off her body there and then, leaving it where she stood – a taffeta puddle in the centre of the lawn – the harrowing prospect of having to leave the party early overriding her proprietorial feelings towards the gown.

Sensing my chance, I carefully placed my unfinished cake down on the side, ran out to the garden, scooped up the dress as nonchalantly as I could and lunged for the door to the summer house, which was really an old garden shed with a few windows, caked-up with dirt. The shed smelled of damp blankets and was home to a couple of old tennis rackets and

some long unused camping equipment. I carefully placed the
dress onto one of the few clean surfaces in the shed and pulled
the door closed. The handle, which was made of smooth black
Bakelite, felt cold in my hand and the rusting shaft jerked
slightly as I yanked it shut.

I crouched on the floor of the shed so that no one could
see me and pulled the dress on over my jeans, lifting the
taffeta swathes up and over my shoulders. The fabric felt soft
and cool against my skin and the fluff of the skirt instantly
filled the postage stamp-sized floor space that was available. I pulled at some of the beads, admiring the way the
light refracted through them; radiating a smattering of tiny
amethysts against the ceiling as they moved.

Buoyed by my victory, I stepped tentatively back into the
garden. Daisy was nowhere to be seen, but Romy was practis-
ing reverse parking in a canary yellow and cherry red Cozy
Coupe on the patio. When she saw me, she jumped out of
the car, ran over and tapped me hard on the arm.

'You're it!'

The dress caught under my feet as I ran after her, flying
around the gnarly old pear tree positioned in the middle of
the lawn. The warm air of the afternoon rippled through
the skirt, making it swirl like the wings of a sycamore seed
as I flew along. I lunged at Romy and we both fell on to the
grass, which was still damp with dew thanks to the dappled
shade provided by the tree. She jumped on top of me shouting,
'It!' between giggles, our frocks moving as one.

After catching my breath, I looked up to see Dad walking

out of the French doors clutching a full plate of food in one hand, and his pipe and red wine in the other. With beard freshly trimmed and donning his favourite Ray-Ban Aviators, he had changed out of his post-flight gear into a pair of chinos (pulled quite high), his oxblood penny loafers and a bottle-green knitted polo with fine white piping on the collar and sleeves. He looked much more elegant than the other men at the party.

Staying low in the fabric like a cat in the long grass, I continued watching as he strode purposefully over to the wooden garden table towards the gang of uncles, all sat picking at cake and drinking from tall cans of Tesco's own lager. Though the front room was where most of the action happened at family parties, the uncles liked to keep themselves separate. In the winter they could be found in the kitchen, far enough away from the melee to assert their independence but close enough to the fridge to easily replenish their drinks. In the summer, their territory was the outside table; the carcass to their pride. They were always kind to me and my cousins, nuzzling our heads with grizzly kisses, but, somehow, they were distant too. We were as much part of them as we were our mothers and aunties, which rendered us the equivalent of double agents who might 'tell' on them for their excessive drinking and lewd comments. We were to be loved, of course, but never fully trusted.

Sensing my opportunity, leaving Romy on the lawn, I gathered up the skirt of the dress and made a beeline for the doors at the back of the house. The gathered fabric suddenly felt heavier than it had before, and the warm air of the afternoon thicker. I pulled down on the right sleeve of the dress, the one facing towards the table, in a bid to minimise the full Cinderella effect and I did my best to walk a little bit faster as I reached the patio where Dad was sat with his back to me, smoke puffing up from his pipe like chocolate-scented cumulus clouds.

As I reached the door, I heard one of my uncles ask, quietly, 'Doesn't that that bother you, Jan?' – a question that was met by a round of muffled laughs and a shifting of beer cans. I ducked into the house before Dad had had a chance to turn and see me, pulling the back of the dress sharply in as I jumped up the last concrete step. Hidden from view, I ran through the buffet room, into the hall and past my grandma who was carrying a pile of used plates back into the kitchen.

Desperate to get the dress off, I powered up the stairs and ran into the pink bedroom at the back of the house, which was still scattered with dressing-up clothes. Pulling the gown up and over my head, I jammed it into the suitcase and zipped it firmly shut.

I couldn't stop the tears this time; hot streams poured down my cheeks as my fists curled into tight balls and a slick wave of frustration washed over me. I knew that I shouldn't care as much as I did about what my dad and my uncles thought of me, but a tight bubble of embarrassment – an abstract sense of not feeling good enough, manly enough, normal enough – swelled in my stomach, pushing against my oesophagus and thrusting all the cake I'd just eaten up into my mouth.

I felt like I was going to be sick. The harsh metallic taste of shame singed my soft pallet. I sat on the bed and hung my head, rubbing my eyes until they were sore.

I lay down on my side and curled my knees into my chest. My eyes were shut tight against the brightness of the sun as it set beyond the window at the back of the room; and the soft orange light spread like a blanket across my retinas. Eventually I needed the loo, so I crept into the hall, treading lightly on the carpet as I went. I could hear the manic strains of the 'Birdie Song' chirruping out from the front room, which was a failsafe sign that the party was reaching its peak. I rubbed my face hard – attempting to conceal the fact that I had been crying – before I set off slowly down the stairs, though I didn't much feel like joining in.

Rozy was leading the charge, demonstrating how to do a demented form of the 'Hokey Cokey' to Daisy, Beatrice and Romy. Grandma was looking on indulgently, her head cocked against her hand, only occasionally becoming animated when it looked as though her youngest daughter might accidentally high-kick one of the porcelain figures that lined the top of the heavy York stone fireplace; and my mum was sitting on the gold and blue brocade sofa, jigging her leg irritably.

'Change the bloody song, Rozy,' she shouted.

'No fear, Janey! Da Da Da De De De DA, Da Da Da De DA DA!'

'Oh, for God's sake.'

While I watched on, relieved that none of my uncles were in immediate evidence, Mum rushed forward, pushing her younger sister out of the way like a bull coming for a sangria-soaked matador, and Rozy fell on her back, landing square on a plate of trifle. As quickly as Mum had made it over to Grandma's hi-fi, the 'Birdie Song' fell away and the house-infused bips and bops of Whigfield's 'Saturday Night' bounced on instead.

As I stood in the doorway of the room, Mum gyrated over to me doing her statement Cleopatra hand dance, wiggling her bum like Donald Duck. 'Come on, darling! Dance with your mother!' She pulled me over to her, despite my protestations. Once I was in position, she held my face in her hands, looked down and asked, freshly anxious, 'Have you been crying, Teo?'

I placed my chin in the warm vacancy above Mum's collarbone, between her neck and her left shoulder blade, and observed the affable chaos playing out behind her. Part of me wanted to tell her what had happened, but another part of me – a more dominant part – just wanted to stay in the front room, away from the male members of the pride, and pretend the whole thing had never happened at all.

CHAPTER 2

The White Socks

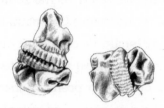

I woke to the sun streaming through the curtains in my bedroom, throwing bright shards of light that fell between the looped ribbons of fabric that attached them to the rail. Mum had made the curtains and a corresponding quilt for me out of vermilion cotton. It had golden suns printed onto it, and the colour matched the hue of the walls, which had been painted yolk yellow at my request.

I could feel one of the shards inching its way across my face and into my eye, willing me to wake up and go downstairs for breakfast where Mum was whistling the tune to *The Archers*, fudging the higher notes with a raspy half whistle that landed too low.

'Good mornin', good mornin' duh duh duh duh duh duh duh.' A pause at the bottom of the stairs. 'Come on, kinders! Get your skates on! We're going to Polesden Lacey.'

The former home of society darling Margaret Greville

– who famously left all her jewels to the Queen Mother, not a relation – my favourite thing about Polesden wasn't the enormous gardens that surrounded the lemonade-hued house, concealing grand rockeries and Rapunzel bridges, but rather the small graveyard at the back of the Georgian building in which Mrs Greville had buried her favourite pets: seventeen toothlike headstones for seventeen tiny canines.

'Mum, can we go and see the dogs when we get there?' I asked as we swung out of the cul-de-sac and on to our road, my back pushing low into the seat as we went. I secretly knew that, at the age of nine, I was probably a little bit too old to be excited about the dog graveyard, but in the excitement of the moment, I didn't care.

'I want to see Caesar!' piped Romy.

'I want to see Cho!'

We drove quietly for a little while as Mum took in the end of her radio show, intermittently complaining about how boring it was. Pootling through the neighbouring village, we eventually pulled up to a temporary traffic light. There was a long train of cars in front of us and, as we slowed, I looked to the left out of my window, which I wound down as we came to a standstill. The sudden rash of sun against my arm made the hairs pull up, and I shivered slightly.

Next to the traffic lights, I noticed three figures turn the corner of the street and begin walking towards the car. The bright sun streaked behind them so I could only see their silhouettes at first, until the boy at the front of the group stepped forward, arm raised to make a joke before doubling over with laughter. It was clear that he was the leader because the two behind him copied his moments with practised synchronisation.

When the trio edged closer, a prepubescent bait ball, I could see that the leader's hair was closely cropped; dark curls plastered to the oval of his skull like shavings on chipboard. Their soft lacquer of grease half absorbed, half reflected the brightness of the sun and his skin was pale save for a smattering of spots at the corner of his mouth. His eyes matched the colour of the trees' rustling leaves reflected in Mum's rear-view window. As the boys came even closer to the car, I realised I was staring, so quickly averted my gaze before looking back again, nervous to be seen but eager not to let the thrill of the moment pass unchecked. At that second, our eyes connected as his lips continued to move, finishing an unheard joke.

There are some moments in life that remain lodged in the carousel of our memories, forever stuck a few frames behind the very thing that's happening in front of our eyes. Sometimes the slide can be flicked into view by an unanticipated trigger – autumn light filtering through the fronds of a pine tree, angular and hazy – other times it can just appear out of nowhere, like a negative at the bottom of a drawer. This was one of those moments.

Rather than look away again, which was my first instinct, I held his eyes for a second longer than felt comfortable. He smiled a broad smile – the kind you'd expect to receive from someone you knew – and turned back to his friends as we started to pull away; the traffic light had flicked from red to green and Mum was shouting at the car in front. She was much coarser in the car than she was in company.

'Move, you bloody idiot! Come on!'

I turned to look through the window as we drove away, the curve of the boy's upper thigh barely perceptible through the loose sheen of his Adidas popper trousers. Light seemed to be emanating from the mouth of his grubby Reebok classics, where a pair of bright white socks, which were finished with a tick, had been pulled high. I shivered again as my arm fell into shadow and my stomach flipped as though we had just gone fast over a hill and as we turned the corner, the trio falling out of view. I looked over to Romy to see if she had noticed my excitement, but she was too busy silently mouthing the words of her book, *The Magic Roundabout*.

'That's it!' she suddenly piped, blowing a puff of air from her cheeks, 'I want to see Dougal's grave too!'

*

'You're wearing them.'

'I am not.'

'You're wearing them, Teo!' It was a few weekends later and we were preparing for my Aunty Rachel's wedding.

'I said no!'

'You're wearing them even if I have to force them on to your feet and drag you down the aisle myself.'

I felt the familiar rush of heat surge up from my stomach, battery acid curdled in cream. My eyes felt tight and my fists clenched involuntarily, but I refused to let myself cry. Instead, I stamped my foot on the dense jade-green pile of the rug Dad had brought back from Hong Kong a few weeks before and began pulling down the itchy grey shorts I had just reluctantly put on. They had a crease down the front, which made them look like scored cardboard, and the pale-blue shirt I had just tucked in was beginning to come loose. My skin was itchy where the elastic of the shorts pinched at my hips.

'Fine. Suit yourself. Don't come,' said Mum, shrugging her shoulders as she pulled her hand through her blown-out hair, which no one would actually get to see until later because she was intending to wear an enormous hat to the ceremony. I secretly thought it looked like a pavlova.

I threw myself down on the sofa, which was covered in moire silk the colour of pigeon feathers, and paused the business of undoing my fly to contemplate the prospect of not actually attending my Aunty Rachel's wedding that afternoon. It was an eventuality I knew was unlikely to occur – Mum would never be able to get a babysitter at such short notice – but there was a good chance that Dad might seize the opportunity of not going and opt to stay with me instead.

Although the thought of sitting around all afternoon rewatching my favourite VHS recording of the Spice Girls' performance at the Brit Awards filled me with joy, I knew the reality was that Dad would never let me spend the day on the sofa watching television – and he certainly wouldn't allow me to gyrate like Geri, wearing a Union Jack tea towel in front of it (particularly as my dad was Dutch). 'It's a beautiful day,

Dao, go outside and do some exercise,' he would inevitably say, settling deeper into his chair.

Mum looked at me side-on as she raised one perfectly sculpted eyebrow, freshly plucked in anticipation of the afternoon's festivities, before stalking out of the room. She was wearing a grey suit, not dissimilar to the colour of the sofa, which was finished with meaty shoulder pads and buttons that looked like miniature cameo brooches, fringed in gold. On her feet were a pair of patent court shoes, which didn't quite fit me yet. She looked elegant and otherworldly from where I was sitting, like a dark-haired Princess Diana, or Joan Collins if she wasn't so mean. I felt a warm rush of pride and something like envy, only softer, as I took her in, but it didn't stop me being furious about the socks.

I stayed still on the sofa, sitting on my hands before moving them out from beneath my mohair thighs; it was a hot August morning and they were getting sweaty. Gradually, I came to the grim realisation that I was probably going to have to pull on the white socks that were lying in front of me, curled on the rug like a pair of Dad's freshly clipped toenails.

As I picked them up, the socks were lighter than I imagined. Made from fine gauge cotton, lightly ribbed and designed to be pulled up high on the calf, they were the translucent kind of white that resembles the surface of a pearl. Smart white, not sports white, though whether that made them any more palatable I wasn't entirely sure. A sense of dread mingled with the bile that hadn't yet left my throat. It was bad enough that I was being forced to wear shorts, which I hated because they made me look even younger than I was, like a spoiled princeling, but I was also being made to don a pair of T-bar buckled shoes and a bow tie. I felt like the bastard lovechild of little orphan Annie and Daddy Warbucks, which to nine-year-old me was an entirely unacceptable state of affairs.

I pulled the socks on one by one, taking as much time as possible to ensure that my protestations were registered; it didn't matter that no one else was in the room. I'd just eaten two 'grab bags' of beef Hula Hoops – the packets of which I'd hidden down the side of the sofa in mine and Romy's personal snack wrapper graveyard – and the salty oil of the crisps left a satisfying print on the surface of the leather of the shoes as I pulled them on.

I stood back up on the less dense, slightly threadbare pile of the mud-brown carpet that my parents were always planning to replace but never seemed to get round to, and slowly did up the buttons of my shorts. Partly in protest and partly for the look, I purposely left the back of the shirt untucked. My cousin Hamish always wore his shirts untucked and he was the coolest person I knew. The socks remained puddled around the tops of the shoes and I silently swore to myself that there was absolutely no way I was pulling them up. No way, no how. No.

'Pull those socks up, Dao,' said Dad flatly as he walked into the room without looking at me. He had a short-sleeved white shirt on, and a cornflower-blue kipper tie loosely knotted beneath the outsized collar. His hair was longer than usual and he'd combed it, which I could tell because the greyer strands had gone static. I thought he looked like Noel Edmonds when his hair did that.

The creamy acid came rushing back with a vengeance as I inched the socks up my calves as slowly as I possibly could, glowering at the stupid carpet. It was Dad's fault, after all, that I hated white socks as much as I did.

Ever since I could remember, Dad had worn the same uniform while he was home from a trip. It was an outfit that consisted of a pair of stained navy-blue Lonsdale tracksuit bottoms – the kind that have a cheap bit of elastic at the hems rather than proper ribbing – an oversized paint-splattered sweatshirt in a darker shade of blue that clashed with his trousers and one of twenty-odd pairs of white socks, which he kept like sacred objects in their own special drawer.

Oh, the socks. There was something so calculated in their slovenliness, so brazen in their vulgarity. Where Dad's black work socks seemed to happen by accident – dragged, in the dark of the morning from the depths of his gloomy underwear-storing cave – his white socks, in all their crystalline brilliance, were worn entirely by choice: garishly bright on-foot beacons to his bullyboy masculinity and, in turn, his dominance of our house.

Whenever Dad returned home from a flight and interrupted the clumsy harmony into which Mum, Romy and I had quickly fallen, he would invariably pull on a pair of socks, stomp out of his jet-laggy lair and start shouting about one thing or another. He took great pleasure in shouting if there was a mess or if something got broken – especially if it was me who broke it – and he particularly loved to shout if I was playing the piano, an instrument Rozy had started teaching me when I was six. Dad being away meant that I could play the piano as much as I liked, but when he was home, the sound of his white sock-coddled feet stomping down the stairs as I played the halting strains of Michael Nyman's 'The Heart Asks Pleasure First' (Mum's favourite piece) meant only one thing: trouble.

*

'It's hor-ri-ble!' cried Romy upstairs, her breath stuttering as she sobbed.

I sloped into the hall and swung off the bottom banister, be-socked feet crossing one another, feigning nonchalance as I looked up to see what was going on. Dad had shut the glass-panelled door to the living room and was sitting on one of the grey armchairs, pointedly reading his newspaper high in front of his face.

'You look lovely, Romy,' cooed Mum with a vague air of panic as she attempted to pull her out of her bedroom.

'I'm too HOT!' said Romy, following the last word with a low moan, her bright-pink face matching the hue of her dress – a high shine magenta confection that rendered my sister wider than she was tall, the dress featured myriad gauzy petticoats beneath its sugared surface. There were two puffball sleeves on each side and the elastic dug into the pillowy skin of her upper arms. On her head sat a flower garland finished with white daisies, cream forget-me-nots and a heap of chrysanthemums, which had been dyed the same shade as the fabric. Any envy I had earlier felt for Mum's outfit was not replicated for my sister's.

When we later got to the church in Surbiton, both Romy and I pointedly refused to smile for any of the photos. I must have seemed particularly grumpy because people kept breaking away from the throng to try to console me. The priest, who was apparently a family friend, made the first attempt. I was around halfway down the bridal procession, behind Rachel in her enormous white dress, which was embroidered with gold lilies, and Daisy and Beatrice, who looked surprisingly happy in their garish gowns. As I stamped past him into the church he chirruped, 'Cheer up young man! It may never happen.' I scowled at him hard and grabbed the hand of Hamish, who was standing next to me in a matching outfit, and stalked into the church.

'What's the matter?' whispered Hamish loudly behind his hand, the flax of white-blond hair on his enormous head almost alight in the afternoon sun.

'Nothing,' I demurred. Furious.

Hamish giggled. Hamish often giggled when I spoke.

'You only have to wear them for a few more hours,' soothed Aunty Rozy in my ear as I stepped into the pew, a few rows back from the main action. By the time the last of the dried petals had been thrown and we'd left the church for the short drive to the reception at my grandparents' house I was just about willing to be mollified by Mum, who promised that

I could have at least four profiteroles from Aunty Rachel's towering croquembouche wedding cake. I picked at the socks, which were making my legs itch.

'Careful on the road, Teo . . .' I slammed the door and jumped out of the car as quickly as I could.

Not stopping, I careened across the crazy paving, ducked through the door, slipped under the arms of cheers-ing uncles and swished past dresses in my grandparents' crowded hallway, straight up the stairs and into the pink room where I sat down on the bed. Now safe, I pulled the shoes off without undoing the buckle. They'd started rubbing against my heel and small red patches had formed where the edge of the shoe met the sock. I threw them hard against the wardrobe before peeling the cursed sheaths off my feet.

I wiggled my toes back and forth as the first wisps of 'what a goooorgeous wedding' and 'didn't she look beautiful?' swirled their way through the window and into the bedroom, where minuscule flakes of dust caught the light, like confetti in the air. The soft warmth of the afternoon mingled with the platitudes like they were old friends.

Rid of the socks, I felt ready to rejoin the party. Once I had sloped downstairs, attempting to avoid the attention of my mum, Rachel or anyone who would make put them back on, I slipped out of the back room and into the wet heat of the marquee, which my grandparents would erect for any party that exceeded forty people. I felt the rough hessian of the floor between my toes as I went about at speed, dodging between merrily drinking adults as I searched the space for

Hamish, my hairy blond balloon. In my haste, I managed to land my bare heel squarely on a nearby red toenail that was pointing daintily from a gold shoe.

Before I realised what was happening, I collided with Grandma and my face hit a wall of navy viscose. Jumping back, I saw her fist become lodged in her mouth, the enormous lemon opal she wore for parties glinting next to her nostril. While attempting to steady myself, the crown of my head jutted up into the base of my Aunty Catherine's glass of red wine, instantly decanting the entire thing over her cream calico skirt suit. The event unfolded in a matter of seconds, but, from my perspective, seemed to happen in slow motion. In a desperate attempt to rectify the situation, I immediately thrust my hands up onto Catherine's top, dragging at her chest to try and magic the wine away.

Before she had an opportunity to respond, Dad pushed through the throng of older strangers surrounding my grandma, a sea of smokey Deirdre Barlow spectacles and plastic flutes of Freixenet.

'What the BLAHDY hell are you doing, Dao?' All I could see were the whites of his eyes.

'I'm sssorry, Aunty Catherine,' I stuttered. 'Sorry, Grandma.'

Catherine looked at me flatly before moving indoors, presumably to find some salt (though I didn't imagine there'd be enough sodium carbonate in the whole of Esher, let alone in my grandma's pantry, to remove the stain). Garnets of Merlot dropped languidly on to the greige living-room carpet as she disappeared through the crowd and into the kitchen.

I could feel Dad's glare burning through the shoulders of my shirt.

'Where. Are. Your. SHOOOS?' he shouted, and the last few strangers who hadn't yet clocked the commotion turned around to rubberneck. Grandma was soothing the toes of her damaged foot and was jigging slightly, looking at me with a mixture of care and pain behind Dad's back. I stumbled backwards, tears welling as countless judgmental eyes stared down at me.

I hated it when Dad shouted at me in front of other people. He had a tendency to save his most volcanic outbursts for those moments when enough of a crowd had gathered that his ire would make you feel sufficiently small, and he only ever went for me, never Romy. His favourite sport was to tell me off when I was being clumsy. 'Slow down, DAO, you're going to break another leg.' (I had broken my leg the first time by jumping onto a concealed child's head in a ball pool, which I hotly felt had little to do with my clumsiness.) 'Take it BLAHDY easy.'

Dad took me by the arm, pulled me out of the marquee and into the dining room, where the buffet lunch resembled Miss Havisham's before the decades of decay. Mum came running in after us, almost colliding with Dad before spinning to save her glass of Chardonnay – my unsteadiness of foot, I noted at that point, had not been inherited from her – as Dad let go of me, like a disgruntled fisherman discarding a tiddler, surrendering me to Mum.

'You talk to him,' he glowered, then shook his head and

stalked out of the room and back to his pipe, his wine and the uncles, who had gathered beyond the confines of the marquee, which billowed like a flag of surrender in the afternoon breeze.

'You've just not quite grown into your limbs yet,' Mum soothed as she hugged me; I was almost as tall as her but didn't feel it at that moment. 'He just sees himself in you, don't worry.'

*

A few weeks later, when Dad was away in Nairobi, I set about seeking my revenge.

It was a bright Saturday morning in early September. Mum had positioned herself out in the garden to soak up the last of the rays and Romy was pottering around in her room, quietly humming the bubblegum strains of 'Barbie Girl' to herself. From under my bed, I pulled one of the plastic lock drawers where I stored all the old toy animals I didn't know how to play with anymore, but couldn't yet bear to part with.

Being a relatively old house, there were certain floorboards which I knew would creak or groan if I stepped on them, so I pulled the drawer onto my purple dressing gown and began carefully dragging it towards my parents' room. One step on the patch next to the radiator, which was firm, one next to the upstairs banister, another on to the gold ridge of metal that marked the doorway to my parents' room and . . .

'What are you doing?'

Romy peered out from behind her bedroom door with

a Barbie in one hand and a purple felt-tip in the other. She had been giving the doll a makeover and things clearly hadn't gone to plan, as Barbie's entire face was the colour of a bruise.

'Nothing.'

'Tell me or I'm telling.'

'Go away, Romy, or I'll cut off all her hair.' A pause. 'And then I'll cut off all of yours.'

She slipped back into her room with a squeal. I could hear the soft creak of her seven-year-old weight leaning against the door in a bid to prevent me from coming in. She knew I wasn't one to make empty threats when it came to her dollies.

Quickly, I slunk into my parents' room and pulled open the bottom drawer of the pine dresser, which had been stained a shade of off-teak to make it look more expensive than it was. The shrill cry of wood being dragged against wood made me wince. Inside, layered up like freshly rolled snowballs ready for a fight, were a sea of white tube socks. Some had turned the soft shade of diluted urine, coloured by time and excessive washing, others were still bright – finished with ankle straps in the colours of the American flag – and garish in their look-at-me masculinity.

Although Dad wasn't blokey in the 'football and fags' kind of way that many of my friends' fathers were, there was no questioning his silverback status in our house. He loved to watch Formula One at full volume on a Sunday, he had no compunction about farting loudly whenever the mood took him, and he could easily get through a bottle of Campo Viejo most evenings. He was also never without his pipe. He smoked it in his study, he smoked it in the living room, he even smoked it in the cockpit of the planes he flew until they told him he wasn't allowed to anymore. 'Blahdy ridiculous,' he had said, eyebrows raised incredulously. 'It's not like we navigate by looking out of the window!'

One night, not long after he'd been banned from puffing on the job, I slipped out of bed and downstairs to inform him that I could smell the smoke billowing up through the ceiling and into my room, where my bed was positioned directly over his favourite chair. He barely spoke to me the week after that. I'm sure he thought I was in cahoots with Mum in her campaign to stop him smoking indoors.

Slowly, relishing the moment, I picked up each pair of socks, one by one, placing them gently into the box, piling them up, counting them until all twenty-six balls had been transferred. Quickly, eager for Romy's fear not to have rubbed off too soon, I dragged the box back into my bedroom, snapped the lid back on – pulling down the bright blue handles until they clicked – and pushed it deep under the bed. The socks concealed within looked like freshly proved bread rolls, squeezing seductively against the semi-translucent lid. As further cover, I pushed the wooden drawer where I kept all my most precious things – the rubber Mickey Mouse ring I'd found on a Floridian beach and my Pog collection – in front of the box. Dad had finished it with castors on each corner, so it slid easily under the slats of my bed. Then, I padded the gaps with my old cuddly toys: Panda, my favourite, whose black left eye had begun to chip away to a flaky white under-layer; Lion, which had belonged to my great-grandfather and looked like it might be an incubus for smallpox; and bigger lion, which Dad had bought for me in South Africa a few years before. I felt a bit guilty as I shoved his mane down the right-hand side of the drawer.

Sloping out of the room – the yolk-yellow walls of which now gave me a headache – I failed to notice Romy's bright little eye peering up and out at the keyhole of her bedroom, her shoulder still pushed hard against the white gloss of the door in case I decided to make good on my threat.

When Dad eventually returned home from his trip, I was disappointed that he didn't immediately realise that the socks had disappeared. I'd imagined he would start filleting his work shirts out of his wardrobe in a rage as he searched manically for his beloved foot friends; my mum's knickers being turfed from the chest of drawers one by one into the hallway as he rampaged through their bedroom; his paint-stained sweatpants lying rejected, unsuitable now that their dazzling ankle-companions had been displaced.

It wasn't until five days after he returned that the penny dropped. As I padded down the stairs that Saturday morning, it was clear that he and Mum and had both stayed up late the night before. I could see that they both had slightly stretched, pale looks on their faces, like the waxworks of Charles and Diana at Madame Tussauds, half alive, half not. Mum was wearing Dad's oversized navy-blue dressing gown, making a cup of tea at the counter as he slammed the door of the washing machine in the utility cupboard at the back of the kitchen. He was wearing nothing more than a pair of black Marks and Spencers boxer shorts, at least as old as I was, and a baggy white T-shirt.

'Where the hell are they, Jane?' he asked, irate. Mum put her left hand to her head, the jumbled stones of her engagement ring winking at me, and padded out of the kitchen, the soft pebbled soles of the backless slippers I'd bought her for Christmas shucked gently against the floor. 'I don't know, Jan, did you take them on your trip with you?' she muttered, used to his temper flare-ups but in no state to manage one.

'Why would I do that?!' he shouted, his eyes widened and his already quite wide nostrils expanded as they eagerly sucked in oxygen to counter the effects of last night's wine.

I backed out of the kitchen and went across the hall into the living room. My heart was ricocheting around my chest and my spit had turned into glue, sticking my throat together and pushing my tongue into the roof of my mouth. I positioned myself on the sofa, which was farthest away from the door and looked at the TV without really watching it. Romy, wearing a blue nighty with a picture of the Care Bears printed on the front, sat next to me. Nibbling on the edge of a strawberry pop tart to avoid the burned icing at its centre, her face was still flushed with sleep, straw-like strands of hair protruding at all angles.

'Have you looked in Teo's room?' she said quietly, her eyes not leaving the screen.

I turned to her, aghast.

'What was that, darlin'?' Dad asked, grazing the warmth

of her cheek with his salt and pepper beard as he bent down to kiss her, a brush against the delicate upper of a new shoe.

She looked at me, biting her bottom lip with her one good front tooth before turning back to Dad and saying, more quietly, 'Have you looked for the socks in Teo's room?'

Dad looked up from Romy to me, eyes narrowing, before he jumped to his feet, stormed out and stomped heavily up the stairs to my room. I waited a beat before grabbing the Pop Tart out of Romy's hand, casting it to the floor and throwing myself up the stairs two at a time behind him. As I reached the landing, he was already pushing his way back out of my bedroom, unable to turn the door handle due to the fact that both his arms were full of white socks. He looked down at me with a mix of confusion and anger, both eyebrows raised, but said nothing.

I waited until he was in the bedroom before heading back down to the safety of Mum in the conservatory, where she had the papers spread out around her on the sofa.

When Dad eventually joined us, freshly showered, face a little less waxy, he was wearing the tracksuit bottoms with a particularly bright white pair of socks pulled up as high as they would go. He didn't look at me until he had lowered himself into my great-grandma's old armchair, which was positioned directly opposite my mum, the red velvet at the front of the seat faded from years of leg crossing. Eventually he asked quietly, 'Why did you take my socks, Teo?'

I looked up at Mum, who had a look of perplexity on her face, and back at my dad, the hot surge of shame – now more familiar – rising in my throat once again. The heat of his gaze bored like sunlight through a lens as I searched the floor, suddenly unsure why I had done it. My anger at Dad for his explosion at the wedding had waned and all I could think about was the boy on the way to Polesden Lacey, the bright white fabric of his socks pulling gently at the nape of his calf. All of a sudden, the socks seemed to bear down on me menacingly through the ceiling, white hot coals against paper. Confusion and a cavernous sense of embarrassment flooded over me; I didn't even want to be near Mum, who was pulling me in closer to her.

'Why did you take them, Teo?' she asked. Romy – sheepish – was standing at the door.

'I don't know,' I said, quietly. Still looking at the floor.

'But sweetheart . . .' said Mum.

'I said I don't KNOW!' I shouted, levering myself up and off the sofa. I saw Dad roll his eyes at Mum as I pushed past Romy and out through the door, creamy battery acid quickly turning to lava.

'Get back here!' Dad shouted up the stairs as I threw myself into the centre of my blood-red bed spread. I waited a breath to be sure that I hadn't been followed, before digging my hand down the side of the frame and pulling up a solitary white sock ball, the pair finished with the blue and red stripes. I lay them next to me on the pillow so that they were close enough to my face that the primary hues of the stripes blurred languidly into the white; close enough that I could almost smell the synthetic tang of the fibres intermingled with something more bodily. The faces of the yolky suns smiled down at me from the curtains above, judgmental in their perfectly spherical positivity, so I bounced up from the mattress and pulled the films of fabric open wide, encouraging the late morning sun to flood the darker crevices of the room.

CHAPTER 3

The Fisherman Jacket

I woke to the sound of Mum pushing at my bedroom door, the metal of the latch clicking loudly against the bracket as it opened. Through my sleep-clotted eyelashes I could see that the clock on my bedside table read 8.05 a.m., which was far too early to be roused on a Saturday.

'MUUUM, can you knock, please?' I groaned as a thimble of Tropicana appeared around the edge of the glossy white door. Mum saved her smallest glasses for servings of orange juice. 'And WHY are you waking me up so early?'

'Sorry, darling,' she said, not sounding sorry at all, pushing a white plastic Marks & Spencer carrier bag ahead of her – along with the juice – in the mode of a peace offering. She was wearing her favourite haemoglobin-hued dressing gown, which had a hood and made her look like a young Mrs

Santa Claus, and she sat on the edge of my bed. Her eyes looked even kinder when they were burdened by the weight of recent sleep.

'I thought you'd like to wear this to go fishing with Dad today, darling,' she said croakily.

'What is it?' I asked, interest piqued by the prospect of a gift, though my stomach fell at the reminder of the trip. A few weeks before, I'd overheard Dad tell Mum that he thought we needed to bond ('he doesn't like any other blahdy sports, Jane, so maybe he'll like fishing') and the trip was to be his last-ditch attempt at filial galvanisation.

'Open it and see.'

Out of the mouth of the bag I pulled a blue, white and grey plaid shirt jacket. Cut from a heavy fleece fabric, it had two bellows pockets on the front, in line with each pectoral, and it was filled with a thin layer of down. Inside, the lining was made from quilted black nylon, which – Mum told me proudly – meant it was waterproof. The stiff newness of the thing coupled with its aesthetically pleasing practicality spoke to me in volumes and I wanted to wear it immediately.

'Try it on for me then.' She smiled, sensing my excitement.

I jumped out of bed, not yet deep enough into puberty, at twelve years old, to be concerned about wearing my boxer shorts in front of my mum, and pulled the jacket on; the nylon of the lining felt cold against my skin. I looked in the mirror, which Dad had recently put up on the wall facing the bed, and took myself in. I resembled, I thought, a young Grizzly Adams, or the lead dinosaur in Jim Henson's nineties animation of the same name. I felt masculine. Impressive in my broad-shouldered, plain-coated blokeishness, and even began to feel quite excited about the impending trip.

'Come and sit down, darling,' said Mum, pausing as I arranged myself on the bed. 'You know you can talk to me about anything, don't you?'

'Ummm, yes?' I said, feeling my face flush.

'OK,' she responded, looking at the floor as she brought her index finger up to her lips. 'Well just remember that. Now get up, you're going to be late for your father,' she said, suddenly officious. 'And we wouldn't want that now, would we?' she added, smiling wryly.

I groaned again and flopped back on the duvet, jacket still on. I didn't want to take it off, but I needed a wee and didn't want to risk sullying it. Once Mum had left the room, I slowly peeled off the jacket, took a hanger out of the wardrobe, and carefully placed each side on the shoulders of the hanger before zipping it up so the nylon interior wouldn't fall off.

Our upstairs loo was the place where old magazines were sent to die. In it was a tall pine dresser that housed dozens of dog-eared copies of *Hello!* and *OK!*, which had retired there like papery Chelsea pensioners once they'd served out their glory days on the shelf under the conservatory coffee table. The dresser enabled direct and convenient access to the stack while you were doing your business, which was useful as my favourite issue – a worn-out copy of *OK!* featuring a 'world exclusive' shoot with the Beckhams at home in Hertfordshire – had recently been relegated upstairs. David had just shaved his head, he had two giant diamonds plugging the lobes of his ears and he was pictured doing odd jobs around his house, which looked like an engorged version of one of those Magnet show kitchens advertised on telly at Christmas time.

Each and every time I went to the loo, sometimes because I actually needed to, others because I wanted to admire how the sparkle in David's eyes matched that emanating from his ears, I would thumb through that issue. Stopping briefly on one particular shot of David wearing a yellow T-shirt and a boyish side grin, I would swiftly make my way to the back where there was a special featurette on the boy band 5ive. One picture of Abz (Richard Abidin Breen, in all his tanned and tattooed bad boy glory, was my favourite 5ive member, closely followed by Scott. I always thought Ritchie looked a bit like my Aunty Rozy) had quickly become my favourite to spend time with. In it, he wore an oversized, unbuttoned denim vest with nothing beneath it, torso fully oiled – his rolling abdominals winking at me from beneath the varnish of the page – and he had his tattoos out on display. My favourite was the one on his right wrist, which spelled out the word 'DREAMER' in Old English lettering. Like the swoops of white pigment painted suggestively onto a geisha's neck, the tortoise head of that Shakespearean 'R' peeking out from beneath a cuff made my tummy go funny.

On the day of the fishing trip, I'd hoped to have some time alone with the magazine before Dad and I set off. Just as I had landed on that picture of Abz, my stomach flipping like I'd gone over a particularly lumpy hill in a hatchback, there was a bang on the door and I shoved the magazine back into its designated position, tearing the top corner as it slotted in behind an issue I rarely looked at with Dame Shirley Bassey on the cover.

'Dao, are you in there?'

'Yes, sorry, Dad. Give me a second.'

I knew that Dad wouldn't go away and wait for me to finish in his bedroom, but would instead stand jiggling outside the door in his pants until I let him in, so I pulled up my boxer shorts, willing away whichever lustful stirrings had occurred beneath the waistband, shimmied up my pyjama bottoms and unlocked the door.

'What were you doing in there?' he said, eyeing me suspiciously.

'Nothing,' I lied, as I inched around him to go into the bathroom, which was across the hall, a rectangle of sludge-brown carpet separating the two rooms like a miniature Suez. 'I've got a bit of a funny tummy,' I lied again, as I splashed some water onto my hands, pretending to wash them.

'What colour was it?' asked Dad, suddenly forgetting how much he needed a wee. 'Was it watery or more like a custard consistency?'

Dad loved talking about poo. He said it was because he was Dutch; Mum said it was because he was kinky.

'It was fine, Dad, just a bit gurgly,' I mumbled as I went back into my room, shutting the white weight of the door on the conversation, eager for a few minutes alone before our odyssey to the Thames. Making doubly sure that it was firmly closed, I went to the pine dresser that lined the back wall and retrieved my favourite Christmas gift from that year: a large, old-fashioned-looking book.

Every year for Christmas, my parents would buy my sister and me our presents in a kind of feudal tier system. At the bottom of the pile were stocking presents. There would be around twenty of these, which Romy and I would still dutifully pretend had been delivered by Santa. They were small gifts like books, toothbrushes, satsumas and packets of Spice Girls collector's cards.

The second tier consisted of presents that we were allowed to open on Christmas morning. There would usually be around three of these: things considered too big or important to go in the stocking, but not quite essential enough to be classed as a 'main present'. A picture frame, for instance, or a packet of colouring pencils. At the top of the Christmas present tree was the one big gift, which we were only allowed to open after lunch in that flaccid, slightly disorienting stage between the Queen's speech and pudding. My main event present that year had been a bright-red remote-control Ferrari, which had clearly been chosen by Dad for Dad, given how much more excited about it he was than I was, and how anxious my mum looked behind him as I opened it.

'Thanks!' I smiled, swallowing down the childish lump of disappointment fast growing in my throat.

'Let's get it going!' Dad said.

'But there aren't any batteries in it,' I said, secretly relieved that the car could wait for another day.

'I'll go and look for some in the workshop,' he responded, furrowing his brow.

It wasn't uncommon for my favourite present from the haul to be one of the middle tier ones. That year Mum, who had obviously twigged my new-found craving for privacy, had achieved the masterstroke of giving me a miniature safe, which was designed to look like an old book. Made from burgundy plastic that had been roughed up and gilded, it only had room enough for a coke can inside, but I couldn't have been more pleased with it.

It had taken me a few months to figure out what to store in the book, which looked as discreet on my shelf as a drag queen at an accounting convention. I started by putting a few of my favourite things in there – a fake emerald brooch, which Oma had given me when I was little, the Mickey Mouse ring – but somehow it seemed like a misuse of the space. So, instead, I'd started using it as a receptacle for cut-out pictures of men in various stages of undress.

Confident that Dad was still in the loo, I unlocked the book to reveal the pages concealed within. Amongst them was the one of Paul Cattermole from S Club 7, wearing naught but a black vest and a grin, and one of Gianni from *EastEnders* glowering furiously in a black leather jacket and a Nehru collar suit. He looked like a sexy version of one of the priests at my Catholic secondary school, which, in order to get me into a few years before, my parents had been forced to begrudgingly attend church for six months.

I thumbed through the pictures, being careful not to tear

the edges, feeling both excited and unsure about why I was so preoccupied with looking at them. I veered between a surging sensation of exhilaration – as though a high-pressure hosepipe had been let off in my stomach – and flat-out embarrassment, attracted to the men in the shots but somehow repelled by them, too. One by one, I laid the pictures out on my bedspread before removing a sheet of white plastic, which was embedded into the base cavity of the book and concealed another space beneath it. Inside sat a folded-up piece of white A4 printer paper, the creases as clearly defined as the reticulate veins on a leaf, embedded deep from repeated folding and unfolding. Opening up the page, it revealed an image of a muscle-bound man, all lubed-up lumps and bumps. He was leaning against a hay bale with a soft smirk on his face, a kiss curl hanging down from his hair, which looked like it had been moulded from plastic, and in his right hand was a penis so big you'd have been forgiven for thinking it was an off-colour cucumber.

My stomach flipped again at the exact moment the toilet next door let out a low gurgle. As the lock scraped open, I quickly folded the piece of paper up as carefully as I could and secreted it into the depths of the book, clumsily fitting all the composite parts back into place before shoving it onto the shelf without locking it. My heart thwacked against my ribcage as I heard a soft knock on my door. 'Shall I do a fry up for brunch, Dao?' asked Dad. Mercifully, he was much better at not barging in than Mum was.

'Yes please!' I shouted, silently willing him not to turn the worn brass handle.

'OK then, see you downstairs in a minute.' A pause. 'Fancy some sausages too?'

I took a sharp lungful of breath. Was he making a joke? 'Yes please! Crispy please!'

After a few hours spent allowing our meal to digest, Dad and I got in his car, which had recently been upgraded from a white BMW 3 series to a white BMW 5 series, and drove to Teddington lock, a quiet, scrub-surrounded patch of the Thames around ten miles from our house.

We trundled along in relative silence, the subtle purr of the German-made engine punctuated occasionally by Dad pointing out one of the more expensive cars on the road, naming the make and model with an impressed upward inflection ('there's a Mercedes SLK!'). He would then glance over, expecting me to nod along, and raise my eyebrows approvingly; it was only after he'd looked back at the road that I could resume gazing back out of the window at the hedgerows fleeting by.

When we eventually arrived at the lock, the sky was moody and it was cold, even with my new jacket fully done up to the top. I was consoled, however, by the fact that I looked the part – the bruised blues and greys interwoven through the check of the jacket perfectly matched the slate of the clouds above and the deep indigo of the sluggish river below. I looked as though I belonged there even if I didn't actually feel as though I did, and there was something comforting in that.

'Come on, Teo, let's go over here,' said Dad briskly, as he gathered our kit into his arms. He was wearing his favourite Aviator shades despite the lack of light, and he had wellies on despite the fact that the entire area around the lock was paved in broken slabs of stone and gravel.

We walked for a while, crunching down the path as the autumn sun pushed weakly through the quilt of the clouds above. The wind was sharp against my cheeks. Eventually we stopped at the edge of a stagnant-looking bit of water, ten metres or so down from one of the locks. There was another pair of fishermen a few spots away in front of us and the leader, an older man with a beard bigger than my dad's, looked both furious and bemused by our presence.

'It doesn't look like there's much in there, Dad,' I said, as we stopped.

'It'll be fine.' He paused, looking more sceptical than he sounded. He glanced over at the other fishermen, who had retreated into the shelter of their tent. I thought better of asking Dad why we didn't have a shelter of our own. 'Here's your rod,' he said.

Dad handed the line to me, knowing full well I wouldn't have known how to string it myself, and together we went about preparing it for the business at hand. After attaching the reel with his big square hands, which reminded me of spades, he gently guided mine as we threaded the clear line up through the shaft of the rod. Job done, Dad attached the lure as he was worried about me hurting myself on it. A glistening feather the colour of blue glass, the evil-looking curve of steel glinted in the gloaming as Dad took out an old tobacco tin from his fishing bag, which was really an old plastic toolbox he'd repurposed for the trip.

'What's in there, Dad?' I asked, anxious for him not to start smoking.

'Maggots,' he said proudly, smiling at the screwed-up face I made as he opened the tin and showed me the mass of white larvae within, writhing together like a screensaver from hell. With surprising delicacy, Dad removed a single maggot from the receptacle and quickly skewered it onto the hook, the fleshy pellet wriggling helplessly against its sharp metal edges. I couldn't help but feel sorry for the maggot as it jolted and jigged, not least because it brought to mind an incident that had happened a few months before our trip, in which I had played the role of the squirming larva.

*

Dad had recently replaced our old Amstrad computer with a brand-new PC, which took pride of place in the downstairs study. Consisting of two giant grey boxes – a screen and a processor – Dad had even bought a new bespoke desk from IKEA to house the thing in. Finished with specific slots for the keyboard, the mouse and the many bootleg CD-roms he'd bought on trips to Hong Kong – including my personal favourite, the Encarta encyclopaedia – it looked, I thought, like the control desk at Chernobyl (which I'd seen many times illustrated on the aforementioned programme), albeit clad in pine-effect laminate.

To access the internet on Dad's new toy was a task. The modem, which he'd installed at the same time as the computer had been winched in, was treated with a certain mad reverence ('you haven't touched the modem, have you, Dao? You must never touch the modem') and it would churn, grind, whistle and squeak its way through its connectivity mating call, meaning that you'd need to wait at least three or four minutes for the homepage to appear. Perhaps more importantly, however, it also told everyone in the house, in squealing tones, that you were diving head-first into the brave new territory of the world wide web.

As far as my dad knew, the main reason I wanted to go online was to use MSN Messenger. Each evening, Romy and I were permitted one hour of chatting, her at 5 p.m., me at 6 p.m., during which we would sit at the screen typing manically to the friends we'd last seen at school just a few hours before. The conversations tended to go something like this:

Ilovewomen87: Hi! Text back

Lozwozere: Hi Tb

Ilovewomen87: brb, dinner

Lozwozere: k

Ilovewomen87: Back! TB

Lozwozere has logged out of MSN Messenger

In order to use MSN Messenger, I was required to create an email address, so instead of picking something simple – my name @ hotmail, for instance – I had opted for ilovewomen87@hotmail.com. Perhaps it was a bid to conceal my burgeoning sexual wonts, perhaps it was a way of making me seem more masculine than I was. Suffice to say, it didn't achieve either goal.

Johndinage4: Hi Gayo

Ilovewomen87: Hello

Johndinage4: Why is your name Ilovewomen Gayo?

Ilovewomen87: I dunno, I love Geri...

Johndinage: GAYO, GAYO, GAYO van den POOPER

Ilovewomen87 has logged out of MSN Messenger

The real reason I wanted to use the internet was to access porn. Luckily for me, my mum had just started doing an Open University degree in English Literature, which meant she was out at the library several evenings a week. On those days, when they fortuitously coincided with Dad being away on a trip, Romy would sometimes be sent to her friend Robin's house to have tea (Robin had lost most of her teeth from eating too many sweets and her mum smoked heavily, but Romy liked the fact that they fed her Findus Crispy Pancakes) and for the odd afternoon I would be left at home on my own for a few sweet, solitary hours when I would have the computer all to myself.

On such a day, the excitement would build: the second I got home from school, having caught the bus as early as possible, I would career through the front door and into the study to power the thing up. During the wait, I would have time to double-check both upstairs and the garden, in case Dad had secretly returned from a trip without revealing himself. Only once I was absolutely sure that the coast was clear, would I then start up the modem, all the while keeping a furtive eye out in case someone had entered the house without me realising. The entrance to the study was finished with three plate-glass panes, which faced directly onto the front door, around four metres away. On the left of the door was a window that looked directly out onto the driveway and allowed me to see whether any cars were pulling up, so long as I kept my neck craned and my eyes peeled at all times.

Once in position, like a lusty teenage contortionist, I would type into the AOL search bar – this was in the days before Google – 'Gay Men Penis'. Truth was, it had taken me a long while to build up the courage to type those words. I had tried 'Gay Men Willies' a few times before and the results had been nearly as tame as the images I'd sourced from my mum's magazines, so I knew I needed to up the ante somewhat. The problem was that the more explicit the words became, the more I grew aware that I was on the hunt for something that was – in the eyes of my parents, my family, the world – wrong. Simply tapping the letters into the keyboard was enough to induce a flash of nausea at the base of my oesophagus, and I would flick my eyes furtively toward the door with each letter I struck. P – flick – E – flick – N – flick – I – double flick – and S.

Slowly, like a Roman blind being lifted by a half-awake octogenarian, the white space of the window revealed count-less tiny pink- and brown-hued thumbnails of men holding their own penises, men grabbing other men's penises and men putting their penises in places which, to teenage me, looked very uncomfortable indeed.

On the day of the incident – that still makes me squirm, maggot-like, every time I think about it – I scanned the page searching for a thumbnail that spoke to me. Eventually I alighted on one of a man that – if I squinted – looked a bit like Abz. He had sallow Iranian skin, dark features and tattoos up and down his arms. His eyes were bright blue and his manhood was almost cartoonish in its girth.

Arching my neck round the edge of the door, I did a quick check that no one was coming, kept my ear out for the crunch of driveway gravel against the aircraft-like hum of the processor fan, and clicked on the picture. My mouth became increasingly dry as I waited – one second, two seconds, three seconds, four – before finally the image revealed itself. Quickly, I turned on the gigantic printer and clicked 'print page'.

WHIIIIIRRRRR, CLLLICCKC, GGRHRHRHHHG. The enormous electronic box crackled into action and slowly started to print out my chosen picture line by line. I couldn't take my eyes off the mouth of the machine, watching the boy – who must have been a good nine years older than me – gradually materialise in ribbons of ink. Just as the cartridge reached his navel, the printer paused in its activity, as if taking a breath, and I heard from the corner of my ear the distinct crack of rubber on gravel as my mum's car pulled up to the brick step off the porch.

In a flash, I grabbed the piece of paper straight from the

printer, making the thing scream like a puppy whose paw had been stepped on, before stuffing it into my blazer pocket, quickly exiting the screen, switching the giant grey box off at the plug in a bid to muffle its moans, and opening MSN Messenger, which I'd had poised, ready and waiting at the bottom of the screen.

'Yoohoo!' whistled Mum to no one in particular as she came through with her arms full of lever arch folders. She slipped out of her black suede heels, slightly scuffed at the front, before pushing her way into the study and looking down at me with a mix of affection and irritation. 'What are you doing in here, darling? I've got so much work to do. I need the computer tonight.'

Obediently I shut MSN Messenger and vacated the room without a word, praying silently that she wouldn't notice the great lump of scrunched printer paper protruding beneath the fabric of my blazer, and that – in turn – she wouldn't notice the bright flush of pink beneath my beading skin.

Safely ensconced in my room, I opened my book and hid the half-printed picture inside, locked it back up and returned it to the shelf, before shedding my uniform and heading downstairs to have a Tunnock's Tea Cake, a packet of Hula Hoops and to watch *The Simpsons*.

Dad came home at around eight that night, just as we were polishing off a dinner of Mum's smoked haddock pie and peas. He was tired – he'd just finished a day flight from Shanghai – and he wanted to check his emails. 'They've changed my roster without telling me, Jane; they want me to fly to New York the day after tomorrow,' he said, looking enraged. 'I'm blahddy knackered!' he barked and stomped out of the room, as Mum and I tried and generally failed to pick up the slightly overcooked peas on our respective forks. Romy had been excused from the dinner table because she was full up on pancakes and smelt a bit like a bonfire.

The familiar chirrup of the modem brought me out of my stupor. The hair on my neck and arms stood up and I felt my eyes widen.

'What's the matter, darling?'

'Nothing,' I lied.

Just as the primordial machine finished its siren song, I heard the click of the plug socket in the wall next door and the printer crunch into action. The whir of paper being pulled through the plastic gears whooshed through the door of the kitchen, and before I knew what was happening, the familiar chug of the cartridge began churning out ink on to paper.

'May I be excused?' I asked, panicked.

'You haven't finished your peas.'

'I don't like peas.'

'Fine, I'm sure your father will have them.' She shrugged. The Claw hadn't left her hair for a few weeks now.

I quickly kissed her on the cheek as I leaped out of the room and took the stairs two at a time.

'JANE,' I heard Dad shout as I pushed into my room. He sounded equal parts perplexed and angry. Slightly scared, too. 'Come in here!'

'What is it, Jan? I'm trying to eat,' she responded with

a sigh. Her chair scraped as she padded out from the parquet of the kitchen and onto the carpet of the study.

'Oh my GOD!' she shouted, stifling a laugh. 'Is that a . . . willy?!'

I had forgotten in my haste that afternoon that the printer had a habit of printing things which had been cancelled halfway through when it eventually came back to life. It had happened only a few weeks before, when my mum thought she had lost half of the first draft of her essay, and it had happened today, with the half-printed male porn star.

I brushed my teeth quickly so I wouldn't have to encounter my parents again that night and barricaded myself in my bedroom: lying on top of the bedspread with my clothes still on, attempting to put the image of my dad waving around a half-printed picture of a penis, by reading *Harry Potter*. After what seemed like hours of failing to take in a word of the same two pages of *The Chamber of Secrets*, I fell asleep.

When I woke early in the morning, in desperate need of a wee, I noticed that someone had pulled the cover up over my legs and taken off my socks.

*

Back at the river, the maggot eventually stopped squirming on the hook and I looked up at Dad to see if he'd made the same cognitive connection between me and the beleaguered baby fly, but he was staring out at the water intently, looking for a spot suitable to cast the poor creature to its final resting place. I shivered slightly as the hook broke the oily surface around a metre from where I had positioned myself. Dad threw his line out a little further and then we stood, not really saying much as our hands became bluer and the roiling liquid below us grew darker.

After a few hours without even a hint of a jerk on either of our lines, Dad suggested – with a hint of disappointment – that we go back to the car and eat our sandwiches. Mum had made smoked salmon with cream cheese for him and peanut butter – with strictly no butter – for me. It was getting dark and I was starting to lose the feeling in my fingers, so I didn't need telling twice. With a rod-based dexterity I had hitherto failed to demonstrate, I skilfully reeled the line back in, helped Dad dismantle it and made for the car at a pace.

We sat chewing our sandwiches in silence until eventually Dad, who had started to fidget uncomfortably, turned to me and said in one breath, 'You know, Dao, it's OK to think about sex, but it's not good to look at dose kind of pictures on the internet.'

I froze, my mouth hanging open mid-mastication. We'd not spoken about the printer debacle since it happened, and I was hoping against hope that he had forgotten about it. Or at least that we would never talk about it again, forever and ever amen. I didn't know what to say, so I didn't say anything.

'Sex is a part of life,' continued Dad, looking down at the steering wheel. 'It's how we made you, for goodness sake!' he blurted out with an awkward smile, which quickly turned back to a frown.

I nodded slowly.

'The most important thing is, though, that you have to respect people, you have to respect women.'

Women?

'It's the most important thing, and those pictures on the internet are not respectful. You have a mum and a sister and you need to think about them.'

Why was he talking about Mum and Romy? I was looking at penises! Hundreds (and hundreds) of penises.

'Anyway, I've put a lock on the computer now so you can only go on the internet when you have my permission,' he said, eyes once again fixed on the steering wheel, fascinated by the tessellating blue and white triangles of the BMW logo. 'I don't want you looking at those pictures again,' he said firmly.

My stomach plummeted. No matter how embarrassed I was by those pictures, they were also a lifeline: a pixel and paper route out of my heteronormative suburban life. These were the days before hook-up apps, *Queer as Folk* had yet to air on TV and Mum and Dad still laughed when Dale Winton came on the screen. Without access to this physical semblance of my desire – a sexual future I did not yet fully understand was eventually to be mine – I felt unsure what I would do.

The fisherman jacket suddenly felt more than a little silly. The weight of testosterone-infused armour it had provided me with dissipated and I felt like a daft kid playing at being a man. I was desperate to take it off, and I threw it onto the back seat with the rods.

'Can we go home, Dad?' I asked quietly. 'I'm tired.'

Dad looked at me then, his eyes slightly drooped as he pulled one hand through his thick thatch of silver-speckled black hair, screwing up the tin foil, which had contained his sandwiches with the other.

'Um, yes, OK,' he said. 'Your mum will be getting worried.' The fishing trip had lasted three and a half hours to the minute.

Dad's eyes burned holes in my neck every time I went on the computer after that. He had even positioned his chair in the living room so that he had a full view of what I was looking at whenever I was on it, and he had taken to sitting in said chair with far more frequency than usual. So, after several weeks of only being able to access the internet to go on MSN Messenger and look up the fall of the Soviet Union on Encarta, I decided that enough was enough.

My generation was the first to be raised on computers, we were weaned on the language of bites and ram and code, and – as a consequence – our parents didn't stand a chance when it came to policing our digital activity. Case in point, I downloaded a spyware programme, which niftily promised to record every stroke the keyboard made at any time, meaning Dad had no idea it was on the computer and I could discover his password as quick as a flash.

My window of opportunity to find out came the very next day when Dad went on a drive to the tip. 'Do you want to come with me, Dao?' he asked. 'You used to love the tip.'

'No, I'm OK, Dad. I've got homework to do.'

Mum was at the library and Romy was at Robin's again, so, as soon as Dad was gone, car piled high with a broken IKEA wardrobe, I whisked my way into the computer room and logged in using the password I'd digitally divined (Jet123 – Dad has always loved a speed-themed password), feeling immensely proud of my new-found deviousness. Quickly, and with practice, I printed out four new pictures, which I weighed, on balance, would be enough to keep me sated until Dad next went away on a trip. This time, not willing to make the same mistake as the last, I printed the pictures off in black and white, which meant they were ready more quickly, and I hid them away in my book long before he returned home with Romy in tow.

I was reclined on the sofa as they walked through the front door. I quickly rearranged myself to look as nonchalant as possible – one hand trailing down to the floor next to a half-eaten packet of Hula Hoops, the other behind my head – while internally panicking that I'd not sufficiently deleted the browsing history, or that I'd left a picture of a big hairy bottom in the mouth of my printer. Before I had a chance to triple check, I heard Romy trill, 'It's MY TURN on MSN!' as she threw her shoes onto the shoe rack in the hall and skipped to the study.

I shrugged at her from the sofa and screwed up my face, sticking out my tongue. 'Fine with me!' I shouted.

Having entered the password for her, Dad walked into the kitchen to make a cup of tea as Romy settled herself at the desk, long legs hanging loosely over the edge of the leather-bound office chair. She must have been looking at the screen for no more than two minutes when a shrill scream ricocheted out of the study. 'ARGH!! YUCK! DAD!!! WHAT'S THAT??'

Dad ran out of the kitchen and into the room, spilling milky sloshes of Earl Grey from his mug. 'What da FUCK?' I heard him shout as a cold trickle of panic tumbled down my spine.

I got up to see what was happening and, on the screen of the computer, managed to catch a glimpse of two muscular men rubbing each other's penises beneath an animated banner that read: 'Want to meet horny guys in your area? Click here!'

Dad switched off the monitor and ushered Romy, who had turned pale and was crying dramatically, out of the room and into the hallway.

He turned to look at me with disgust as he hugged her. Her head was nuzzled into his shoulder and her sobs became louder the more attention he showed. Before I had a chance to run upstairs, he screamed at me, nostrils flared and brow fully ridged, 'What da FUCK is wrong with you?' Barely pausing for breath, his face quickly turned the colour of overripe cherries. 'Why da FUCK are you looking at that shit?!' he shouted again as I tried to move past the two of them and out of the door. Dad's arm shot out at me as I went, the spade of his hand fanning the fabric of my sleeve in his attempt to grab my arm.

I jumped out of the way with uncharacteristic nimbleness

before running for the front door and slamming it behind me as quickly as I opened it, the tentative threads holding together our relationship snapping smartly between the heavy wood panels as they met.

CHAPTER 4

The Baggy Jeans

'Have you done any practice at all?' I asked Lauren with an air of faint exasperation. Sitting beside me on Mum's recently reupholstered piano stool, she looked sheepish. I'd positioned myself next to her on one of the rattan-based dining chairs, which had once belonged to my great-grandma. The overlapping fibres were pinching at my bum through my new jeans, which were making my legs sweat. It was a hot summer's day and Lauren's clankingly unrehearsed rendition of 'Für Elise' was adding to my feeling of claustrophobia.

'Um,' replied Lauren, chewing the ends of her fingers. 'Not really,' she said, pausing. 'Do you like my hair though?'

Lauren knew I had a weakness for her hair, a thick slap of bright blonde keratin that would have made Barbie envious. Lauren and I had first become friends four years ago, when, one Saturday afternoon, I had taken a paddle brush to it as we sat around our bikes on the communal patch of grass in front of our houses. Lauren had been playing with Romy before my sister had invited me to join the two of them; it was a warm day and I was at a loose end. I spent three hours dragging at Lauren's (rapidly diminishing) follicle count in the pursuit of making her 'look like Baby Spice'. She hadn't complained once.

Lauren had decided to crimp her hair for our lesson that day, which might have been because she knew it would make it harder for me to come at her with any kind of taming implement, but the more likely reason was that she was trying to look like Melissa Joan Hart from *Sabrina*. I didn't have the heart to tell her, but I thought she more closely resembled the Cowardly Lion. 'It looks lovely, Lau.' I paused before trilling out an upbeat chord on one of the lower octaves of the piano. 'Shall we go and pick our outfits for tonight instead?' I asked, looking at her side-on with a mischievous half smile. 'It's too hot for this.'

Ever since the incident with the hairbrush, Lauren and I had been nurturing our friendship like a pearl in the oyster of Fetcham, the Surrey village which constituted the sum total of our early adolescent world. As we went to different schools – Lauren, the scary local comp and I, the Catholic school further afield – she was my officially designated out-of-hours friend. Or, as my school gang referred to her: 'home a-Lau'. I was thirteen and she was twelve, which I had decided was a gap in age sizeable enough to allow me to give her excessive life advice, whether it was requested or not.

'You know, Lau, smoking Mayfair Dark Blues is really bad for you.' I would tell her, as I puffed away on the combusted insides of a Mayfair Sky Blue.

'Oh, OK, Tay.'

'You know, Lau, Vivienne Westwood's *Vive la Cocotte* (mispronounced as vivah la cocotteee) collection was full of bustiers and cinched waists, nothing like the minimalism all the other designers were showing at the time. You would look amazing if you dressed like that.' Sartorial guidance was high on the agenda, my interest in fashion having been piqued the year before, when I'd started devouring Mum's *Vogue* magazines and books from the library. There was something captivating about the way the women moved on the page, like birds of paradise parading their finest feathers for all to see. It wasn't something I talked about with my friends at school, for fear of being judged, but with Lauren it seemed OK.

'Oh, really, Tay? Wow!'

'You know, Lau, your hair would look even nicer if you let me brush it for just a little bit longer . . . please?'

'Um, OK, Tay.'

I'd been giving Lauren piano lessons for a few weeks at her mum's behest, but instead of actually playing any tunes, we'd spend the time chatting about our lives at our respective schools and the dramas that played out daily within our friendship groups. She spoke about her parents, who had fallen out of love and lived in separate rooms in their three-bed semi-detached house. I told her about mine and the many altercations they would come to when Dad returned home exhausted from a trip. Tentatively we shared our chains of experience, garlanding them around our burgeoning bond, like friendship bracelets encircling a wrist.

Lauren's mum clearly knew that we never actually did much piano playing, because on that hot Saturday morning in late August, she'd suggested that we 'put on a show' for the parents that evening. 'Let's see what you two have been up to, eh?' said Jo, her eyes a few shades darker than Lauren's own saucer-like sky blues. As luck would have it, Romy was already planning a garden-based presentation for the local children she had been 'teaching' to dance, so Lauren and I jumped on the bandwagon.

Mum, always up for a party, thought it was a wonderful idea and invited both Jo and Martin, Lauren's dad, round for drinks prior to our performance, which was to be at 7 p.m. sharp.

'I'm going to dance in the show.' Romy asserted from the top of the stairs, her Bugs Bunny front teeth glinting in the morning sun. She was wearing a pair of candy-pink pedal pushers and there was a mass of acid hued clips caught in her hair, like Quality Street wrappers stuck to fly paper, which Mum had pulled back tightly from her face.

'Yes,' I agreed. 'You do a dance, I'll play the saxophone and Lauren can sing,' I stated, knowing full well that Lauren wasn't anywhere near up to playing the piano in public. Lauren seemed relieved to accept her newly designated role and Romy looked a bit irritated that I'd attempted to take charge.

The arrival of the evening was announced by the fat sub-urban wood pigeons cooing softly in the cluster of firs that sat at the centre of our garden. We set up chairs for our parents on the lawn near the house, facing outwards towards the trees. They were already quite Chardonnay merry as we positioned ourselves in front of them. Romy had kept on her outfit from the day, because she thought it made her look like one of the members of B*Witched, and I had decided to wear my school shirt, untucked, with my new pair of baggy Bleubolt jeans.

The jeans were the first item of clothing I'd ever bought with my own money. I had first seen them being worn by Travis from Blink-182 and after 'All The Small Things' came out, anyone who was anyone at school started wearing them. This, of course, meant I needed a pair too. David, year nine's unofficial oracle on all things skate wear, had told me that a shop in Guildford called Pony Express was the best place to get my hands on them. Full to bursting with vast shelves of artfully worn-in hoodies, seas of mountainous skate shoes and great piles of freshly folded Bleubolts, the place was a treasure trove of awkward teenage clothing. The jeans – in all their soft-handed floppiness – had cost £50 (the entirety of my birthday money), and quickly became the only things I wore, even when it was far too hot to be wearing them. They made me feel cool and urbane, despite the fact that I looked a bit like Olive Oyl in a denim maxi skirt.

Lauren, who had gone home to get changed because she couldn't find anything in our dressing-up box (primarily because I'd ripped everything which was suitable for a teenage girl by squeezing into it myself at one point or another), had yet to materialise in the garden. 'Come on, Lau!' I shouted up to the house as I lubed up the reed of the saxophone in my mouth, train tracks making the task considerably more slobbery than it already was. I looked down at the keys, the lustre of which had worn over the few years due to all the Haribo-induced sugar in my spit (or so my teacher had suspected) before Romy shouted, 'Wowza! Look at Lozza!' midway through performing a cartwheel for the parents.

Lauren was slowly shuffling through the French doors that backed out of our living room and into the garden wearing a floor-length column gown made of bright magenta velvet. So tight around her legs that she could barely walk, it had spaghetti straps on the shoulders and bursts of bright maribou feathers around the top and the bottom. The effect of her hair, still crimped in a style not dissimilar to the feathers, combined with the gown made her look like one of my mum's favourite Christmas tree decorations – specifically, a bright-pink diamond-shaped bauble with a puff of fuchsia fluff out of the top. She was clearly wearing a push-up bra, and I had a sneaking suspicion that the whole junior courtesan in a Westwood runway look was designed, in part at least, to entice me.

I felt myself begin to blush and I tried hard not to make eye contact with either Lauren or with Dad. We'd not really interacted in any meaningful way since penis-gate – certainly not about penis-gate itself – and our exchanges were kept to a bare minimum. It seemed to me as though we had reached a rocky impasse in the landscape of our relationship, and neither of us could quite figure out a way to cross it. I was of the firm belief that he, as the grown-up, should make the first move, but he seemed to think the opposite.

Pulling myself together and focusing on the task in hand, I shouted over the heads of the gathered parents, who were craning their necks between sips to smile indulgently at my friend. 'Come on, Lau, we were meant to start five minutes ago!' Although I knew I didn't really fancy Lauren at that point, I also felt drawn to her somehow, so I decided to plough my confusion into my performance.

Romy, who had grudgingly accepted her role in our specific micro autocracy, clicked play on the old Sony boombox, which was nestled in the grass, and started jigging wildly. The backing track to Britney Spears's 'Baby One More Time' came on with crackly force, and, as Lauren eventually made it over to the grassy stage, stumbling over the train of her gown, I started blaring the notes of the melody like a maimed goose as she sung over the top, 'Mah loneliness is killing me', heart clutch for dramatic effect. 'AAAAND III, I must confess, I still beleleilieieve.'

When the first part of the show had finished – our parents looking shell-shocked, Lauren laughing in relief, Romy panting heavily from her exertions – it took a while for anyone to remember to clap. Eventually when they did, they were led slightly raucously by Jo who didn't often drink, and Mum, who had the look of a Victorian gentlewoman gathering herself after a fright. 'Um, that was lovely, sweethearts.' She glanced at my dad who was attempting to stifle a giggle. 'More wine anyone?'

Alarmingly they seemed to have gleaned the idea from somewhere that the performance was over, so before I allowed them to drown us out in the reservoir of their inebriation, I picked up the saxophone and began playing the theme to *The Pink Panther* forcefully, at full volume. It was a piece I'd recently learned off by heart and I was keen to show it off. Lauren and Romy dutifully resumed positions and began dancing like seductive panthers, clawing and snarling at the warm summer air as I puffed and squealed my way through the notes like an asthmatic tabby.

Lauren smiled broadly at me once I had finished. 'That was amazing, Tay!' she shouted from across the lawn where she had ended up, her chest heaving beneath the tufts of maribou as her eyes flicked in my direction. I knew she was only saying so to make me feel better about the fact that the parents still didn't seem remotely interested – apart from Mum who was looking at me with an air of soft-eyed sympathy – but it wrapped me in a blanket of approval nonetheless; the self-same blanket I curled into whenever a teacher complimented my work, or Grandma asked me to play a piece on the piano for a second time, and I was thankful to her for it.

As the parents quickly fell back into their Wolf Bass Creek-soaked intimacy, relieved to be absolved of audience duties, Lauren ran over to me as fast as her dress would allow. Her arms were flapping around like a fledgling flamingo and one of her front teeth overlapped the other, loosely mirroring the cowlick at the front of her hair. Perhaps it was the glint of her tooth in the evening sun that spoke to me, or maybe it was the kindness she had demonstrated, but either way, before I knew what I was doing, I had blurted out, 'Do you fancy going swimming together tomorrow?' She and I had often gone swimming together before, but somehow this time the invitation felt more loaded. 'Yeah!' Lauren replied brightly, her face turning a similar colour to that of her dress before she ran inside to get changed.

As I lay in bed the next morning, contemplating our trip to the pool, I thought about Lauren. I didn't want to have sex with her per se, but I did love to be around her. I felt completely at ease, able to talk about things that I wouldn't dream of discussing with anyone else. Plus, if we were to go out with each other, we'd be able to spend even more time together, and it might make the atmosphere at home a little less fraught following penis-gate, as Dad would surely think more of me if I had a woman in my life. Even though she obviously looked nothing like Abz, I'd never had a girlfriend before and I wondered if trying the idea out for size was such a bad idea.

Just before lunch, I called in at Lauren's house. I had left Mum groaning on the sofa in her radish dressing gown. Dad was still in bed and Romy was crying in her room because Mum had ignored the fact that she'd been sick the night before. The parents had bought us two gigantic Domino's pizzas – a sure sign that they had been absolutely hammered – and there had been something wrong with the mozzarella, according to Romy, who had a sensitive stomach.

'Mummmmm's horrible,' moaned Romy, her lower lip firmly downturned, fists clenched. 'She didn't care at all.'

'I know, Ro,' I said. 'Don't worry, she'll feel guilty about it later.' Romy and I were at our best when we were in cahoots against our parents.

Jo answered the door wearing a pair of very black, very oversized sunglasses before giving a vague wave of her hand and shouting Lauren's name up the stairs of the house. Lauren, dressed in royal-blue Adidas popper trousers, a pair of grey Nike Air Force Ones and an oversized black hoodie from Kappa, looked more like herself and less like the walking, talking bauble she had yesterday, and I was relieved.

'Hey, Lau,' I said, suddenly feeling shy as I shoved my hands into the pockets of my Bleubolts. I'd worn my swimming trunks beneath them because it seemed silly to carry a bag when they were so roomy.

'Hey, Tay!' she chirruped, bopping out of the white uPVC front door and onto the driveway, linking my arm with easy affection.

We walked along, chattering about the night before ('I've never seen my mum drunk like that!' said Lauren. 'Welcome to my world,' I said) until we reached the sheltered bus stop next to the common.

'Shall we stop here for a second, Lau?' I said.

'OK ... why?'

'Sit down if you like?' I continued awkwardly.

'Um, OK.'

Once her Air Force Ones were sufficiently dangling,

I pulled up the front of each leg of my jeans, being careful not to graze the fabric, and got down on one knee. I was suddenly acutely aware that I was kneeling before my friend as if I was about to ask her to marry me, but it was too late to back out, so with a deep breath I picked up her hand, soft with youth, her nails nipped down to their beds, and looked up into her eyes.

'Lau,' I said, haltingly, 'um.' Pull it together, Teo. Come on. 'Will you go out with me?'

Her eyes wobbled like the surface of the swimming pool to which we were heading . 'Yeah, all right then!' she laughed, as easily as if I was asking whether she fancied one of the Black Jacks that were burning a hole in my pocket. Dusting my jeans down as I stood back up – like a teenage Tudor queen reprieved from imminent cranium removal – we carried on walking side by side without saying very much else.

When we eventually got to Leatherhead Leisure Centre, I went and bought us a packet of deep-fried oven chips, which were slathered with too-sweet ketchup that definitely wasn't made by Heinz, and presented them to Lauren as if it was lobster which I'd personally caught and encrusted with caviar and gold leaf.

The relationship blossomed haltingly over the days that followed, without a great deal of change to our dynamic. But a pivotal moment came on our two-week anniversary when I walked Lauren home after a particularly arduous hair-brushing session. Lingering against a wall a few doors down from her house, we stood chatting for a while; Lauren leaning against the brickwork looking coy, me knowing full well what was about to happen, trying not to fall on top of her.

Eventually, clumsily, we locked lips. I'd never properly kissed anyone before, so the moment I felt Lauren's tongue push against the fortifications of my front teeth, I froze. We stood like a pair of washer dryers with their doors open for a good ten seconds before I pulled away, trying not to swallow because we were at the height of a meningitis scare that year and I'd heard that snogging helped spread the disease.

As we walked back to the house, the gloopy puddle of intertwined saliva grew ever deeper at the base of my mouth. I felt a sudden sense of certainty that what we were doing was wrong, that perhaps our relationship wasn't destined to be a romantic one after all. The kiss had not made me feel the 'butterflies' they talked about in romantic comedies, nor had it felt worthy of having a long song written about it. In fact, it made me feel more repulsed than it had turned on, which I knew couldn't be a good sign. Struggling to move my tongue, absolutely determined not to swallow, I said, 'Maybe we shouldn't do that again, Lau.' A pause. 'It's a bit like having a slug in your mouth, don't you think?'

Lauren glanced up at me with a look of shock that quickly melted into a smile. 'Um . . . OK, Tay!' she laughed with a slightly panicky upward inflection 'Ha!' before looking at the floor and jumping up to kiss me on the cheek. 'Night then!'

'Night, Lau,' I waved, before I turned to walk back to my house, subtly emptying the contents of my mouth onto the grass verge when I was sure that she was safely ensconced inside. The backs of my beloved jeans, my on-leg comfort blankets, scuffed under my skate shoes as I shuffled home. Wondering what might be for tea, I pushed our oral tryst to the back of my mind. The twilight sky had turned an incandescent shade of amethyst behind the roof of our house, and all I could think about was an interaction I'd had on MSN the week before.

> **DazBick87:** Hy
>
> **Ilovewomen87:** ... hi, how did you get my email?
>
> **DazBick87:** How ru? Found it.
>
> **Ilovewomen87:** I'm OK, u?
>
> **DazBick87:** gd. WU2?
>
> **Ilovewomen87:** just home, u?
>
> **DazBick87:** home

Darren Bickle was a boy who lived a few streets away from me. The kids in the neighbourhood were often heard referring to him as 'a poofter' at the same time as demonstrating the universally recognised floppy wrist signal for 'homo', in case I hadn't initially grasped what they were talking about.

At the time, the fact that I knew Darren was gay and that he was talking to me on MSN was terrifying. He was the first boy who liked boys I'd ever come across in real life, aside from poor Arun in my year who was mercilessly tormented for his sibilant 's'. But in the wake of my kiss with Lauren, it started to feel crotch-botheringly exciting. And this excitement quickly began to eclipse any fears I had about being tarnished with the poof brush should anyone find out about our exchanges.

Indeed, following the disastrous kiss, the conversations increased in frequency. Darren and I were arranging to talk most evenings, and the guilt I was feeling about my duplicity was intense. So deep was the sense of shame that I felt permanently nauseous and I'd started biting my nails again – a habit I'd stopped years before. After a few weeks, things reached a crescendo.

DazBick87: mbe we should meet?

That familiar surge of bile – a soupy mix of anxiety and exhilaration – gurgled up from my stomach and into my throat. My heart started racing at the thought of meeting this faceless character; something that had once seemed so out of reach, suddenly felt within grasping distance. A real boy! With a penis! My shoulders started to ache from the adrenaline surge.

Ilovewomen87: You couldn't tell anyone
DazBick87: I knw
Ilovewomen87: U promise?

As much as I was worried about my relationship, which, somewhat miraculously, seemed to be trundling along nicely, minus any sexual activity, of course, I was also concerned about the other kids in the area – the boys more than the girls – the vast majority of whom dressed and behaved as though they were part of So Solid Crew, and terrified me as much as they made me want to fold them up and put them in my plastic book for safe keeping.

DazBick87: promise

Ilovewomen87: k . . . when?

I waited a good ten minutes for him to answer, looking to and from the computer screen with such a forceful rhythm that I accidentally cricked my neck.

DazBick87: 2mrw?

Ilovewomen87: OK . . . I have a free hs 2mo. Come here?

In school the next day, I could barely concentrate. I'd always had unusually restless legs but I could have foot pumped 500 blow-up mattresses that afternoon as the clock edged its way to 3.30 p.m. with terminal slowness. It was difficult to imagine what Darren and I might do together as I'd never actually seen him, so instead I substituted one of the boys from my book box in his place, Kai Cruz – an angry-looking hard body with a gold belcher chain and a French crop – who was easily my favourite of the characters I'd encountered during my online odysseys.

I envisaged Kai arriving on my parents' doorstep wearing a pair of grey marl tracksuit bottoms, some Nike TNs and a smirk. Every time I thought about it, the saliva in my mouth turned to syrup and it became increasingly tricky to swallow. By the time the final bell trilled and our teacher screeched at us that it was time to 'get the hell out' of her classroom, I felt like I'd spent the day gargling with superglue and I could barely walk because my legs were ricocheting so vigorously.

As soon as I got home, I did my usual scan of the house before heading up to my bedroom to get changed. Mum had freshly laundered my Bleubolts despite my repeated requests for her not to in case they shrunk, and I threw them on with one of my gazebo tees before heading into my parents' bedroom to survey myself. Although I was almost certainly no one Kai Cruz would fancy, I thought that the jeans made me look somehow less gawky and lumpen than I felt, and my T-shirt did its job of covering up the puppy bumps.

Studying my face, I flashed my teeth at the mirror – there was nothing I could do about the braces – so instead I rubbed at my hair with a certain floppy-fingered fatalism. It had both the look and feel of a piece of brown fuzzy felt. Dad kept his three sole grooming products – a half empty bottle of Polo Sport for men, a pair of angry-looking toenail clippers and an ancient pot of Brylcreem – on the side next to the mirror, so I scooped up a sizeable handful of the latter and flattened it onto my hair, willing myself to look more like Kai but really giving my head the look of a Lego Liza Minnelli. I spritzed on some of the scent just as there was a soft knock at the front door. The final atoms of fragrance made landfall on my neck as I turned to face the sound.

Our door was embedded into the red-brick front of our house by way of a metre-deep porch, so I knew there was little possibility of me being able to see Darren from the window of my parents' bedroom. As I peeked over the ledge with my heart in my mouth, I craned my neck but could only spy one solitary school shoe on the driveway, the other having already been planted on the front step. From what I could see, it was a slightly scruffy-looking Kicker lace-up, which didn't bode well. The fact that Darren had come in his school uniform – which was an ugly shade of electric blue – made my stomach tighten uncomfortably, but I pushed the feeling away, slipped down the carpeted stairs on my socks and rushed to open the door.

'Hiya!' said Darren, in a reedier voice than I had expected. He didn't sound anything like Kai.

I didn't respond right away, but stood in the doorway and took him in. Just like me his hair was fluffy and there was a certain chipmunk-y air to his mouth. There was a smattering of facial hair loosely scattered – like crumbs on a breadboard – around his jaw, which was soft and his uniform hung loosely on his frame. He most certainly wasn't wearing a gold belcher chain or, indeed, a smirk.

Not wanting to be rude, I opened the door a little wider and ushered him in. Both of us stood in the hallway for a moment before I took the lead and walked up the stairs like a soldier beginning his march toward the front. I heard Darren dragging his feet behind me, panting slightly, until we got to my room and sat on the bed spread a good metre apart from each other.

'Um,' I said, 'how are you?'

'Fine,' he replied, looking at his hands. His nails were long.

The silence continued for what felt like an hour, so in a bid to diminish the awkwardness I leaned forward and kissed him on the lips. If kissing Lauren had been like sucking a washer dryer, this was like snogging the wave machine at the Guildford Spectrum. Unlike Lauren, however, Darren's saliva was disconcertingly cold, and his teeth kept bashing against mine.

After twenty seconds or so had elapsed, I pulled away, desperately thinking of ways to get Darren out of my bedroom. I didn't want to do anything else with him, and I was determined that my first time wouldn't involve doing stuff with a man who I fancied less than I fancied the girlfriend I didn't fancy. I suddenly felt like my space was being invaded by a foreign entity, an unclean being, which was acutely unfair given that I'd invited him in and I was just as much of a speccy spotty teenager as he was.

I didn't want him looking at the photos of my family on holiday in Spain, or at my collection of Goosebumps books, or at the Mickey Mouse ring. I didn't want him to be sat in the same spot that Lauren had been sitting just a few nights before. I didn't want him there at all. In a moment of inspired improvisation, I looked up at my old Lion King clock on the wall and studied it. A cut-out figure of Rafiki, the wise old baboon, acted as the hour hand while baby Simba, who was currently turned fully upside down, was the minute hand. Theatrically I shouted, 'Oh no! It's half past five! My mum's going to be home soon!'

'I thought you said you had a free house until eight?' queried Darren. A look of disappointment fell over the soft planes his face, like a wet towel on an air dryer, as he wiped his nose against the sleeve of his blazer.

'No, no, she changed it to five thirty,' I said, maintaining the air of panic in my voice. 'Sorry but you need to go!'

'Oh . . . OK.' He paused. 'You don't want to do anything else then?'

'No, sorry, let's go, she's going to be here in a minute.'

Darren's look of confusion hardened as he pushed himself off the bed. The shoulders of his blazer hung grumpily off his frame and he stared at me intently from behind his glasses. I could see for the first time that his eyes were the colour of frosty moss.

'If you're not interested you can just say, Teo.'

'No, it's not that, my mum's coming back. Please.' I said the last word a little more desperately than I intended, as I gently shoved him towards the door.

Once he had left and I'd watched him turn the corner out of the driveway, I went back up to my room and smoothed down the bed spread carefully, checking the surface for signs of what we'd done – for any microscopic remnants of Darren. I felt embarrassed that my second snog on this earth had been equally as unsuccessful as the first, but I also felt ashamed – as guilty for kicking him of my house as for breaching Lauren's trust.

Satisfied that no physical signs of Darren remained in my room, I took off my jeans – which suddenly felt dirty – and I put them into the washing basket, hoping that mum would end up shrinking them so I never had to wear them again.

Still feeling queasy, I returned downstairs and logged into MSN Messenger.

Lozwozere82: Hey, Tay! Hw woz ur day?

Ilovewomen87: Fine! Nothing exciting to report! How ws urs?

Lozwozere82: OK! You wanna go to the rec l8r?

Ilovewomen87: Can't. Homework

Lozwozere82: Oh OK. Friday? Will be fun!

Ilovewomen87: Yeah maybe! Brb! x

*

After a week had passed, I began to let myself believe that maybe no one was going to find out about the Darren incident. It was a warm Friday night and instead of going to the rec to drink bottles of WKD Blue with Clara and Lisa, as had become our weekly ritual, Lauren suggested that she and I go for a walk around the block instead. I was disappointed at first because I wanted her friends to see the new Adidas Popper trousers, which I'd bought at TK Maxx to replace the Bleubolt jeans I no longer wanted to wear, and then I started to panic because I thought she might want to kiss again.

The moment I clocked the anxious look on her face as she came down her driveway – the pop in her bop a little less energetic than usual – I realised that she had something more serious on her mind.

We talked lightly about Clara ('she's being a bitch') and

Lisa ('she's seeing a guy who's thirty, Tay!'), until we reached the house that belonged to the grumpy lady who'd screamed that we were 'demons' when we'd tried trick or treating there a few Halloweens before. Lauren must have realised that she only had a few more minutes to say what she needed to say before we arrived at my house, so she suddenly slowed down, scuffed the toes of her trainers on the loose diamonds of tarmac and looked intently down at the floor.

'Tay . . .'

'Yes, Lau?'

'I need to talk to you about something . . .'

Oh shit. I felt my neck go red and my heart started beating like a drum & bass track. I looked down at my feet and waited for the blow to land.

'Um, well, there's this guy called Tony at school.'

Wait, what? I'd met Tony. He looked like a sloth who'd been punched in the face.

'And, well, he's told me that he really fancies me . . . and has asked me out.'

She looked terrified. Was she asking my permission to go out with him?

'Well . . . what do you think?'

'You're asking me – your boyfriend – what I think about you going out with someone else?' I asked, trying hard(ish) not to show my indignation.

'Well . . . yeah.' She suddenly looked like she might cry. 'But I won't if you don't want me to.'

By now we were at the mouth of my parents' driveway

and I didn't have a clue what else to say. A big part of me felt relieved that Lauren was doing the inevitable for me, for us both: that she was breaking the charade so that I didn't have to, but another part of me felt hotly betrayed. Not because I cared about this new arboreal paramour sleeping with her or anything, but rather because I didn't want her to start spending more time with him than me.

Thinking on my feet, I took Lauren by the arm and slowly walked us across the gravel towards the front door of my house. I looked pensively at the ground, as if I was mulling her proposal seriously until we reached the porch where I stopped and said, 'You know, Lau, let me make this easy for you . . . ' I pulled my arm out of hers swiftly, the static crackling between our respective polyester sleeves. Less smoothly than I intended, I put my key into the lock, positioned myself in the frame and shouted dramatically, 'You're dumped!' before shutting the door in her face.

I sat down on the bottom of the stairs, from where I could look out of the lead-framed window at Lauren. She was crying on the step, her head buried histrionically in her lap. As much as I felt a crashing sense of shame – hatred at myself for deceiving her, hating my dirty secret – I also felt some grim satisfaction, vindicated by the fact that although I may have let Lauren down by my ten minutes with Darren, she'd let me down, too. Lauren stayed where she was for a little while before she got up and started walking down the driveway, looking back wistfully at the house every few seconds as she went.

Following her revelation about the sloth, Lauren and I didn't speak for a few weeks. With no one to spend my evenings with at home, my time spent on MSN messenger naturally increased, mostly with inane chat with my school friends. One evening, however, an unknown user named PaulP06brah popped up in my inbox.

PaulP06brah: U fucking faggot

Ilovewomen87: what?

PaulP06brah: I know what you did you dirty fucking gay

Ilovewomen87: I don't know what ur talking about

PaulP06brah: You and that Darren kid, I know what you did. You'd better watch yourself van .den Pooper.

Ilovewomen87: What?

PaulP06brah: I know where you live.

Ilovewomen87 has logged off MSN Messenger

Frozen to the spot in Dad's black leather office chair, I glanced out to the garden where my parents were sunbathing and Romy was playing in the sprinkler. Not knowing what to do, I shut down the computer and ran out of the study into the downstairs toilet, where I felt as though I was going to be sick. Nothing came out of my mouth bar a pathetic metallic trickle that stung the back of my throat. I felt a bubble of panic rise up in my chest as I sunk to the floor next to the loo with my arm resting on the seat.

Paul was one of the scarier kids in the area; he had spoken to Lauren a number of times in the past, and hated me since I'd started going out with her. It was something that had worried me before – he had a reputation for beating up everyone from year sevens to sixth formers – and now I felt like I might be in serious trouble. I remained on the floor of the loo, unsure of what to do, hot tears building in my eyes as I slapped my cheeks to stop myself crying. Darren Bickle must have broken his promise.

Listening to check that there was no one outside the door, I slid open the brass lock and sped upstairs into my bedroom, where Mum had placed the folded pair of Bleubolt jeans on my duvet, exactly where Darren had been sitting a month before. Hyperventilating now, I grabbed them and took a pair of scissors from my desk, cutting raggedly down each leg before throwing them in the mesh bin beneath it. As I deflated onto the bedspread, my new Nokia 3310, with its Spice Girls-themed fascia, started beeping wildly next to me. I picked it up with the same care one would treat an armed grenade, and peered down at it from within the pillbox of my panic. 'Lauren D New' read the blocky black text on the sea-green LED square.

'Hello?' I said.

'Hi Tay. You OK?'

'Um, yea. You?'

'I've missed you.'

I paused. 'I've missed you too.'

'Tay ... I heard something today and I don't think it's true,

but I just wanted to tell you so you heard it from me first, OK?'
She sounded slightly nervous, which made me feel worse.

'OK.'

'Darren Bickle, you know that gay kid who lives around the corner?'

'Yeah,' I responded, almost whispering.

'Well, he's gone around telling everyone that you and he, um, well, messed around.'

I didn't say anything.

'Tay? You there?'

'Yeah, I'm here.'

'Did you hear what I said?'

'Yeah, I heard.'

'It's not true is it, Tay?'

I didn't say anything.

'Tay?'

'We didn't have sex, but . . . we kissed,' I said, hating the cold of the phone against my cheek, hating the stupid spots on my face, which were itching, hating the fact that Lauren now thought less of me, hating myself. Tears had started trickling down my face but I was determined not to let my voice break.

'Oh, Tay,' she said, 'but you're so much more handsome than he is!'

I blurted out a drain-like gurgle of a laugh.

'I don't know why I did it,' I said.

'Do you think you might be gay, Tay?' she eventually asked.

I paused, unsure of what to say. 'Yeah. Maybe.' My voice caught on the second word.

'Oh Tay,' cooed Lauren down the phone. 'Are you at home?'

'Yeah,' I said; my head was hanging, I could barely hold up the phone.

'Wait there, I'm coming over.' She paused before saying gently, 'It's all going to be all right.' Another pause. 'I love you, beauty.'

CHAPTER 5

The White Nike Cap

Coming out to Lauren had certainly made some things easier. I could finally talk to someone about the boys I fancied, for one thing. 'Do you think it's weird that I think Paul Cattermole from S Club 7 is hot, Lau?' I had asked her tentatively in the rec on a sticky Thursday in late July the following year. We were at the start of our summer holiday before year eleven began, and we'd been picking the brownest-looking grass with a plan to take it home, dry it out and use it to make a joint with torn-up printer paper. Neither of us had actually smoked weed before and Google didn't yet exist.

'Ummm,' she replied, a small smile betraying itself by the dimples that had suddenly appeared in her cheeks.

'Or . . . what about Gianni from *EastEnders*?' I responded hurriedly. 'There's something quite sexy about him, isn't there?'

'I guess so . . . yeah!' she said, unconvincingly.

What coming out to Lauren hadn't helped with, however, was the fact that I had still not managed to gain any real sexual experience to speak of. I had yet to kiss anyone who didn't look like a cast member of *Fraggle Rock,* and the notion of being with a man was abstracted to the point where I wasn't even sure if I could figure out what to do when the time finally came.

And although there were certain people from my real life, as opposed to my digital one, who I fancied, I'd never dared to look at them head-on, let alone talk to them. They were invariably the almost-men from the upper sixth who drove souped-up Honda Civics and Subaru Imprezas into school, wearing white Nike TN caps high on their heads and Reebok Classics on their feet, soft brushes of stubble bothering their top lips and voices just broken.

There was something about the caps in particular, in all their priapic posturing, which I found specifically affecting. Perhaps it was due to the erect way they were worn, or maybe it was because they imbued their wearers with the look of laddish jocks, ready and raring for action on the field or otherwise; either way, a white Nike TN cap was like catnip to me – the one issue being that the people who wore them would most likely kill me if I so much as looked at them, let alone tried to flirt with them.

The only opportunities I had to potentially meet other boys like me, therefore, were on our Friday night boozing sessions in Guildford, which were all the more enjoyable during the summer holidays, when the warmth of the long evenings added to the intoxicating sense of possibility. The problem was that the last handful of times we'd been out, I'd been left standing on the sidelines like a dumpy debutant as my friends spent the evening snogging strangers, snogging each other and searching for, well, anyone to snog before last orders were called.

'Bye, Mum! Bye, Dad!' I shouted into the house as I made my way towards the front door. It was a warm evening and I was wearing a black Eisenegger shirt, which Mum had bought me in the sale just a few weeks before, paired with my black school loafers because they were the only smartish shoes that I owned. I was trying – and most often failing – to evolve my own style from saggy demi-grebo to something a little more sophisticated. Beyond their seductive smiles and rippling pectorals, I'd begun to notice the ways in which the men dressed in Mum's magazines – from David Beckham's immaculately appointed Dolce & Gabbana suits to Robbie Williams's Adidas tracksuits – and they were looks I tried, usually in vain, to replicate. I had swapped my skate jeans for slightly slimmer Levi's 501s, and the surf T-shirts had been replaced with slim cut bowling shirts in dark enough shades to conceal my lumpy bits, which were proving persistent as the years went by.

Pulling the door shut behind me, I could feel the Brylcreem I'd slicked through my hair beginning to trickle down the sides of my forehead, like glaciers of Mr Whippy melting through a clenched fist. 'I'll see you at the statue at ten thirty!'

Dad refused to pick me up from anywhere else in Guildford. Parking his car next to the statue of George Abbot (a former Archbishop of Canterbury) meant that he avoided getting sucked into the town's convoluted one-way system.

'OK, darling!' shouted Mum on Dad's behalf, who was sitting silently next to her on the sofa. He pretended not to enjoy the thirty-two-minute drive (not accounting for waiting time) to collect me on a Friday, but I knew that he secretly did because Dad loved spending time in anything that moved fast – be it a plane, a train or a car – more than he did anywhere else. 'Dad'll see you there then, sweetheart.' I heard Mum jump up out of her seat so I hurriedly made my way out of the house in the hope that she might not catch me.

'What film are you watching, darling?' she shouted breezily through the open window, as I speed-walked down the drive-way, taking care to keep my feet facing forward as I turned my head back.

'Um ... *Minority Report*, I think,' I shouted, batting back the breeziness. 'I dunno, Lauren booked the tickets.'

'OK,' she said, with a hint of scepticism. 'Well, give that girl a kiss from me.' I'm pretty sure Mum knew, by that point, that there was nothing going on between Lauren and me, but she was kind enough to maintain the charade.

I started the three-minute walk up the road to Lauren's house, hoping to avoid the same grilling from Jo, who was prone to ask as many – if not more – questions as Mum, so I prepared the response in my head in case she answered the door.

'Hi Jo, yes, don't you worry, Dad is picking us up at ten thirty sharp. Of course! She'll be in bed by eleven. Haha! No, thank you, Jo, for letting Lauren come out, of course! Yes, we're seeing *Minority Report*. Would you like to come? I'm sure we could get a ticket. No? OK then, well, have a lovely evening!'

Like my parents, Lauren's mum must have had a strong inkling that we didn't always make it to the cinema on those bright, optimistic Fridays – not least because we'd often return raucous and ripe with the scent of cheap vodka. But also, like my parents, she must have realised that if we wanted to drink (which we did) then we were going to find a way, and it was better that we were doing it together in a pub than in a ditch somewhere.

'Hey, Tay!' said Lau cheerily as she emerged from her house. She had straightened her hair to pencil points and she had clearly spent a while working on her cowlick, which was very nearly flat, but not quite. She was wearing an Aero-brown jersey halterneck dress with a kind of frilly flamenco bottom that stopped diagonally midway down her thighs. It made her look like someone impersonating Christina Aguilera on *Stars in their Eyes*.

'Ready, Lau?' I asked.

'Yeah, let's go,' she said, pulling the door behind her. 'BYE DAD,' she shouted, slamming the plastic against its frame with a meaty thwack. So, her mum wasn't there after all. I exhaled deeply.

We started walking down the road, the early evening sun still warm enough that trickles of sweat began to run from my temples. Reaching the end of Nutcroft Grove, I started to turn right towards Cobham station, as Lauren went left.

'Come on, Tay, Lever'ead's closer.'

'But what if we see Paul?' I asked. I had managed to avoid seeing him since he'd tormented me about Darren Bickle the previous year and was in no hurry to bump into him anytime soon.

'We won't; I saw him last week. He's at a day rave in Vauxhall.'

'Are you sure?'

'Yeah, I promise,' she said, soberly.

I walked across the road in Lauren's direction, mollified in part by the promise that I wasn't going to be beaten up, and in part by the fact that the shorter walk to Leatherhead station might prevent my already quite large sweat patches from growing any bigger. 'Fine, but you're buying the cigs.'

Lauren didn't like spending any more money than she needed to, but she agreed before grabbing my hand and dragging me across the road towards the field of sweeping couch grass, which filed like a leggy garrison down toward the station. The new seeds atop the canes reacted lazily to the shifting sunlight, glinting like bottle tops in a soft sea of Gordon's gin greens and Lambrini yellows. We walked in companionable silence for a while. Lauren had hooked her arm through mine and her hair was swinging loosely in the breeze.

'Do you think there'll be anyone I can snog there tonight, Lau?' I asked eventually, being careful to look straight ahead.

'Maybe, Tay!' she chimed optimistically. 'We might be better off going to a gay bar for that, though.' She paused, before adding more quietly, 'I'd definitely go to one with you if you want to?'

'Umm.' I paused. 'Maybe another day.' The only gay bar in Guildford was called the Elm Tree, which smelled like bleach on my occasional, furtive walks past it. And although I knew it was just a pub, which served drinks and peanuts like any other, the thought of visiting it made the truth of my sexuality feel all too real. I didn't yet feel ready to take the plunge.

'The music they play in Bar Kick makes it feel like it should be a gay bar,' I said as we entered the cool of the brick archway that led up to the station.

'Don't worry, Tay,' said Lauren kindly, 'Tony would kill me if I pulled anyone, so I'll be with you if you don't', before quickly adding, 'but you never know!'

Diligently ignoring her comment about sloth face, a Rizla of hope fluttered gently against the sides of my stomach. A warm wave of possibility and unfettered potential rushed over me – a heady sense of absolute freedom – and I felt excited for the evening ahead.

Having managed to avoid buying tickets for the train, we arrived in Guildford and manoeuvred our way down the high street at pace, passing the restaurants we would sometimes pretend to our parents that we'd patronised if we'd seen all the films at the cinema that month. Stopping briefly at the corner shop to pick up fresh packs of Mayfair Light Blues and Clipper lighters, we arrived at Bar Kick, our sticky-floored temple to too-warm plastic beakers of booze. At only fifteen, we were far too young to be legally served alcohol, of course, but these were the days when the UK's less salubrious drinking establishments didn't really care how old their punters were, so long as they paid up. Fortunately, the £20 note my parents would give me each week for a film and some nachos from TGI Fridays was more than enough to ensure that I was served every time.

'Hi, guys!' Lauren shouted happily, waving at my friends as she walked ahead of me into the bar, which was already thick with the scent of Joop and pheromones. 'How you all doing?' The roster of reprobates in attendance was pretty consistent week-on-week. There was corkscrew-headed Jess Jones, who was far too liberal with her curlers and seemed to be perpetually at war with her brother Andy from the year above, though they insisted on going everywhere together. He was sitting on the other side of the bar with some of the older boys from his year. Adam, who looked like a handsome meerkat and loved ice hockey and beer, and Anna and Vicky, two of my newer friends from school who were in constant competition with each other for the attention of all the men who entered the bar. They had no interest in flirting with any of the boys in our group, of course – we were far too young, none of us had any real income to speak of and, most importantly, none of us were yet able to drive.

'So good to see you girls!' smiled Lauren, as she plonked herself next to them on a sticky banquette, oblivious to the fact that that they viewed her as a dangerous rival for the affections of mid-Surrey's choicest men.

'Yeah you too, Lauren,' they said in unconvincing unison.

The beginning of that night at the bar passed much like any other but by 8 p.m., I was already quite drunk, having been forced to down three pints of snakebite-and-black by Adam. Jess was on my lap, and I found myself telling her between sweet, cidery breaths that I thought I might be bi-sexual (the term 'bi' seemed less committal than 'gay'). I hadn't planned on revealing my secret; in fact, I'd made a promise to myself to tell absolutely no one else now that I'd told Lauren, but there was a heady feeling of potential in the air that evening, and it made me want to share.

I trusted Jess. We'd only been friends for a few months, but in that time we'd spent hours chatting on MSN which had fostered a sense of closeness that felt even more pronounced on this evening thanks to the alcohol coursing through my veins. I reasoned, therefore, in my semi-inebriated state that the bigger the cohort of people who knew about my sexuality, the smaller my secret would become – and that couldn't be a bad thing.

'Oh my God! That's so cool,' said Jess. 'I've always wanted a gay best friend!'

'Bi,' I repeated, 'but please, please, promise not to tell anyone, Jess.'

'Yeah, yeah, of course!' she shouted loudly into my ear. Andy was shooting me daggers from across the bar; the slit he'd recently shaved in his left eyebrow was magnified by his bottle of Desperado.

'I think he's annoyed with us, Jess,' I said, as I attempted to spit out the blonde curls of her hair that had become caught in my mouth.

'Who cares?' she said, looking over at him seductively between whispers into my ear. 'I love yoooououu.' She laughed. 'You're my new best bi friend!'

In a bid to extricate myself, I went to get another drink. As I turned the corner into the room where the bar was situated, I could see that Anna and Vicky had positioned themselves in front of the TV and that they were attempting to attract the attention of a figure standing at the bar. Vicky was twirling the straw in her vodka cranberry, eyelids lowered seductively, and Anna was doing her best Jordan impression – her upper arms pushing her not insignificant cleavage closer together. I tried to see who they were looking at, but the lights whirring above prevented me from getting a clear perspective.

I walked a little further into the room, the soles of my school loafers sticking to the floor. The robotic lights swung their gaze, like a drunk being diverted by a pretty girl, and it was then that I was afforded a full view of the figure. Each of his elbows was resting on a beer mat to protect them from the sticky, dehydrated alcopop beneath and he was wearing a pristine navy-blue polo shirt, which hung loosely around his conker-brown arms. As he talked in profile to the barman, I could see that his smile was warm. He must have been around my height, at least six foot, and his legs were long and slim beneath the close-cut of his denim jeans, which sat neatly on the top of a pair of white Reebok Classics on his feet. On his head, revealing a little of the softly curled brown hair beneath, was a white Nike cap, deliberately pushed back to match the angle of the tick on its side.

He must have noticed me at the side of the bar, because before I could look away, he glanced over, caught my eye and smiled without breaking his gaze. My stomach flipped again, only this time it was because I was about to vomit on the floor. Not wanting to move but propelled forward by my gut, I ran behind the bar and up towards the toilet.

I must have had my head in the bowl for a good five minutes when, just as I was using the last piece of paper to wipe the sticky soup of bile and snakebite away from around my mouth, I heard the door open and footsteps approaching the urinal. Tentatively I looked out from under the stall and saw the peak of a perfectly white Nike cap hanging languidly in his hand, next to a pair of denim-clad legs. In front of them, the back of the chrome trough was gradually turning the colour of golden syrup behind a steady trickle of urine.

I was aware that I probably smelled of vomit, but thanks to the amount of alcohol flowing through my blood stream, an unexpected sense of confidence overtook me. Opening the door widely, I walked out and stood at the flimsy metal receptacle next to him. He turned to look at me with a beer-softened smile on his face before pulling up his flies quickly. As he turned to go to the sink, his crotch rubbed gently against the side of my jeans. Forgetting to pee, I followed suit and once again we were standing next to each other, only this time we were adjacent in the soap-splattered mirror.

I could barely bring myself to look at him, convinced that he must be able to see my heart beating like a bouncer's tally beneath my voluminous black shirt, which looked childish and tent-like in contrast to his perfectly cut polo. When I eventually looked up, he was staring at me. Lightly and as if we hadn't just engaged in an awkward kind of mating two-step, he said: 'I'm Tim.' Before I had the chance to respond, he leaned forward and kissed me.

It was unlike anything I'd experienced before. Tim's full lips felt warm and familiar but also totally, intoxicatingly new. The sweetness of his breath filtered up pleasantly into my nostrils as he breathed gently into my mouth and a jolt of electricity ran through me as the tip of his tongue met that of my own.

Tim lingered a little before pulling back and reversing out of the bathroom. It took me a few minutes to regain my composure. Looking at myself in the mirror, I checked that there was no visible sick on my chin before running down the stairs, slipping on some unknown liquid as I went.

Anna and Vicky had given up on the hunt and were talking to one another. Tim, on the other hand, was nowhere to be found. Disheartened, I went back around the corner where Lauren had been flopping around with Adam before. She was considerably drunker than when I'd left her.

'Wooohoho, Tay! Where have you been? Want a drink? Yeeeaaaa!' She laughed as she threw her head back and hung her arms loosely around my neck, like a cider-sozzled farmer placing a yoke on a shire horse. 'Oh shit, Tay, I feel like I'm going to be sick . . .' I looked down at my phone and saw that we only had twenty minutes before our allotted pick-up time, which sent an unwelcome jolt of anxiety through my brain. I didn't want to leave the bar and risk never seeing Tim again, so I looked around wildly for him as I planned out our route to Dad's car in my head. It took at least fifteen minutes to walk to the top of town, and that's if you weren't completely paralytic, which left me just five minutes in which to track him down.

As we elbowed our way through the bar, which was now full to bursting with muscular lads wearing shirts, chains and porcupine hair do's, I lengthened my neck and scanned the room like a defective periscope, searching desperately for any trace of a white cap. I couldn't see anything that resembled Tim's head among the sea of frosted spikes, so, instead, I started searching the floor for his trainers, praying that the blue lights above might make the white panels of his shoes shine even brighter, but the flash of luminescence never came.

Outside, we gulped in the warm night air, which had been gently coddled by the heat of the day. 'Where we going, Tay?' Lauren asked, more alert. 'Where's Adam?'

'I thought we should leave quickly. Easier. I'll call them all tomorrow,' I said. 'Dad's picking us up in ten minutes.' I kept glancing over my shoulder and back to the bar, searching to see Tim's cap bobbing up the hill behind me. I hadn't even told him my name.

'Where did you go earlier, Tay?' Lauren asked, suddenly more lucid. 'I bought you a double vodka Red Bull.' She paused. 'But then I drank it.' My friend, who was still hanging heavily around my neck, let out a cackle, which made the middle-aged couple ahead of us turn round and glare. 'I went to the loo, Lau,' I said. I considered telling her about my encounter with Tim but reasoned she'd likely just forget.

As we arrived at the statue, Dad was standing on the pavement next to his car, inspecting the roof with as much intensity as if he was contemplating purchasing it from a dodgy salesman. 'Some blahddy idiot just ran over the top of my blahddy CAR!' he shouted as we staggered towards him. We pulled up to the side of the vehicle and both feigned sobriety by inspecting the invisible damage to the paintwork. It looked fine to me, so I tried to usher Lauren into the car before he noticed how drunk we were. 'You get in the back, Lau!' I shouted merrily. 'I'll go in the front because of my legs.'

Lauren fell into the car like a sack of sand, slamming her cheek into the seat before slowly steadying herself. I was starting to feel a bit spinny again too, so I closed my eyes and thought of Tim's handsome face, framed perfectly by his brilliant white cap, with a soft smirk falling lightly across his lips.

*

By the time we started back at school three weeks later, the first chills of autumn were beginning to spark in the September air, but the change in weather did little to extinguish the heat of my tryst with Tim. I'd spent hours reliving it, over and over again in my head. Each time I re-remembered our meeting, I subconsciously embellished the encounter with new details – the hoppy taste of beer on his lips; the hard ripple of stomach against his shirt; the furry landscape of the back of his head as I stroked it. Far from diminishing with the passage of time, the technicolour clarity of my memories of that night grew with a determined intensity.

Although I'd resigned myself to the fact of never seeing Tim again, a glimmer of hope came in the shelves of one particular corner shop en route to school, which sold the best gay magazines. I was never brave enough to pick up the pornier titles on the top shelf and besides, I could just access that stuff on the computer from the comfort of home. But I would – on occasion – muster the courage to pick up *Gay Times* or *Attitude*, before slipping the title into a copy of *Top of the Pops* magazine in a bid not to attract the attention of the shopkeeper.

A glossy scrapbook of half-naked B-listers, features on the ins-and-outs of other men's sex lives and gay escort ads, *Attitude* magazine was the first place I learned a little about what being gay might entail, at the very least sexually. I learned what the word 'rimming' meant for instance, in an article about the opening scenes from *Queer as Folk* – and I couldn't help but think it sounded a bit disgusting – while the Agony Uncle column, which was full of horror stories about cheating partners, threesomes, and nymphomaniacs, taught me that I was meant to be having 100 per cent more sex than I currently was.

On one particularly intensive browsing session, I spotted an advert for 'Gaydar' in the classifieds at the back of the magazine. Promising 'friendship, dating and relationships' for 'men like me', Gaydar was a hook-up website, a bright multitude of pixels that enabled users to chat directly with other gay men in their areas.

Over the ensuing weeks, my visits to Gaydar became a regular occurrence because tracking Tim down, which had become my teenage raison d'être, was no small feat. These were the days before most people felt comfortable putting pictures of themselves up on the internet, and very few users used their real names. Or at least they didn't if they were anything like me, fitsurreyboi87 (Ilovewomen87 no longer seemed entirely fit for purpose).

I set my parameters, shrinking the net to no more than a three-mile radius from central Guildford, narrowing the age criteria to one that was within the realms of my own, and refreshed the results on a daily basis, scanning for names that could potentially have been Tim's. Eventually, one day – several weeks after our encounter – I stumbled across 'TimBoiGford86'. Not wanting to get my hopes up, I sent him a message:

'Hi, I think we kissed in the toilet of Bar Kick a few weeks ago. Is that you?'

His response came within an hour.

'I think so. You were the tall lad in the black shirt, right? Sexy.'

My knees flipped up in an overexcited reflex movement and I flew back in my chair. The black leather back hit the wall behind with surprising force. My mouth as dry as the piqué of my polo shirt, I typed as quickly as I could.

`'Yup. That's me.'`

`'We should do that again sometime, boi. That was hot.'`

`'Yeah, definitely.'`

I hesitated as I wrote the next words, because I didn't want to seem childish, but I also didn't want to inadvertently get entangled with anyone twice my age. `'How old ru, btw?'` Btw made it sound breezy.

`'15. Well. Almost. U'`

`'14.'` I let out a small sigh of relief as I typed.

`'So, when shall we meet?'` I added, when he didn't respond immediately.

`'Come to my mate's place in town tomorrow. He'll be out most of the afternoon.'`

`'K.'`

My fingers were shaking so much that the single letter affirmative was all I could manage. Tim sent me the address and suggested that I come at 4 p.m.

I couldn't stop thinking about the lifted peak of the hat Tim had been wearing on the night we met. Like a spray of peacock feathers spread in search of a mate, it demonstrated a subtle virility which I was eager to emulate. I'd never owned a cap but I knew Dad had his own white one, which he wore to play golf. That evening, while everyone was in the living room watching television, I sneaked out into the garage where the bag was kept, in search of the cap. When I eventually found it, it was covered in spiders' webs, the peak was bent out of shape and it didn't properly fit my head. Although the cap was undoubtedly a shadow of the Nike one that Tim had been wearing on that day, it was the right colour, and if I pushed it back far enough, it didn't really matter that it looked more like it belonged to Nick Faldo's grandad than it did a testosterone-charged teenage boy.

When the final bell rang at 3.30 p.m. sharp the following day, I ran out of the classroom, down towards the bathroom, and slammed the door of the cubicle behind me. Rushing, I changed into my jeans and black Eisseneger shirt, the same outfit I'd worn on the night we met – my reasoning being that if he wanted to kiss me while I was wearing it then, he'd most likely want to kiss me wearing it now – and ran out of the toilet, my school trousers flying out the back of my rucksack like a windsock as I sped through the car park, up the lane, and out onto the main road. I made it to the bus stop just in time and jumped onto the first one that passed, which meant I missed all the other students. As I fell panting into a bucket seat near the back of the bus, which was still warm from someone else's weight, I pulled the cap out of my backpack and fitted it onto my head.

I was ten minutes early by the time I reached the address Tim had given me. My heart was racing as I walked towards his friend's house; I had no idea what our meeting held in store. I'd never had sex with anyone and I wasn't sure if I was ready to with Tim, but I knew that I wanted to kiss him, to be near him, and it was a primordial urge that spurred me on as I walked down the street, and enabled me to push any anxieties to the back of my mind.

I hung around in the street a bit, not wanting to appear too keen, and then I panicked that he might see me, so I hid behind an old Morris Minor, which had clear windows around the top. I then realised how much weirder it would look if Tim found me hiding from him behind sheets of plate glass, so I stood up, stroked down the front of my top, and stepped out as nonchalantly as possible towards the house that matched the address he'd given me, a small detached terraced cottage with a teal front door.

After a brief hesitation, I lifted my hand, closing my fist to conceal the shakes, and knocked with less surety than I would have liked. After about thirty long seconds of silence, I heard the faint but definite sound of footsteps. It was undoubtedly Tim who opened the door, but somehow he looked different. The change of context hadn't diminished his attractiveness, by any means, but somehow the reality of facing him one-on-one, outside this domestic setting, felt a little less dangerous, a little less sexy than our original toilet tryst.

His hair was darker than I remembered. He was wearing a white T-shirt with a pair of grey tracksuit bottoms, and the cap was nowhere to be seen. I suddenly felt an intense need to take my own hat off. Tim smiled slyly and his gaze flitted up to the top of my head.

'Come on in, pal,' he said.

I followed him into the house, which was small. The salmon velvet curtains in the living room were closed, it was stuffy inside, and there was a single pink sofa positioned looking out of the French doors at the back, where another set of curtains were similarly drawn.

'Take a seat,' said Tim. He was less smiley now and he swallowed loudly, which made me wonder if he was nervous too.

I sat down on the front edge of the sofa. 'Do you want me to take off my hat?' I asked, punching myself in the face internally.

'Ha, no, don't worry, pal.' He smiled as he came and sat next to me. His movements were fluid and before I knew what was happening, he was kissing me hard. I was shocked by how quickly he had pounced, but also relieved that we'd skipped any awkward two-stepping, which would absolutely have occurred had the reins been handed to me. His hand was holding the back of my head and his tongue was penetrating my mouth like a muscular eel. I resisted initially but I quickly acquiesced, allowing him to hunt its crevices. His hand shifted from behind my head and found its way into my crotch with slippery speed, which was where it stayed for several minutes, shifting searchingly. A jolt of anxiety shot through me; beyond the cartoonishly engorged penises I'd seen online and the few fleeting glimpses I'd had of Dad's when he neglected to shut the bathroom door properly, I had very little to compare mine to. I had no idea how I measured up and the thought that Tim was disappointed made me momentarily feel like

I might vomit in his mouth. I forcibly pushed the thought from my mind and, in turn, pushed my tongue from behind my teeth until it met his.

We stayed in that position, static aside from our vigorous inter-mouth activity, for at least two minutes and then, as quickly as it started, it was over. The whole thing felt more perfunctory than our previous kiss, somehow less tender: the giddy sense of excitement which had accompanied our communion in Bar Kick had been replaced by something more urgent but also less intimate. One part of me want to stay and carry on, and another wanted to run out of the house, down the road and back behind the Morris Minor. The decision, however, was about to be made for me.

'My mate will be home soon, pal,' said Tim. 'And I need to feed his cat,' he added, awkwardly. The skin around his mouth was red and his eyes shifted to the door. 'Thanks for coming over. We should do it again.'

'Um, OK,' I said, dumbly. The image of Darren Bickle sitting on my bed, dejected after our ill-fated encounter, flashed through my head, and I felt a surge of nausea as I realised that might be how Tim was seeing me now. 'Can I have your number?' I asked. Despite the palpable awkwardness of the situation, I was desperate to see him again. The moment the request left my lips, a wave of embarrassment overtook me and I looked down hard at my feet, which were still shod in my scruffy school loafers.

'Um, yeah, sure, pal,' he said. He grabbed a half-chewed pencil and an opened envelope from the sideboard, which was strewn with fliers for pizza delivery services, and scribbled down eleven digits before thrusting the paper into my hands.

'Thanks for coming round,' he said, and before I knew it, I was standing on the doorstep. I turned back to say goodbye but was met by a wall of glossy blue. I looked at my watch. It was 4.15p.m. It didn't particularly matter that it had been so brief, nor did it matter that it had been a little awkward in the aftermath. We'd kissed; and this time we'd spoken too.

I trotted the ten-minute walk down to the bus station in a haze. I sat on the jutting plastic lip beneath the bus shelter, took my phone from the pocket of my backpack, switched it on and quickly punched in the numbers before I lost the piece of paper. I still didn't know his surname, so I saved him instead as 'Tim Sexy'. With at least half an hour to wait before my bus was due to arrive, I decided to text him. He didn't have my number, so it was only the polite thing to do.

'Hi Tim. Teo here. That was amazing. PTB'

I pressed send and attempted to relax my hands, which had transformed into a kind of gnarled frame around the edges of the phone. I shoved the plastic cuboid back into my backpack, determined to ignore it until I felt it vibrate, and I pulled the cap off my head.

The twelve-hour period that followed felt a bit like spending an entire day on the Vampire ride at Chessington World of Adventures: a successive series of soaring highs and crashing lows with regular bouts of gut-churning nausea thrown in for good measure.

On the journey home, I was still high on the endorphin surge from our brief time together, though the good feeling didn't stop me checking my phone every two seconds, silently willing him to respond.

By the time I sat down to dinner of Quorn mince lasagne, two hours had passed since I'd left Tim's friend's house. I could barely eat anything ('but I put dried apricots in it this time, darling ...') because my stomach felt solid, like a lump of wood petrified by the ignominy of the experience. All I could think about was the fact that I'd written 'PTB' at the end of the text, and how desperate it must have seemed to Tim. Urbane, handsome Tim, who kissed strangers in toilets and would never, ever plead with someone to text him back.

By 9.15 p.m., some five hours after sending the text, I had already been sat at the computer for an hour, where I refreshed Tim's Gaydar page every twenty seconds or so, checking for signals that he might have been online, all the while pretending to chat to my friends on MSN messenger. I had tried to find Tim on there too, but I didn't know his email address.

'Darling, what are you doing in there?' called Mum. I could hear from the tone of her voice that she was craning her neck back lazily, which meant she'd probably had a glass of Chardonnay and was unlikely to come in and check on me.

'Just talking to Lauren! Be done in a minute,' I riffed in my breeziest voice, despite being at the point in the ride where I might involuntarily evacuate the contents of my stomach at any moment. I'd given up checking my phone and instead I'd turned the ringer up to full volume and shifted the vibrate setting to its highest, just to be 100 per cent sure that I definitely wouldn't miss a message if one arrived.

'It's getting late, darling, you've been on there for ages ...' she shouted again, this time more insistent.

Begrudgingly, I logged out of the bright orange site, being careful to delete the specific entry from the internet browsing history. I'd learned not to remove the entire catalogue of visited websites, as that aroused suspicion, and I had been sure to look at a few pages of GCSE Bitesize before shutting the computer down. I pushed myself away from the desk, the black plastic castors squeaking sullenly against the carpet, and dragged myself up the stairs to bed.

'Aren't you going to come and give us a kiss goodnight, darling?' cried Mum with merry indignation.

I tossed and turned for several hours before eventually falling sleep. I woke twice in the night, jerking into conscious- ness from dreams that involved Tim and me being on two separate rollercoasters, each coming within millimetres of crashing into each other before veering away. Both times, I checked my phone, switching it on and off just to be sure that a wayward text hadn't gotten lost in the ether. Nothing came through on either occasion, and by the time I woke up in earnest at 5 a.m. I was exhausted, sweaty and more than ready for the ride to be over.

I sluggishly prepared for school. As I searched my wardrobe for my uniform, I remembered that it was still screwed up in my backpack. Angry with myself because I was in no mood to iron the creases out of my school trousers, as Mum would insist that I did, I grabbed the bag from under my desk and pulled at the wad of fabric within. As my shirt, tie and trousers fell to the floor, a bright flash of white surfed out from the open mouth of the backpack and landed next to my feet. The brim of the cap was still bent as I placed it on to my head and pushed it back as far as it would go.

I took myself in as I stared at the mirror above my desk, the cap hardening the angles of my face and making me look more self-assured than I felt. I pulled on my school uniform with a fresh shirt, and positioned the hat back on my head, more deliberately this time, but, despite the intensity of the act, I felt like a fraud.

As I continued observing myself my eyes swam until I saw nothing more than a cobbled together composite – a simulacrum of the men I wanted to be with, and the men I wanted to be more like. I threw the cap to the floor and turned away from the mirror, distracting myself with the search for my form journal, a lodged golf ball clogging my throat as I rummaged through the detritus of my bag, desperately trying not to think about how much I lacked in the eyes of the other boy in the white cap.

CHAPTER 6

The Puma Mostros

'What time do you call this, Teoooo?' Mrs Thallow chastised. 'Sit yourself down and don't even think about talking to Victoria.' She glared over at Vicky and then back at me as I manoeuvred away from her through the sea of grey desks, which were pockmarked by years of biro-inflicted abuse. Mainly by virtue of our proximity to each other in registration, Vicky and I had become closer in year eleven than we had in any other year prior. She had a dry sense of humour, which I liked, and she seemed to find me hysterical – though I think that was more down to my clumsiness than anything else. I fell into my usual seat next to my friend, who put her small, freckled hand on my arm.

'Right, class, pay attention,' shouted Mrs Thallow in a tremulous register. 'We've got a new student joining us today,' she continued, lifting the inflection at the end of the sentence so it sounded like the person was in trouble before they'd even walked through the door. 'Please make Marcus Frederickson feel very welcome.' The last part was levelled at the room like a threat.

I'd never met anyone called Marcus before: the name sounded exotic, even by way of Mrs Thallow's Celtic squawk. Marcus was the kind of moniker only men with full moustaches and even tans could ever hope to pull off. It was a name befitting an emperor or gladiator. I found myself looking up expectingly: imagining a teenage Russell Crowe, all bulging bicep and glistening French crop, to walk triumphantly through the door.

Though I could see some movement behind the glass porthole, I couldn't quite make out the face behind it. Momentarily, the door opened and through it strolled someone familiar: a praetorian from my recent past. I registered the pale skin – lightly smattered with spots – the dark hair cropped close to the perfect pale egg of his head. Suddenly it clicked. It was the same boy I'd seen all those years ago on that bright Sunday morning on the road to Polesden Lacey. My surprise was so intense that I could barely look at him. My heart began to race.

After my ill-fated interaction with Tim a few months before, at the end of year ten, it had taken a while for it to stop feeling like a cigarette had been stubbed into the cavity of my chest, and only in that moment did I realise that it might be healed from the singeing. I looked down at the desk in front of me, at the same time praying that my face hadn't flushed, before glancing up again to check that my eyes weren't deceiving me.

Marcus. So that was his name. He wasn't wearing tracksuit bottoms and ice-white tennis socks this time, but his school uniform – our school uniform – which fit his frame as though it had been cut by a Savile Row tailor. The trousers fell straight and the arms of his blazer – which were a deep inky black in contrast to the faded greenish-grey of my own – hugged close to the curve of his bicep like a toga on a tyrant.

'Marcus joins us from George Abbot,' drawled Mrs Thallow. 'Where I understand they couldn't quite cater to his talents on the football field,' she continued with an undisguised note of distaste. St Peter's was known county-wide for its football team, so it wasn't the first time that an athletic student had moved to our school to take advantage of the fact.

Having been careful not to gawp, I suddenly became aware that I was staring at him – this golden-footed Adonis – and I reddened in panic that everyone in the room had noticed. As I looked away, Marcus turned to face the class – a gaggle of grunting heathens – holding the room with a clear gaze and a straight-backed confidence. I thought I noticed a flicker of recognition hurry across his face as he looked in my direction. His eyes were as clear as I remembered, bright green tidal pools, flecked at the edges with sandy yellow, and there was a ripple of electricity across the room as the boys registered a potential new football partner and the girls recognised a prospective new conquest.

'He's SO fetch,' whispered Vicky.

'Welcome, Marcus, you will be sat next to James, over there,' said Mrs Thallow as she pointed at the only spare seat in the room, which was as far away from me as it was possible to be within the five-metre square space.

'Thanks, Mrs Thallow,' he said, in a smooth voice dipped in a smidge of syrupy obsequiousness. 'That seat over there?' He raised his eyebrows in question and flashed a bright smile at her. If Mrs Thallow hadn't been in her fifties with the ageing appropriate for her forty-a-day cigarette habit, I could have sworn he was flirting with her.

'Yes, Marcus.' She smiled, out of character. A flush rose in her sallow cheeks, though it disappeared just as quickly. 'That seat over there.'

Marcus turned smoothly on the heel of his shoes, a pair of perfectly polished black loafers from Pod – of course his school shoes didn't come from Marks & Spencer, like mine – with steel plaques on the tongues. They looked brand new. I had wanted a pair of the same loafers since year eight but Mum wouldn't let me because she thought I would grow out of them too quickly.

There was something about the immaculate way in which Marcus was put together – the manner in which the hem of his trousers didn't puddle around his shoes but rather kissed the tops of them tenderly; the perfect line of his blazer hugging the curve of his back – which made me feel even more drawn to him now than I had all those years ago. His unbothered elegance calling directly to me, and me alone.

Though the weeks of school that followed Marcus's arrival were outwardly consumed by preparation for my GCSEs, the vast majority of my time was spent plotting ways to befriend him. I encouraged Vicky and Anna to flirt with him so that he might be more inclined to come and sit with us at lunch. I subtly attempted to position myself near him in lessons where seating was unassigned, and I would quite literally fall over myself in bids to leave the classroom at the same time as him, so that we might have a chance to chat as we filtered out through the bottleneck of the door.

It quickly materialised that Marcus preferred to be referred to as 'Marc' and he had soon gathered a gang of the most popular boys in school around him. There was reptilian Aaron, who wore his trousers below his bum and never smiled; there was aloof Luke, who was as tall as me but thinner and good at football; there was chubby Atif, who rarely spoke; and there was athletic Rich, who thought nothing of grabbing girls' breasts as they walked past, a lascivious tick, which meant all but the most intimidating female students went around with their hands across their chests whenever he was in the vicinity.

Together, the group moved through the halls of the school with a slick, gyrating ease. They jostled and joked, of course, doling out dead arms when a member of the gang said something soppy about a girl (though Marc, I noticed, never seemed all that interested in members of the opposite sex, other than to comment on how well dressed one was, or how much he thought their haircut suited them) and pats on the back when they intoned something disgusting.

Each morning as they made their collective way down the school corridors, Marc would move at the centre of the group like a nucleus, steadfast and perfectly proportioned. Luke, Rich, Atif and Aaron pin-balled like wayward electrons around him, each one attempting to get closer to the core with more highly charged fervour than the other, while Marc's uncommon sensitivity and poise did little to push them away. It was an extraordinary dance to observe.

When Marc and I eventually collided, it happened entirely without warning. It was one of those rare muggy days when autumn was still struggling to shift the sun-crisped chrysalis of the summer just past, and I was walking out of the dining hall, where I'd been buying a Raisin and Biscuit Yorkie from the vending machine with Anna. Descending the steps towards the playground, I was explaining why the glossy purple brick in my hand was my favourite of the chocolate bars available, when I felt a hand on my shoulder. I was carrying my blazer over my arm due to the heat and my back was damp.

'Hey, Tay.' I recognised the voice immediately and turned round quickly to face it. I was slightly shocked by the intimacy demonstrated by Marc as we'd barely spoken before, despite my best efforts. 'I was wondering if you wanted to hang out this weekend,' he continued. His eyes, like coins of jade set into the milky oval of his face, seemed surprisingly earnest and open. 'Maybe you could come over to mine or something?'

'Um, yeah, that sounds, er, great, Marcus . . . I mean Marc,' I said, stumbling.

'Great!' He flashed a smile again and for the first time I noticed the perfect white spread of his teeth, arranged like miniature pellets of chewing gum within the bow of his mouth. It was then that I smelled him for the first time, too: a balsamic mix of Carolina Herrera's 212 and a soft, tobacco-tinged body odour. It was how I imagined Abz from 5ive and Paul Cattermole and Gianni from *EastEnders* might smell. 'Let me give you my number,' he said, taking my phone and tapping the digits quickly. He'd saved his name as 'Marc School'.

'Oh, great, sure,' I said, thickly. My tongue seemed to have doubled in size. 'Thanks!'

As quickly as he'd pulled me in, he disengaged, swallowed up by the crowds of blazer-clad students milling their way through the playground towards one of the many coaches that lined the tarmac in front of the school.

'That was weird,' Anna said. 'Are you even friends?'

'Um,' I muttered, 'not really.' I was trying hard not to smile but I was elated: I had been waiting for this moment for months and finally here it was: not only had I been touched by this loafer-adorned deity among Clarks-shod serfs, but I was going to God's house! I looked at Anna, frowning concertedly in a continued attempt to conceal the grin. A surge of endorphins flooded my brain as it computed what had just happened. 'He probably wants me to help him with his English homework or something,' I busked, willing it not to be true. 'I can't imagine why he'd bother inviting me over.'

'Yeah,' said Anna, suddenly disinterested. 'He's really hot though.'

'Is he?' I replied, my inflection a little too high. I hadn't yet revealed the truth about my sexuality to Anna or Vicky. I was anxious enough about the information being in Jess's possession and I was eager to mitigate the risk of anyone else discovering my secret. 'I hadn't really noticed.'

Marc and I didn't speak again in the days leading up to our weekend together. I didn't want to jinx it or risk being uninvited, so I actively stayed out of his way. I hadn't texted him since he'd given me his number either, for fear of a repeat of the Tim experience.

When the Thursday before the big date finally arrived, I decided that it was close enough to the event to risk texting Marc to confirm, but that I would wait till after tea; my theory being that texting someone at around 8 p.m. felt like the grown-up thing to do. I'd spent the entire day planning the perfect text, writing and rewriting it, saving it in my drafts and being sure not to put Marc's name in the 'to' box just yet.

```
'Hey, Marc. Teo here. Hope all well. We
still on for the weekend? Let me know. Teo'
```

Shit, I'd said my name twice. And does 'let me know' read a bit like 'PTB'? I couldn't risk another PTB.

```
'Marc! It's Teo. We still on for the
weekend? T'
```

Better, but a little non-committal, perhaps.

```
'Marcy boy, it's Teo! Can't wait for the
weekend. What are the plans? Tay.'
```

Shit.

In the end, my hands shaking involuntarily as I typed, I went with:

```
'Hey, Marc, it's Teo. Looking forward to
the weekend. What's the plan? T'
```

I read the text over and over again and finally built up the courage to press the send button. A greasy ooze of paprika-infused crème fraiche and difficult-to-pronounce mushrooms (Mum had cooked her patented stroganoff for dinner) swilled dangerously in my stomach. In turmoil, I turned my phone off and threw it onto the bed. There was no way I was looking at it until the morning. No way, no how, no.

I turned my phone back on at 9.02 p.m. At 9.03 p.m. there was nothing. 9.05 p.m. Still nothing. Here we go again. 9.10 p.m. . . .

```
1 message received
```

I looked down at the glowing green screen, my heart was racing and the spasms in my hands had returned. Summoning the courage to open the message I half expected it to be from

123

Lauren or Mum. The latter had recently developed the habit of texting me to tell me she loved me (usually after a glass of wine), even though we lived under the same roof.

```
'Hey, Tay! Great to hear from you. Yeah,
definitely. Let's go have a look at the
shops in town on Saturday and then you
can stay at mine? Marc.'
```

It was happening. I dropped the phone on the duvet, furnished with the same vermilion cover I'd had since I was six, and jiggled my arms up and down in a private victory dance. My smile stretched so wide that it hurt my cheeks.

School was a blur the next day and the usual Friday evening routine of *The Simpsons*, *Hollyoaks*, *EastEnders*, *Friends*, *Frasier* and *Smack the Pony* zipped by in a flash of muffled technicolour. 'So, who is this Marc?' asked Mum, clearly bored of the drama playing out on the screen in front of her. She was sat on the sofa on the opposite side of the room from Dad, who was positioned like a sentinel in his armchair. 'You've not mentioned him before.'

'He's a new kid at school,' I said, attempting to infuse nonchalance into my voice. I didn't take my eyes off the television. 'I thought it would be nice to make him feel included.'

'That's kind of you, darling.' She smiled benevolently as she took a sip of Wolf Blass Creek and turned her eyes back to the bigger Mo berating the littler Mo for some muck-up on the market stall.

The plan was to meet Marc outside Burger King at the bottom of town at eleven on Saturday morning. From the little I knew of him, the way he sported his school uniform, his polished shoes, I could tell that he cared deeply about the way he looked, so the fact that we were going to go shopping together worried me. Thankfully, I still had £40 left from my fifteenth birthday money and the savings I'd scraped together that summer teaching local kids how to play chopsticks on the piano, so at least I would be arriving with ready means.

I went straight to bed after *Smack the Pony*, mainly to allow myself plenty of time to make the decision on my outfit for the next day. I already knew that I would wear my black ribbed DKNY jumper as it was the only item of designer clothing I owned, and I hoped that it would impress Marc in a way that my dad's cap, which I'd long since returned to its cobwebby grave in the garage, hadn't seemed to impress Tim. The jumper featured the brand's logo knitted across the breast and it was slightly oversized. When I wore it, I felt somehow more held together, the voluminous tube of ribbed cotton providing me with a of soft-edged definition – a fuzzy sense of self – which I sometimes struggled to muster on my own. I also decided that I would wear the pair of Levi's twisted jeans Mum had bought me in the sale at Madhouse, and, finally, that I would pinch a pair of black boxer briefs from my dad's underwear drawer as none of mine were clean.

Shoes were trickier. Having gone off Reebok Classics

since my meeting with Tim, what I really wanted to wear was a pair of Puma Mostros. Ever since I'd seen a pair in Mum's Littlewoods catalogue, I knew I needed them in my life, but both my parents thought they were ugly and, as a consequence, neither party would buy them for me. The shoes, which had a futuristic quality, resembled the shape of a foot in a slick, undulating way that the chunkier trainers of my early childhood hadn't, and the velcro straps, which wrapped around them, holding the shoe onto the foot within, resulted in a contouring quality that made them look sexy somehow, like miniature torsos wrapped in gaffer tape.

Bereft of the shoes I really wanted to wear, I decided instead that I would sport my old pair of Dunlop plimsolls, which Mum had bought a few years prior for the handful of ill-fated tennis lessons she'd made me embark upon. She thought I had the physique to be 'the next Pete Sampras', though it had in fact turned out that I had the hand-eye coordination of a dyspraxic Stretch Armstrong. The shoes didn't really fit me anymore, but they looked just about passable with my jeans.

The next day, I set off for Guildford. To get to the bus station, the 479 was required to navigate the town centre's convoluted one-way system, which took it directly past the street corner where Burger King was situated. As we got closer to the restaurant, I could see that Marc was already standing outside. He was ten minutes early and my heart gave a jolt in thanks for his small act of punctuality.

He was wearing twisted jeans too, but a slightly more

fitted style than mine. On his feet were a pair of cream Puma Speedcat trainers and, on top, he was wearing a tight white T-shirt with a navy-blue bomber jacket. Perched effortlessly on the straight slope of his nose was a pair of mirrored Aviators. He looked like one of the models I'd seen in the copy of *GQ* I'd bought for the first time a few months before. I loved the way the clothes hung on the bodies, angular and unexpected but also seductive and luxurious. It was a glossy world I was desperate to be a part of, even though I had no idea how to access it. Marc, on the other hand, seemed like he was already there. His perfect level of polish suddenly made me feel entirely inadequate. It was definitely still too warm to be wearing the jumper; I had six months to go before my braces would come off; I had yet to buy any of my own gel; and Dad's Brylcreem had made my hair far too stiff . . . I felt like a lumpen, remedial Ken doll. With spots.

Alighting unsteadily from the bus, my too-small shoes pinching my toes, I took my time walking over to Burger King. I stuck close to the edge of the buildings on the same side of the street as the restaurant in order to remain in the shade, so that the morning sun wouldn't make me perspire any more profusely than I already was. As I reached the corner I took a deep breath, stroked my over-crisped hair one last time and patted down my jumper, attempting to smooth away the body bumps, which were (still) going nowhere fast.

'Hey, Marc,' I said as I walked up behind him. He turned around quickly, smiling broadly. The bow of his upper lip spread lightly over his teeth and I could see my reflection in his glasses. I thought I looked nervous as he pulled me in for a hug.

'Hey, Tay!'

As far as I was aware, I hadn't told him that the abbreviation of my name was what my parents, Romy and Lauren called me, but the intimacy fell on me like a blanket. 'How are you? Love your jumper.' We had started walking across the road towards the high street and my heart flipped in my chest at the same time as the sweet scent of freshly baked dough entered my nostrils. A branch of Millie's had recently opened nearby and you couldn't move around that part of town without getting a whiff of the company's signature white chocolate and raspberry creation. 'Shall we go to Blackson's?' he said, putting his hand on my shoulder in a smooth movement and guiding me into the arcade. 'I've got some birthday money to spend.'

Blackson's was a designer menswear boutique, which had opened in town just a year or so before, though I'd never been brave enough to go in on my own because everyone I'd ever seen working inside looked so intimidatingly cool. A small white cube filled with sparsely hung rails of ultra-expensive clothes from brands like Daniele Alessandrini, Diesel and Maharishi, there were £400 cotton cargo pants embroidered with silk dragons, there were funnel neck cashmere coats with off-centre fastenings, and there were voluminous poplin shirts entirely devoid of collars. They were clothes unlike any I had ever seen in the flesh before, and everything from the soft handle of the fabrics to the perfect thickness of the labels concealed within them, imbued me with a feeling of immense possibility.

It was another high-gloss world to which Marc, who navigated the little store as if he owned it, seemed to be the gatekeeper. As we perused the rails he started chatting to the owner, who was sporting a carefully sculpted beard and Duffer of St George sweatshirt, as if they'd been friends for years.

Moving around the small space concentrically, Marc and I eventually met at the footwear section at the back of the store. The wall had been lovingly punctuated with a series of miniature shelves to display the shoes like rare artefacts, and it was dominated by trainers. There were cobalt-blue Adidas Sambas in fondle friendly suede, retro-looking Nike Cortezes in pastel hues and Puma Speedcats, much like the pair Marc was wearing on his feet.

'You should get yourself a pair of these,' said Marc, casually, gesticulating at his trainers rather than those on the wall. 'They're inspired by the shoes worn by Formula One drivers.'

'I'm quite keen to get a pair of Mostros one day,' I responded tentatively, eager to meet Marc's confidently delivered trainer trivia with some kind of assertion of my own. 'I think they look ace,' I added redundantly.

Before I'd finished my sentence Marc craned his neck in the direction of Duffer of St George and asked lazily, 'You got any of those Mostros in yet, pal?' before turning his gaze slowly back to me. 'What size are you, Tay?'

'I'm a size eleven, I think, but, um, I'm not sure, um.'

'Don't worry—' he winked, placing one of his hands – which

looked as though it had been recently manicured – on my shoulder '—he's here to assist us.'

When the Mostros came out, the first thing I noticed was the smell, which was a heady mix of shoe rubber, sneaker glue and cheaply dyed leather. They were black, and the entwined tonal straps made them look like something Batman might wear if he ever decided to give up the Batmobile and race classic cars instead. I put them on and they made my feet resemble a pair of slick Doberman snouts. By contrast, my Dunlops looked like a pair of mongrel puppies, abandoned and unloved on the carpet next to them.

'How much are they?' I asked Duffer quietly. His porcine eyes were buried deep in his face, which was curiously tanned for the time of year.

'They're sixty pounds, mate.' He paused. 'But because you're with Marc here, I'll give you 10 per cent off.' Another pause. 'Just this once, mind,' he added with a proprietorial sniff.

'Marc,' I whispered, slightly panicked, 'I've only got forty pounds.'

'Don't worry, Tay, I'll lend you the money,' he said, not missing a beat. His hand was on my shoulder again. 'I've got your back.' His face was earnest.

And just like that, the shoes were mine. I'd never been able to buy the things I truly wanted at the price they actually were and walking out of the shop swinging the bag felt good, powerful almost. 'We'll have to go up to London together soon,' Marc said lightly as we walked out of the shop and onto the polished cobbles of the high street. 'Sloane Street has some amazing boutiques.' He emphasised the final word with a French accent-tinged flourish. 'Have you ever been?'

I said that I hadn't.

'Let's go after Christmas, when the sales are on,' he said. 'I want to get a pair of Tod's driving shoes.'

I'd never heard of Tod, or of his driving shoes. But a trip to London to go shopping with Marc sounded like the most wonderful thing in the world.

After a lunch of soggy Zinger burgers from KFC, we took the train back to Marc's. When we eventually arrived at his very large house, Marc's mum, a garrulous blonde woman of Italian descent, gave us beers which we drank straight from the bottle as we played raucous rounds of Shit Head on the patio. Every now and then I would stretch out my legs in order to admire my new shoes against the paving slabs. I liked the way they looked on my feet, and I liked the way they looked next to Marc's shoes, too.

When the hazy autumn sun had finally dipped behind the hedge at the back of Marc's garden, we made our way inside to watch *Bullitt* with Steve McQueen. It was dark and the beer had gone to my head.

'He looks so cool,' I said without thinking, as I stared longingly at McQueen's lips, which were in the process of saying something pithy.

'I love him. Look at the way he dresses. Just amazing,' said Marc, his eyes not leaving the screen.

I turned to look at Marc then, as the soft glow from the television mingled with the twilight diffusing through the French doors. McQueen was surging through the San Francisco streets in a green Ford Mustang and Marc's long eyelashes caught the shifting light like new pine fronds, the soft line of his jaw revealing the first smattering of stubble. I suddenly had an intense urge to reach out and touch him, but even with the alcohol in my bloodstream, I knew that would be unwise. Instead, I continued to stare. Sensing my eyes on him, Marc turned and smiled, the same broad, conspiratorial smile he had flashed on the dining-hall steps just a week before.

Despite the small window of time we'd spent together, it felt in that moment as though Marc and I had been friends for years. The day had passed with ease and the pair of us had quickly fallen into a jocular rhythm as we stalked the cobbled stones of Guildford high street – a subtle jibe at a dodgy hairdo sported by a shop assistant here, a shared moment of admiration for the cut of an unknown man's coat there – and it felt more natural than anything I'd experienced with any of my friends before, perhaps even with Lauren. I was attracted to him physically, I knew, but by the end of our first day together I also felt connected to Marc in a way that felt a hundred times more intoxicating than the effects of the beer, which was slowly warming in my hand.

'We should probably go to bed, eh, Tay? It's getting late.'

I followed him up the stairs, the three Heinekens I'd drunk still warm in my stomach. Given that there were ample rooms in the house and only Marc and his parents living there, I had fully expected to be directed to a spare room. To my surprise, however, Marc led me into his room and started getting undressed in front of me. In a few deft movements, he had changed out of his jeans and T-shirt and into nothing but a pair of perfectly white Calvin Klein boxer briefs. His chest and arms were pale and toned, and the curve of his spine was as smooth as the edge of a willow leaf.

'We'll both sleep in here, if that's all right, Tay?'

I nodded wordlessly and pulled off my jumper. I decided in that moment to keep on the oversized Airwalk T-shirt I was wearing beneath it. I wasn't ready for Marc to see the verticalised foothills of my body just yet, and the tent-like proportions of the tee also helped cover up my boxer briefs.

Climbing into his small double bed, I was half expecting Marc to come to his senses and push me out. Instead, he put out the light, patted me on the arm and said goodnight before turning away to sleep. The small of his back was just inches away from my hand. Lying motionless, I noticed the sodium glow from the streetlamps outside casting abstracted shadows across the smooth white surface of the fitted wardrobe before us. Confused, I turned to face the other way, where a tall pile of *Esquire* magazines formed a makeshift bedside table. I tried to concentrate on the waves of orange spines in a bid to switch off my brain, which was swimming with images of race cars and boxer shorts, boxer shorts racing. I didn't sleep much that night, but I didn't really mind.

*

Over the next couple of months, I stayed at Marc's most weekends, much to Lauren's friendly chagrin, and during the week, I spent every evening on MSN, waiting for him to pop up. He rarely did, though, and although we texted (each product of which I saved on my 3310 at the expense of anyone else's), he thought it was much more 'couth' to talk on the phone. We would spend hours poring over the back issues of *Esquire* in his bedroom, picking out things we wanted to buy when we had enough money – a shearling jacket from Prada here, a pair of Ralph Lauren ecru jeans there – as we listened to playlists of Marc's favourite songs by U2 and Interpol and The Chillis, which I soaked up like sonic sustenance. Sometimes we would spend whole days watching old films like *Breathless*, *8 ½* and *American Gigolo*, revelling in the glorious adultness of it all.

Our conversations tended to centre on the kind of houses we would have when we were older, and the kind of cars Marc would like to own. But we also talked about personal things, like our shared struggles with our respective fathers; Marc's was tricky, and dominated the family home in much the same way mine did. Each would end with the same statement of dedication to one another; an affable tick we'd developed over our six short weeks of friendship.

'Got your back, Tay.'

'Got your back, Marc.'

I talked about Marc all the time to anyone who would listen.

'Mum, did you know that most of Marc's family live in Italy?'

'I didn't know that, Teo.'

'And his dad has said he can have his Rolex when he turns eighteen.'

'Wow.'

'Also, Marc owns six pairs of Tod's loafers.'

'OK, it's dinner time. We're having stuffed peppers.'

I quickly came to realise that I was falling deeply in love with Marc. I listened to K-Ci & JoJo's 'All My Life' on repeat and, in turn, thought about him on repeat. I was Radio Marc's sole DJ. Whenever the first line of the Goo Goo Dolls' angst anthem 'Iris' came trilling into the headphones attached to my CD Walkman – 'and I'd give up forever to touch you . . . ' – I thought of the longing I felt every time I shared Marc's bed, lying next to him like a Queen's Guard, static yet happy in my horizontal coffin.

CHAPTER 7

The Gucci Loafers

Christmas came quickly that year, and the present haul was particularly good. At the top of the three-tier gifting system, Mum had bought me a new pair of Levi's twisted jeans, which were more like Marc's (the new Janet Jackson album, which came as part of the middle tier, was also a high point), and my aunts had collectively given me £120 in cash, aka a veritable fortune to spend in the sales.

The only gift I cared about, however, was the text I received from Marc on Christmas morning. I had forced myself – with the same grim resilience as a child attempting to sleep despite the stocking rustling at its feet – not to contact him first. So when the vibration suddenly came in the pocket of my dressing gown, my stomach flipped up and into my chest and a surge of energy galloped down my back like a herd of tiny stampeding reindeers.

'Happy Christmas, Tay. Fancy going up to London on the 27th? Sales will be on! Got your back, Mx'

I didn't waste any time texting back. There was no point playing any harder to get than was absolutely necessary. My experience of shopping thus far had been limited to sporadic trips to TK Maxx with Dad, the occasional post-Christmas visit to the Next sale with Mum and my recent voyage of discovery to Blackson's, so the prospect of actually going to proper luxury boutiques in London with my new cash haul was thrilling.

'Yeah, definitely, sounds good. Merry Christmas M. Got your back x'

Boxing Day was perhaps my favourite day in the fortnight-long stretch of parties, dinners and arguments that constituted our childhood Christmases. The entirety of my mum's side of the family would gather at my grandparents' house and the usual chaos would ensue. Wearing a tattered felt Santa suit, Grandpa doled out presents to all the cousins from a black plastic bin bag. Aunty Rachel made her famous lemon cream pie and the older kids drank too much Malibu before secretly vomiting in the upstairs loo.

As the day reached its boozy crescendo and everyone lay around the living room in a semi-comatose state, I became keenly aware that I hadn't heard from Marc. Anxious that he might have changed his mind about London, I sloped upstairs to my room to craft a text that, in reality, I knew I wouldn't send for fear of coming across as too keen.

'Are you OK, Teo?' Aunty Rozy asked, poking her head round the side of the door. I must have been upstairs for longer than I realised. She'd straightened her hair for the occasion, and it was hanging loosely around her ears, which meant she was yet to start on the mulled wine.

'Yeah, I'm fine, thanks Aunty Roz,' I said, trying not to sound glum.

'Are you sure, Tay?' she asked, searchingly. I was closer with Rozy than the rest of my aunts, partly because she was the youngest but also thanks to the many years she'd spent teaching me the piano. Perhaps I felt spurred on by the Malibu maraca-ing its way around my bloodstream, or maybe the burden of my secret was weighing more heavily than I realised, but I suddenly felt an overwhelming urge to tell Rozy everything. I looked up at her from my phone and felt soothed by the concern in her eyes. My heart had risen to my mouth and I was on the brink of speaking when suddenly the phone in my hand vibrated.

```
'See you at Waterloo tomorrow at 11, Tay?
Does that work? Why don't you bring Lauren?
Got your back x'
```

My heart returned to my chest and started racing excitedly. Marc had only met Lauren once and, during that meeting, which had taken place at the rec in Fetcham, I had worried that he might think she was attractive after he complimented her on the glossiness of her hair. In truth, I still had no idea whether Marc was gay or straight, and in turn whether he was attracted to me or not. But the thought of spending a day in London with my best friend and the person I thought I loved was too enticing an opportunity to risk ruining by suggesting that just the two of us meet instead.

I was so excited by the fact that Marc had texted me back that I had almost forgotten Rozy was still in the room with me. She must have noticed that my demeanour had changed as she looked less concerned. Forgetting my urge to share my secret, I smiled and, with a note of relief in my voice, said, 'No, I promise, Roz! I'm fine!', before skipping out of the room.

As I descended the stairs to rejoin the party, I texted Lau. 'Do you fancy coming to London with me and Marc tomorrow? We're going sales shopping on Sloane Street. Will be fun x'

The response came immediately. 'Er yer, Tay! Posh shopping! Am pissed!

The next morning was cold, so Dad offered to drop Lauren and me at the station. I was sporting my Mostros – already slightly scuffed from excess wear – with my new jeans and Dad's old flying coat, an oversized navy-blue Melton wool beast with gold buttons, which he had seemed half-miffed and half-proud to lend me. Lauren wore a full grey marl

tracksuit from Nike with a matching pair of her trademark
Air Force One trainers.

We met Marc under the big Victorian clock at the centre
of Waterloo station. He was wearing a pair of slim indigo
jeans from Façonnable, a blue Daniele Alessandrini blazer and
a pair of perfectly polished chestnut-brown Chelsea boots.
As he walked towards us from the platform, I noticed that
there was a boy of around our age, who looked vaguely similar
to Marc, trailing closely behind him. Wearing an oversized
black Melton wool peacoat with black jeans and a pair of
black sunglasses, he looked even more elegant than my friend.
A feat which – until that moment - I hadn't thought achiev-
able by anyone.

I analysed Marc's face as he moved closer, searching its
perfect planes for signs of I wasn't quite sure what, and I could
sense his distaste at Lauren's outfit before we even said hello.

'Hey, mate!' she shouted as she bopped over to him ahead
of me.

'Oh, hi Lauren, nice to see you,' he said, uniformly charming but somehow thinner-lipped than usual. 'Hey, Tay,' he said,
softening, as he pulled me into a tight hug. 'This is my cousin
Fede,' he said, gesturing towards the black clad figure standing
in his shadow, before adding more quietly, 'He doesn't speak
much English . . .'

'Hey Freddy,' said Lauren gamely, making a move to
bump his fist. The boy sniffed before pulling his black leather
glove-clad hand away and shifting closer to Marc, his mouth
downturned.

'Let's go shopping!' said Marc, who seemed to have missed the awkwardness of the interaction. 'I'm in a shoppy mood!' he added, winking at me as he strode out across the polished white marble floor of the station.

We spent the afternoon milling through the sale rails, first in Harvey Nichols, with its incredibly low ceilings, where we found little but tricky-to-wear Japanese suits. Next was Harrods, replete with eye-poppingly gaudy offerings where everything seemed to be covered in crystals. For a brief sojourn from the sales racks, we headed to Yves Saint Laurent on Sloane Street, where each and every garment cost around five times as much as my dad's car. Lauren asked the shop manager, who himself looked like a young Saint Laurent, if she could try on a particularly enormous silver fox coat, which had a price tag of £40,000. Miraculously, he allowed her to put it on over her tracksuit. To me, she looked like a jockey done good, but I could see that both Marc and Fede were spurred on by the transformation.

'Lauren, is it?' asked Fede slowly, replacing the 'au' of my friend's name with an 'ow'. 'You know, you could be *molto bella* if you tried harder with your clothes,' he added in his stalling, Italian-tipped English. His voice had a nasal pitch.

I turned to look at him with my mouth open, not quite believing what I'd heard, but he had already resumed browsing the rails of slim white jeans and tobacco-hued leather bomber jackets, as if nothing had happened. Marc, who was laughing openly at the comment his cousin had made, turned to join

Fede at the rail without a second glance in our direction. I stared at the two boys, who suddenly seemed unpleasant and alien – like the twins from *The Shining* with better shoes – before turning to Lauren. I could see that she had been hurt by the comment. Her chin was tucked into her neck and her shoulders were hunched, and, although I felt angry on her behalf, I knew that if I said anything, I might risk upsetting Marc. So I pushed the feeling to the back of my mind and went to put my arm around her instead.

'You are beautiful, Lau,' I whispered as she peeled off the coat and handed it glumly back to Yves. 'Shall we go somewhere else, Marc?' I said, pointedly ignoring Fede and attempting to shift the mood. For Lauren and Marc not to get on was better than them sneaking off to a changing room to snog each other, but, still, it wasn't part of the plan. 'I can't afford anything here and I really want to buy something.'

Outside, the light was beginning to dim in wintry concurrence and the bright shop fronts lining the street shone with renewed retail promise.

'Why don't we go to Gucci?' suggested Marc.

'Si!' said Fede, more illuminated than he had been all day.

The word rolled around my head like a marble, large and gleaming. I had seen the Gucci adverts in Marc's copies of *Esquire*, which featured angular models holding newborn babies, but I never thought the brand, in all its voluptuous Italian luxuriousness, would be somewhere I might be able to shop. Gucci had famously been given a sexed-up revamp at the hands of handsome Texan creative director Tom Ford and the buzz around the Italian brand was palpable. Most famous for its preppy horse-bit loafers, under Ford, Gucci made a name for itself in slick suiting and sumptuous shearling outer layers. YSL – which had also been given a marginally less successful Ford makeover – may have been beautiful but Gucci was pure sex and even I, a relatively fashion illiterate fifteen-year-old, could appreciate the power of its hormonally charged appeal. 'Yeah OK,' I said, a surge of excitement charging up my gullet. 'Let's go there.'

Lauren, who was dawdling and kicking her trainers, was clearly upset. 'Come on, Lau, just one more place and then we can get some food.'

Arriving at Gucci, the first thing I noticed was just how enormous the space was. All hard metallic edges, low lights and vaulted ceilings, the very mysteries of wealth and success seemed to be concealed within its recesses. As we ascended the wide ebony staircase, a 'sale' rack, which looked more than a little out of place, came into view directly ahead of us. At the very centre sat a pair of pristine suede loafers, shining out to me like a beacon. The colour of clotted cream, they were finished with red and green webbing on their respective tongues and black rubber pads on the soles. And they were huge. Unlike the Mostros coddling my feet, which suddenly felt a bit childish, these shoes honked of money; of expensive leather and rich, fatty tanning agents. On the soles, a discreetly placed sticker revealed that they were within my price range. Down from an eye-watering £150 to an excitingly attainable £75.

'Can I try these on?' I asked the nearby server, a thin woman with hollow cheeks and hair scraped back tight from her face. She was wearing a drawn expression that suggested she had very little interest in being bothered by a spotty teenager with a menial budget.

'Um, yes, sir.' She paused. 'You do realise they're a size fourteen?' She looked down at my feet, which were a size eleven, and back up to my face.

'That's OK,' I said. I felt like Julia Roberts in *Pretty Woman*. 'I can wear insoles.'

Raising one perfectly arched eyebrow, she spun into the stockroom on the heel of a polished court shoe.

'You have to get those, Tay,' said Marc. 'They're amazing.'

'Si,' added Fede gravely. The corners of his mouth were downturned. 'Molto benne.'

'They're quite expensive, Tay . . .' Lauren said quietly behind him. 'And they don't fit.'

'He should get them,' retorted Marc. 'They're Gucci.'

Lauren looked down at her feet. I wanted to hug her again but the wildly conflicted feelings pinging around inside my brain stopped me. I didn't want Marc to think I was taking her side. I felt anxious suddenly, and like I wanted to get out of the shop.

Once both shoes were on, it became abundantly clear that they were, as both women had suspected, far too big for me and that I would never be able to wear them properly. Despite my chunky wool socks, they slipped around like canoes on my feet as I shuffled around the polished marble floor, but I knew instinctively that I needed them. Marc liked them. Marc wanted me to get them. If I got them then Marc, I reasoned, might see me in the same way that I saw him.

'I'll take them, please,' I said to the woman with a note of a defiance. Her look of distaste softened into a wry smile, part indulgent, part pitiful.

'Absolutely, sir,' she simpered. 'Cash or card?'

'Cash, please,' I responded, pulling out the wad of greasy Christmas money, which was wrapped tightly in my wallet.

'Nice one, Tay.' Marc winked at me, as Lauren pretended to browse the shelves behind him. 'Think of them as an investment.' It was a reasoning we'd both read regularly in the pages of *Esquire* but it made me feel good to know that he approved of my purchase, and it made the prospect of wearing my new shoes feel all the sweeter.

From behind the curtain where the cash register was kept, the woman handed me a glossy brown bag. It was debossed with the brand's double-g logo and there was a grosgrain ribbon tying the two sides together at the top. The silky rope handles, the same colour as the bag, felt smooth between my fingers. As I swung it ahead of me and out of the heavy shop door into the cold late afternoon air, I felt suddenly as though I belonged. As if I had been inaugurated into a club to which I'd long wanted to become a member without even realising it.

My back straightened and my stride extended imperceptibly. I could feel Marc beside me and Fede beside him, but I became aware that Lauren had slowed and was walking a few metres behind us. The feeling of pride dissipated as quickly as it came, and I slowed down to link her arm, the white cotton of my jacket rubbing crisply against the marl of her tracksuit.

'Shall we go and get some food, Lau?' I said, nuzzling my chin into the thwack of blonde I knew so well.

'I know a great little place on Pavillion Road,' Marc shouted back to us as he walked ahead.

'I kind of want a Pizza Hut buffet,' said Lauren quietly.

'Me too,' I laughed.

'Oh, shall we go to Sal e Pepe? It's so nice. I went with Mamma and Fede at Christmas a few years ago.' Marc had a tendency to feign Italian informality, particularly when discussing the various high-end restaurants he'd frequented. Ordinarily, I found it charming, but at that moment – perhaps because of the way he'd spoken to Lauren – it struck me as pompous; a means of asserting his cultural superiority. Carrier bag swinging pendulously in my hand, the pleasure of the weight was a welcome distraction from the growing animosity between my two friends.

'Won't it be really expensive?' asked Lauren, anxiously. 'We could go to Subway?'

'We could get a steak tartare to share?' Marc suggested. 'It'll only be around a fiver each?'

'Um, I don't think I like steak tartare,' said Lauren. 'What is steak tartare, Tay?' She whispered so that only I could hear.

'It's uncooked steak, Lau,' I said, smiling as her face contorted in disgust. 'They serve it with a raw egg.'

'Oh my God, NO WAY, that's gross,' she said loudly.

Marc, overhearing, placed both of his hands in the back pockets of his jeans, raised his eyebrows, and tightened his lips.

'I might have to go home soon anyway, Tay,' she said, between gritted teeth. The clouds, which had kept in some of the heat of the morning, had cleared, and it was cold. The ends of her fingers had turned a shade of lavender. 'But you three stay!'

'You haven't bought anything yet, though, Lau!' I exclaimed. 'You could get some gloves? Or maybe a coat?' I knew the last suggestion was futile, however, as Lauren never wore coats because, deep down, she saw the act of sporting an insulating outer layer as a kind of capitulation to a climate she couldn't control. Forget booze and fags (though she was happy to partake of those too), Lauren's true two-fingers-up to the establishment was to dress entirely inappropriately for the temperature outside.

'Nah, Tay. I'm all good,' she said. 'I want to save my money.'

I felt a pang of panic about the day coming to end.

'Yeah, Tay, I probably need to get back too, sorry buddy.' Marc put a hand on my shoulder. 'Trains are shit on Saturdays and Fede's flying home early tomorrow morning.'

'Um, OK. We could go get a coffee?'

Sensing the note of anxiety in my voice, Lauren took me by the arm. 'Come on, let's walk back to the station instead?'

We strolled to Victoria in relative silence. Lauren's arm was linked steadfastly through mine, while Fede and Marc trailed a few metres behind. Marc was playing on his phone.

'We should do this again soon, guys!' I said.

'Sure, Tay,' replied Marc absentmindedly as he typed.

'Who you texting?' I asked, as nonchalantly as possible. Please let it be his mum. Please let it be his mum.

'No one,' he said breezily. 'Just this girl in the year above.' My stomach turned and a sweet acidity began to fizz at the back of my throat. Lauren squeezed my arm gently. In that tender moment of reassurance, I realised that she knew the truth about my feelings for Marc, and I felt a deep swell of gratitude for my best friend surface in my stomach.

*

'DID YOU HAVE A GOOD BLAHHDY TIME?' Dad bellowed over the noise of the hot air billowing from the vents of the car, just as they cut out.

'Yeah, it was fine, thanks.' I paused. I was sure he'd seen the Gucci bag as I got in, but I felt embarrassed to tell him what was in it. I wasn't sure that Dad, being a man who made the vast majority of his footwear purchases from the back pages of the *Telegraph* magazine, would understand the notion of his son forking out the amount he might spend on a fancy dinner for four on some summer loafers, which didn't even nearly fit him.

The gulf of understanding between Dad and I had widened since I'd been spending more time with Marc, and we were talking less than we ever had. I had stopped looking at porn given how diverted my attention had been, which should have made things easier, but my increasingly piqued interest in fashion was not one which my dad shared. 'I bought some shoes.' I paused, before adding, 'They were in the sale.' Dad looked over at the bag at my feet before looking up at me with a single bushy eyebrow raised. 'I should hope so,' he muttered, before turning his obsidian gaze to the road ahead.

We dropped Lauren off outside her house and she was quicker with her goodbyes than usual. I reached back across the seat to give her a hug, but she squeezed my hand and gave me a warm smile instead. 'Thanks, Jan,' she shouted merrily as she slammed the door hard. Dad flinched. 'See ya, Tay,' I heard her shout. I looked out through the back window but could only see a flash of her silhouette against the spooky fog of brake light and exhaust.

A wave of melancholy rushed over me as we pulled into the drive. The lights were off in the front room, and the twinkling of the Christmas tree intermingled with the ocean glow of the television. Domestic warmth settling like a fire blanket over the excitement of the day, the pride I'd felt when making my purchase began to transform into something resembling embarrassment.

I felt bad for not defending Lauren and I felt silly for thinking that Marc might reciprocate my feelings if I bought the shoes. In that moment, I tried to force myself to confront the fact that Marc probably wasn't gay: that he wasn't attracted to me in the way I was to him. But despite my best efforts, I knew nothing could truly dull the persistent pilot light of hope that flickered at the pit of my stomach. The clownish shoes sitting in the heavy carrier bag at my feet suddenly seemed a sad embodiment of my optimism, foolish and naive. I felt an urgent need to be on my own so I went inside and clambered quickly up the stairs to my room.

I shoved the unboxed shoes under the bed and pulled my phone from my pocket, the smooth plastic warm where it had been pressed close to my thigh. There was a text from Marc waiting.

```
'Love you, Tay. So glad you bought those
shoes. We're style kings, buddy! You and
I are going to take over the world. Mx'
```

A warm feeling suffused through me, and the pilot light surged in my stomach, fed by the petrol of Marc's message. He had never said the word 'love' to me before, and, although I knew he probably meant it platonically, it made me feel fantastic. I opened the cassette deck of my sound system and plugged in a radio recording of 'Beautiful Day' that I'd made a few months before. The warmth in my gut soared in tandem with the twinkling notes at the opening of the song and I felt invincible. I mimed along with an imaginary saxophone for a minute or so before pulling out the shoes from under the bed and placing them on the duvet, allowing the box to form a rectangular dent in the fabric. All feelings of shame and embarrassment suddenly dissipated.

With a smile on my face, I carefully unfurled the layers of chocolate-brown tissue paper encasing the shoes, one sheet at a time. I tentatively scooped out the loafers, like a midwife cradling newborn twins, removing the toe-shaped balls of tissue paper from each before placing them on the floor.

I peeled off my thick winter socks and one by one, gently pushed my feet into the smooth leather cocoons. The heat of my feet against the uppers intensified the new shoe smell, and I walked tentatively towards my desk, catching sight of my smile in the mirror, before turning towards the wardrobe. With toes curled, I clung to the insoles to prevent them from slipping as I made my way back to the bed, where I lifted my feet to look at my shoes head on. They were the most beautiful things I'd ever owned.

My phone vibrated on the duvet beside me. Another text from Marc.

```
'Oh, and by the way, one of my friends is
having a New Year's Eve party. Wanna come?
You can stay at mine after. Mx'
```

I'd already agreed to go to Lauren's parents' party, but I knew without thinking that I would tell her I was being forced to go to Grandma's. This year, Grandma was hosting a 'wig party'. 'I'm not wearing a blahdy stupid wig, Jane,' Dad had declared, furrowing his brow.

But, in that moment, there was nothing I wanted more in the world than to spend New Year's Eve with Marc. The idea of us seeing 2003 in together, me staying at his house, in his bed. Us waking up on New Year's Day together, walking the dog in the pine-tree-dappled light that seemed exclusive to his corner of Surrey, was too much to resist, whatever the cost. 'Sure, sounds good. Got your back, M.Tx,' I wrote back, without a moment of hesitation.

'Great, should be fun,' he replied. 'P.S. listen to "Best Friend" by Harry Nielsen; it makes me think of me and you. Night, Tay.'

That night, as Nielsen burred gently in my ears, I drifted off thinking of all the potential outfits I could wear with my new shoes. 'You're my best friend . . .'

The days which followed passed in a sludgy haze of too much chocolate and terrible TV. I pushed any guilt I felt about lying to Lauren to the back of my brain, and instead focused on persuading Dad to drop me off at Marc's on the evening of the party. Eventually he agreed, so long as we arrived early enough that he didn't have to miss any of Grandma's soiree (which had considerably less to do with his desire to wear the Andy Warhol wig than it did with his desire to drink as much red wine as possible).

'Be careful tonight, Dao, and look after yourself,' he said as he dropped me off at Marc's house at 5 p.m. sharp. 'Don't drink too much, you hear?' My parents never seemed to get all that upset about my alcohol-related antics. Perhaps it was because they knew it would be entirely hypocritical if they did, or maybe it was since they viewed my fledgling boozing with a certain level of perverse pride; impressed and surprised by the fact that their offspring had the same stamina as they did for damaging their livers in the pursuit of a party.

'OK, Dad!' I shouted back. Dad could be tricky, but he was consummately good at caring for mine and my sister's basic welfare – the practical stuff, like keeping us alive. 'Happy New Year!'

'Are you going to be warm enough in that?' he shouted from inside the car. 'Where's your blahdy coat?! Stoopeed boy.'

Ignoring him, I kept walking. I suddenly felt a bit self-conscious in my outfit. To accompany my loafers, I'd opted to wear a pair of green cargo trousers, which I'd inherited from one of the uncles, and an oversized Ralph Lauren polo shirt that I'd found for a bargain in Madhouse. It was so large that it fitted more like a muumuu. I was shivering by the time Marc's mum opened the door, the cold night air whistling up around the shirt, making it billow like a sail. I wanted keenly to get into the warmth.

'Don't you look smart, eh?' she said in her lightly accented English. She was holding a glass of white wine in her hand and her slim hips were jutting in a pair of black leggings. Marc was standing a few metres behind.

'Hey, Tay,' he said, pushing past his mum and ushering me into the house, 'the shoes look great!'

I smiled and nodded a little inanely. Marc's mum came back into the hallway with a bottle of beer for us both.

'Should be fun tonight, Tay. Lucy's invited loads of her mates from year twelve. They're so fit.' He said the last word with an upward inflection, which made him sound a bit like Ali G, which I think was the intention.

'Um, yeah!' I said, the hot knife of his comment stabbing directly into my heart and out through the back of my polo shirt. I immediately rushed to the assumption that it was Lucy who he had been texting when we were in London. The thought of Marc messaging her, laughing with her, kissing her, even, made me feel physically sick. In a bid to conceal the pain I responded, 'That Claire is really, um, fit!' The charade of pretending to like girls, whenever I was forced to play it, was roundly exhausting. The only person I really thought was fit in year twelve was Marc's mate Max, though I thought better of telling him that.

The beers went down quickly and, by the time we were finishing our third, it was time to go. The warm feeling of possibility, which I had felt on the drive to Marc's, had curdled into something resembling panic. I couldn't cope with the concept of Marc snogging one of the girls at the party, so, to drown the feeling out, I took a long final pull on the beer until I was sure there was nothing left at the bottom.

'I think that one might be finished, Tay,' said Marc, with a half-smile. My heart leaped in response to his handsomeness and all I wanted to do was kiss him, but instead I said, 'Do you think I can borrow a coat, Marc? It's pretty cold outside.'

Our plumes of frosted breath mingled before us, like a pair of ghosts embracing, as we walked down the bridleway that connected Marc's cul-de-sac to the main road. The mud, churned up by post-Christmas walkers, had frozen into stiff peaks, which felt sharp under the thin soles of my loafers.

Marc was wearing a pair of brown suede Russell & Bromley Chelsea boots that his mum had bought him for Christmas, and I was holding the blue Lyle & Scott pea coat he had lent me tightly around my torso for dear life.

'It was fun in London the other day, wasn't it, Marc?' I said. We hadn't spoken for a few minutes.

'Yeah!' said Marc. Pausing. 'I'm quite surprised that you're into Lauren, Tay.'

'What do you mean?' I asked quietly, attempting to hide my shock at his comment.

'I dunno, I just like more elegant girls. Girls who are a bit more, you know, like Liberty Ross. I don't like boobs on a girl, to be honest. And she goes to a pretty rough school . . .'

'Yeah, I don't like boobs either,' I didn't lie, 'but I love Lauren.' This time, I felt an overwhelming urge to defend my friend, perhaps because of the shame I felt for how I had acted in London, or maybe because I was subliminally annoyed at the prospect of Marc abandoning me for some unknown sixth former during the evening to come.

He turned to look at me with a hint of disappointment in his eyes before walking slightly ahead. He trudged the rest of the way with both of his hands lodged firmly into his back pockets, the starchy clouds of his breath bothering the night air.

Lucy's house was a pretty thatched cottage in a small village on the outskirts of town. Diffused amber light emanated from the front windows and, as we approached, I could see the outlines of people milling around in the kitchen. The occasional shriek of laughter wafted from a solitary open window upstairs, out of which a boy I didn't recognise was smoking. A swell of uninhibited conversation rippled out as Lucy opened the front door to greet us.

'Oh my gaawawd, hi Marc!' she shouted. She was wearing what looked like a half-folded napkin covered in sequins, the points of which hung low as if to direct unwitting eyes to her pierced belly button. Her hair was tied up into twists, and she had extended the reach of each of her Modigliani eyes with a lick of eyeliner. Her nose matched the elongated proportion of her frame, and her nostrils were small. Her features almost made her look like a catwalk model, but not quite. Her eyes were a touch too close together and her jaw had a weakness I recognised in my own.

'Hi, um, Teeeo, is it?' she said, with eyes closed as she hugged Marc tightly.

'No,' I said, 'it's Teo, like Mayo', instantly regretting it.

'Ha! Hi Mayo! That's what we'll call you.' Her eyes flicked to me only briefly as she gazed at Marc. 'Would you like a drink?' The 'you' was aimed solely at him, so I squeezed around them and walked into the house. Looking back, I tried to signal to Marc that he should join me, but he was laughing at a joke Lucy had made.

'Oh my God, TEO!' a familiar voice shouted. It was Jess. I hadn't seen her since we'd broken up from school for Christmas, which in the freshly-tilled landscape of teenagerhood felt like a decade. Her curlers had been used with particular aggression for the evening. In fact, she'd almost given herself a perm the corkscrews were so tight.

'I'm SO drunk,' she added. Her eyes were droopy and her mouth was downturned but somehow it still looked as though she was smiling. She couldn't stop touching her hair.

'Is Andy here?' I asked, slightly relieved that there was another person at the party I knew.

'Um, yeah. Let's go and get a drink.' She nuzzled her head into the curve of my shoulder. I felt the static crackle up my neck as we made our way to the drinks table, where she proceeded to talk at length about how disappointed she'd been by her Christmas presents that year. She'd hoped to get a new pair of GHD curlers but she'd instead been given a pair of Superdrug's own.

'Where's Andy?' I asked, assuming that he would be close by. I secretly hoped he wouldn't be at the party as Jess and Andy always seemed to have something to bicker about. But I knew the question would allow us to change the subject before Jess asked how my Christmas was. I didn't want to have to talk about myself or to think about the fact that I'd much rather be talking to Marc about shoes, watches, music, anything, than talking to her.

'It's OK. He's angry about something again,' she said, glumly, looking at her feet. 'He's so bloody overprotective,' she added, looking sad.

'Want another drink?' I asked, in a bid to distract her. I passed her a fresh bottle of Reef which I thought tasted like orange squash, my least favourite of the squashes, from the drinks table. I needed something stronger, and quickly spotted a 50cl bottle of Glen's vodka, which looked far more appealing. I grabbed it and stuffed it into my back pocket.

'I'm just going to the loo, Jess,' I said.

'OK, see you in a minute. Love you,' she said sloppily, without turning around. She had turned back to the party, a wayward ball of curls which bobbed in a sea of heads moving in time to Fatman Scoop and Crooklyn Clan's 'Be Faithful'.

Safely ensconced in the toilet, I removed the bottle from my pocket and hurriedly unscrewed the red lid. I took a long pull and the vodka felt cool as it hit the back of my throat and coated the length of my gullet. The boldness instilled by the beers was subtly multiplied, infusing me with a sense of confidence that felt bracing, like ice water being poured through the creases of my brain.

No longer cold, I ventured out into the hallway and threw Marc's pea coat onto the pile of outer layers that had amassed on a chair. Heading down the narrow space towards the front door, I turned right out onto the driveway where I hoped to find someone to give me a cigarette. As I walked out towards the parked cars, I suddenly heard an angry voice from behind, 'Oi, Tayo.'

I froze.

'What THE FUCK have you been doing with my sister?'

As I turned around to face the unknown voice, an intense pain hit my temple, jolting my head hard to the side. The punch knocked me onto the cold tarmac and my backside was the first thing to hit the ground. I heard a loud crack followed by the feeling of wet heat spreading across my trousers. My first instinct was that I'd peed myself, but as I came to my senses, I realised the bottle of vodka in my back pocket had smashed. I looked up to see the sole of a trainer come to meet me in the face. Behind it, I could make out the blurred impression of Andy.

'Why THE FUCK did you kiss my sister?' he shouted as he slammed his foot into my face. 'Who the FUCK do you think you are?'

The increasingly blurred outline of his sole came back towards my face once more, and I turned to protect myself from the next blow, wrapping my arms around my head.

'You fucking homo,' he shouted. 'You don't even like girls. Why her?'

'ANDY!' I heard Jess shout. Her tone was strange; partly horrified, but I also gleaned a sense of pride. She must have pulled him off me because the third blow never fell. The taste of hot metal was strong in my mouth, like sucking on the end of a used match, and I turned away as much to avoid Andy's ire as to separate myself from Jess.

'I'm so sorry, Teo,' I heard her say in my ear. I felt the dusting of her curls, like the tufts protruding from a shag carpet, flit across my face. 'I only told him I thought you fancied me a bit. I'm so angry!'

I groaned and tried to push her away as I cantilevered myself up. The bottle in my pocket had emptied the entirety of its contents over my bum and, as I got my feet, my sight still fuzzy, I reached to pull the shards of glass from the pouch of fabric. My fingers stung as the scored flesh met vodka.

'We've called the police!' shouted a voice I didn't recognise. 'Somebody stop him!'

'You're such an arsehole, Andy!' shouted Jess. 'Why would you do something like that?' Her hand fell away from my arm as I felt her shift away from me. Moving as quickly as I could, I headed towards the lights of the house. Inky amoebas danced across my eyes and I struggled to make out the figures surrounding me. I looked back to see Andy, whose face betrayed a mix of bemusement and fury, chasing Jess out of the driveway and down the unlit country lane.

'Where's Marc?' I asked quietly, to no one in particular.

'Um, I think he went outside, mate.' I hadn't noticed that Adam, who looked more like a meerkat than ever – wide eyed and on high alert – was standing next to me with his hand on my shoulder. 'He was with some girl.' My relief that Marc wasn't with Lucy was tempered by the concern that he might have found some other person to kiss who wasn't me. Adam and I hadn't spent much time together since the last night at Bar Kick but I was glad of his presence. It struck me that I didn't know anyone other than Marc, Jess, Andy, Lucy and now Adam at the party and I suddenly wanted very much to be anywhere but there. My eyes were still slightly fuzzy.

I needed to clean myself up but didn't want to use the loo next to the kitchen; it was in earshot of everyone, and I feared I might start crying. As I ascended the stairs in search of another bathroom, I started to take stock of the state of my outfit. There were rips in the knees of my cargo trousers, which I didn't really care about, but the loafers were badly scuffed. There were dark streaks of mud up the sides of each shoe, where I'd been jerking to get free on the tarmac as Andy had been kicking me, and there were dark grazes on the toes from where I'd pushed myself up and off the floor.

When I made it into the bathroom, I looked in the mirror to inspect the damage to my face. My eyes were wide and there was a small cut above my eyebrow. The socket underneath was bruised. I washed away the dried blood and removed the last shards of glass from the back of my trousers. As embarrassed as I was for having failed so dismally to defend myself during the beating, a point which I feared would prove once and for all to everyone at the party that I was in fact gay, I was more mortified about the giant wet patch that had stained my crotch. I used some toilet paper to pat down the remaining spirit, which was cold against my skin.

Once I felt I looked presentable enough, I made my way out into the landing where I noticed a large porthole window looking out onto the garden behind the house. The glass was obscured slightly, the kind usually found in bathrooms, but through it I could just about make out what looked like a large figure writhing around on the lawn outside. Perhaps it was the alcohol still coursing through my veins, or maybe it was the fact that I'd been kicked in the head, but the air in the house seemed heavier, parting around my limbs like honey as I made my way closer to the window. I think I knew what awaited me on the other side, but with robotic smoothness, I turned the brass catch and opened it wide.

On the grass Marc was lying next to a girl I didn't recognise. Her hand, which I could see even from a distance had neatly polished nails the colour of an uncooked chicken fillet, sat on the curve of his thigh. He must have left Lucy inside. Marc's left hand was on the small of the girl's back and he was nuzzling into her neck, lightly kissing her collarbone. Her head was thrown back in a kind of staged ecstasy, while Marc's right hand worked its way around one of her breasts, which were small. He was twisting it with about the same level of force as I'd just twisted the window catch.

Quickly, not wanting to witness anything more of the scene, I pulled the window closed and backed away from it, hoping that neither he nor the girl had seen me. The cut above my eye was beginning to hurt and a lump, around the size of a small golf ball, was growing in my throat. Now I knew the tears were coming so instead of returning downstairs, I went back into the bathroom. Surveying myself in the mirror, I had turned a shade of greyish mauve, which highlighted the injuries on my face. I fought back the hot sting of tears and pulled my phone out of my pocket, which had mercifully not been damaged by my fall or the vodka. Instinctively, I dialled Grandma's home telephone number because I knew Mum and Dad wouldn't have their phones on. The time in the top right corner of the screen read 11.48 p.m.

It took about six rings for someone to answer. 'Hello! Welcome to the pard-y residence!'

I could hear from her voice that she was a good three glasses in. 'Mum?' I said quietly.

'Darling, what's happened? What's the matter? Are you with Marc?' She suddenly sounded sober.

'Mum.' I paused, not able to stop the tears. 'I've been beaten up. Can you come and get me?'

'Oh shit, oh fuck. JAN! JAN! Teo's been beaten up. Oh shit. Darling, where are you? Dad's going to come now.'

'I'm coming, DAO!' I heard Dad shout in the background. 'Don't blahdy move!'

I hung up the phone and sat down on the toilet seat, which was covered with a white fleece finished with lacey sides, a loo-shaped doily. I didn't want to go back downstairs and face the group, and I certainly didn't want to see Marc. I didn't blame him for kissing someone, I just wanted so badly for him to kiss me, to protect me, though that evening it became abundantly clear that was never going to happen. I didn't want to admit it to myself, but the hope which had been growing inside me – the pilot light of tentative, just-whispered belief that Marc might want to be with me one day – had finally been extinguished.

I decided that I would stay in the bathroom until Dad arrived. Ignoring the occasional rattles on the handle made by drunk revellers in need of a wee, the New Year's celebrations came and went. Strains of 'Auld Lang Syne' long since finished, I was hopeful that when I emerged, the effects of the celebratory tequila shots might have kicked in and people would have forgotten that I'd just smashed a vodka bottle with my bum. Eventually, I heard a familiar voice shouting downstairs.

'DAO?'

I was flooded with a sense of relief. 'DAO? Oi, have you seen my son?' I heard him ask someone in the hallway. 'Get your blahhdy hand OFF of my shoulder mate. DAO!'

I walked out of the room and down the stairs. I didn't want to risk bumping into Andy or Marc, so I took the steps slowly, stretching my head around each banister tentatively to see who was there.

'Hi, Jan,' I heard Marc say. He must have abandoned the girl on the lawn and come inside. 'I'm not sure where Tay is, let me help you find him.'

'Where were you when he was getting his head kicked in?' I could hear the anger in Dad's voice, and though his ire would usually be a source of embarrassment, in that moment it made me feel safe. I was suddenly desperate to be in the warmth of my grandma's house, celebrating with my family, so I moved quickly towards the hall.

'Head kicked in?' I heard Marc stammer, 'Who . . . ?'

As I walked into the hall Marc stopped speaking. I tried to avoid his eye as I looked in Dad's direction, but I didn't recognise the furious man in front of me. The body was undeniably Dad's – wide-leg jeans, brown moleskin jacket, white shirt, brown boat shoes – but the face looked more like a mangled Andy Warhol. Perched on his nose were a pair of lensless black spectacles, and on his head, a matted platinum blonde wig that looked as though it had accidentally been ironed.

'Oh, blahdy hell, Dao, look at your face?' he cried. 'Are you OK? Where's the person who did this, Dao? Show me who he is.' It was difficult to take him seriously.

'Honestly, Dad, he's gone. I'm fine. Let's just go,' I pleaded between my teeth. Urging him through the hallway, we passed Marc and the girl, who were now holding hands. I spotted Lucy looking on dolefully from the kitchen and I felt a brief pang of perverse kinship with her, given that she'd been spurned by Marc, just like I felt I had. My friend tried to grab my arm as I passed him, but I kept moving.

'Tay,' Marc called after us. 'Got your back?'

'See you later, Marc,' I said, pulling Dad along as we left the house.

Slamming the car door shut, I sunk as low as possible into my seat. A sea of sadness swelled inside me as I looked down at the ruined loafers. I could probably never wear them again. I pulled each one off my feet and pushed them under the seat. As Dad walked towards the car, I looked down at my phone, hoping that Marc would call or text and ask me to come back into the party. The sea swelled higher as Dad got into the car next to me. Before he had a chance to say anything I said, flatly, 'Dad, I think you forgot to take off the wig.'

He looked at me blankly for a second before reaching up to pull off the flattened albino hamster that was affixed to his head.

'Oh, fucking hell,' he said, his eyes were still wide with anger but the fury was countered by the wide smile which broke out on his face. 'Why didn't you tell me?' he asked, laughing.

'I dunno,' I said, but as the noise left my mouth, I felt the tears start to fall, the hot salty water stung the grazes around my eyes as Dad pulled me into his chest. He hadn't hugged me like that for a long time and I was surprised by how good it felt.

As Dad began reversing out of the driveway, I picked up my phone.

'Lau,' I typed. 'I'm so sorry I didn't come to your party tonight. I was beaten up. Happy New Year.'

Within three seconds of pressing send, the screen of my phone read, 'Lauren D New Calling'.

CHAPTER 8

The Vivienne Westwood T-Shirt

'Teo, we've been walking for hours,' moaned Mum from what sounded like a good five metres behind me. 'Where is this place?' There was a newly sharpened edge to her tone, which hadn't been present the past fifteen times she'd complained, so I considered that it might be the moment to take her a little more seriously.

'Louise said it was in the Eixample district, which is where we are, so it can't be far,' I shouted back over my shoulder. Mum's cousin Louise, who had hair the colour of Campari and a mouth like a kindly platypus, had lived in Barcelona for well over a decade. We were staying with her for a long weekend, during which we'd spent indolent hours eating cheap yet delicious tapas and gawping, crane-necked, at Gaudi's gloopy architectural creations. Louise had recommended a specific vintage shop to visit before we returned to the UK. 'Why don't we get a drink and look on the map?' I suggested, in an attempt to shake my dread at the thought of going home.

After a few minutes, we found a small café with a rainbow flag fluttering outside it. Looking down the road to the left of us, I noticed that the streets were heaving with men. Men holding hands, men with enormous muscles, men with multiple shopping bags and little dogs, young men and old men. I'd caught glimpses of a similar world in London, on fleeting trips to Soho en route to the theatre with Mum, but never before had I witnessed up close this level of unabashed gayness. I felt momentarily embarrassed, concerned what Mum might make of it; that she might align me with these exuberantly demonstrative creatures of a world I didn't yet fully feel a part. But as we took our seats at the small table, the relaxed look on her face stopped me from worrying.

We sat in silence, surveying the activity for a while as we sipped our drinks. A boy who must have been about my age, fifteen or just over, walked past wearing a tight T-shirt finished with a Breton stripe. He had on a pair of chino shorts and some green Havaianas flip-flops and he was handsome, like a young Adam Garcia. His chin was dimpled, his brows were thick and they arched elegantly over his eyes, which were the colour of the coffee being poured at the table beside us. I caught his eye and he smiled at me. I checked to see that Mum hadn't seen and smiled back.

Turning my attention to the task in hand, I attempted to decipher the scrawl of Spanish words littering the spidery map of Barcelona's metropolitan area. 'OK, so apparently it's just down the street,' I said.

Mum, who had quickly thrown back her favoured Iberian refreshment trifecta of '*zumo de naranja y café negro y aqua con gas*' seemed newly invigorated as she brushed herself off and stood up from her chair. 'Lovely, darling, let's get going!' She paused, flapping her arms at her side and smiling. 'Isn't it beautiful here!'

Walking slowly so as not to miss it, eventually we stumbled on what Cousin Louise – a surprise *Harry Potter* fan – had described as 'a gem of a vintage shop, which looks as though it belongs in Diagon Alley'. She hadn't been wrong. With its peeling green painted sign, lack of discernible name and air of ragged eclecticism, it looked as though it belonged in nineteenth-century Montmartre more than it did twenty-first-century Barcelona. Imbued with a glorious air of dishevelled flamboyance you would be hard pushed to find in London, the shop was a world away from the polished boutiques and gilded flagships of Knightsbridge I'd visited with Marc a few months before, and was all the more beguiling for it.

Outside the entrance, countless rails of old theatre costumes, military pieces and designer clothes were hanging in a higgledy-piggledy fashion. There were leopard print jeans from Jean Paul Gaultier, satin jackets from Maison Margiela, unbranded silk shirts finished with ornate baroque patterns, which looked as though they came from Ming-era China, and voluminous military overcoats.

Eagerly, I started rummaging and trying things on: a pair of heavily embroidered silk parachute pants, which were so dear that I didn't even bother asking Mum if I could have them. A navy-blue sweatshirt with gold naval buttons from Gucci, which was even more expensive. A bearskin hat, which looked and smelled as though it had been worn by a soldier in the Crimean War, and a voluminous Ann Demeulemeester overshirt in satin, which I knew I would never be able to wear anywhere other than in the confines of my bedroom.

After what felt like hours, I eventually alighted on a black Vivienne Westwood T-shirt, which, despite its relative simplicity, seemed to shine out like a seam of gold from its place on the jam-packed rail. I knew from reading Mum's old copies of *Vogue* and from doing my own fashion research on Encarta (as much to impress Marc as to satisfy my own curiosity) that Westwood had reinvented womenswear, sending out voluptuous models in eighteenth-century crinolines and towering platform shoes, but I didn't know that she designed men's clothes too.

An expanded print of a blossoming peony was plastered onto the left shoulder of the T-shirt, with a trail of petals littering down to the naval. The back hem was considerably longer than the front, and it was just about bold enough to draw attention without looking, well, too gay. Despite being fifty euros ('for a T-shirt!'), Mum bought it for me and I was elated. It was a perfectly formed piece of fabric, proof that

I'd lived this bold new life, a bright cosmopolitan life full of promise, even if only for a long weekend: a life free from Guildford, free from school and, most importantly, free from Marc. Because shortly before our trip, on an evening like any other, the unthinkable had happened.

*

'Teo, it's Vicky for you,' Mum shouted up the stairs. It was early January, and I was lying on my bed, ruminating over whether to text Marc. We'd not spoken since New Year's Eve. 'But don't be long, I'm expecting a call from Grandma.' Mum was always expecting a call from Grandma.

I wasn't in the mood for gossiping with Vicky, but she never usually called me at home. If we weren't chatting on MSN messenger, we preferred to send each other faxes from our dads' respective machines, purely for the novelty of the medium, so my interest was piqued by the fact that she'd decided to contact me the old-fashioned way.

'OK! I'll get it upstairs,' I responded. I went up to my parents' lair, sat down on their candy-striped bedspread, and picked up the phone. Mum's discarded stilettos, ankle boots and kitten heels were pouring out of wardrobe like jewellery spilling from a box.

'Hello?' I said, tentatively.

'Hey, Tay!' said Vicky. 'How are you?'

'I'm fine,' I said, sensing a note of eagerness in her voice. 'What's the matter?'

'Um, well.' She paused. 'Jess Jones has been telling everyone that Andy beat you up because you told her you were gay.'

I felt myself float out from the confines of my body and up into the cobweb-dusted recesses of my parent's bedroom. From my new vantage point, I watched the boy below, with his sloped shoulders and bad short back and sides, arms angled outward like the truncated wings of a jumbo jet. He looked like a stranger, and I felt pity for him.

'Um, what do you mean?' I heard myself ask.

'Well, you know you said he beat you up because Jess told him you fancied her?'

'Yes . . .'

'Well, she's saying that Andy didn't want her hanging out with you because you're gay and that's why he beat you up.'

The floating version of me stayed exactly where I was, refusing to budge.

'But I didn't tell her that.'

'Yeah, well, she said that you told her and that the way you were with Marc made it obvious.'

An anvil of emotion fell down through my pelvis, dragging me back into my body with a jolt of inertia that made me nauseous. 'Does Marc know?'

'I don't know, but did you hear he's going out with some girl who he met on New Year's Eve?!' Vicky's ability to pivot from one gossip topic to another could have been considered an Olympic event. The anvil went past my toes and down through the floor.

'No, I hadn't,' I said. It was cool in my parents' bedroom

but marbles of sweat were streaming from my temples. My hands were slick. 'I've got to go now, Vik, see you tomorrow.'

'OK, bye, loves ya!'

I hung up the phone and stared down at my feet. I knew I had made a mistake confiding in Jess that night in Bar Kick. I should have been more cautious, but after Lauren's response had been so kind and emboldening, the urge to tell someone else – anyone else – combined with the copious alcohol consumption had clouded my judgment. I wanted to call Marc but I didn't know what I would say. When I walked back into my bedroom, the weight of the revelation made it feel like I was wading through over-refrigerated soup.

As I lay back onto my bed, I willed myself to believe that it had all been a misunderstanding – that Jess hadn't, in fact told anybody, and that my secret was still safe. My brain felt flooded, emotions rushing through my synapses like ferrets down drainpipes. Tears pricked in the corners my eyes, but I didn't feel sad. If anything, I felt numb; powerless to stop the wrecking ball of change that was about to come crashing through my life.

The next morning, I went into school early, long before anyone else was due to arrive. The form room felt safe somehow, and even though Mrs Thallow wasn't in yet, I was sure that her ferocity would protect me from my classmates in some small way. I willed her to arrive before them. As the minutes ticked by, I tore my fingernails down to the beds using my front teeth, collecting each of the shards in a pile on the table in front of me. Eventually, people began to filter slowly into the room.

'Look, there's Gayo,' I heard Carla, a cross-eyed girl with oddly slim legs and scraped back hair, whisper behind her hand to Emma.

'Don't look at my arse, van den Pooper,' said Chris, a red-head with a bum so flat and trousers so baggy I wouldn't have known where to look if I'd wanted to.

I remained as still as I could, sphinx-like, determined not to rise. When eventually Anna and Vicky walked through the door, arm in arm, they both looked over with such an uncharacteristic level of sympathy that I felt the golf ball return to my throat, so I looked down at my neoprene Quiksilver pencil case and waited for the feeling to pass.

'How are you, Tay?' asked Vicky.

'I'm good!' I said, loudly, hoping that everyone would hear.

I continued watching the door for the length of registration, but Marc never appeared. Our first lesson was art and, as I made my way there, I stared at my phone, wondering whether or not to text him. Something inside told me that I shouldn't – that the reason he was off had something to do with me, something bad. I slipped the phone back into my pocket and filed into the art room, which was large and dotted with cubic workbenches in lieu of traditional tables.

'Now, who can tell me about Michaelangelo,' asked Miss Jacobs, the school's raven-haired Head of Art. She had a penchant for wearing paint-covered overalls and often had wayward strands of gesso streaked through her hair. Unlike many of the other teachers, who would crumble and call for the head at even the slightest sniff of disobedience, Miss Jacobs was made of stern stuff. She also had a soft spot for me, I knew, since I'd revealed to her that art was my favourite subject, but I'd quickly discovered that being the focus of her attention could be as much a blessing as it could a curse.

The entire room ignored her question and carried on talking, so she banged the table and shouted, 'Come on! Michelangelo! Who knows anything about him?'

'He was a bender, wasn't he, miss?' shouted Chris, squinting his foxy eyes across the room at me.

'No, he's a turtle!' shouted Lorrie.

'No, you idiot, he's a painter, and he's a poofter,' retorted Alex, adding loudly, 'just like him.' He pointed at me. Sharp as metal, the barb flew across the room and into my ear. Half the class laughed and the other half seemed to collectively pull a sharp intake of breath. I felt Vicky's hand on my arm as I looked down at the table. I was as angry as I was upset, but I tried hard not to let it show.

'It makes not a blind bit of difference what his sexuality was,' said Miss Jacobs. 'But I'll tell you what, I don't know many straight men from history who could match his level of talent. There's no one I can think of, actually,' she said with a downward inflection, winking at me. I think she thought she was being helpful.

Thankfully, the rest of the lesson passed swiftly and without further incident. Nonetheless, when the bell went, I made for the door as quickly as I possibly could.

'Teo, can you stay behind for a minute?' Miss Jacobs shouted over the throng. I hated her with the intensity of a kiln fire at that moment.

'Is everything OK?' she asked once the rest of my classmates had filed out of the room. 'You know you can talk to me about anything. If you're struggling, I might be able to help.'

'No, I'm fine, Miss Jacobs!' I lied.

'OK, then. Well, I'm always here if you need me. We should also discuss your A level options in a few weeks. I think you should consider art.'

'OK, definitely, will do. Thanks!' I said, running out of the room as quickly as I could. Although I knew I should be as concerned about my A levels as Miss Jacobs was, the only thing I was capable of thinking about in that moment was where Marc was and how he and I might be able to get back to the way we were. His response to Andy's attack had certainly damaged our relationship, but the thought of not having him in my life at all felt like too much to bear.

After making it through the day largely unscathed, save for the occasional puerile comment, that evening I lay in bed reading John Webster's *The Duchess of Malfi*. A welcome distraction, it was our assigned GCSE text for English Literature and despite everyone in my class bemoaning the fact that they couldn't get to grips with the language, I loved the bloody tale of murder and revenge in medieval Italy, not least because it helped remind me that things are often much worse for other people than they are for you.

Engrossed by how ruthlessly Bosola encouraged the

Duchess to eat apricots in order to induce her labour, thereby proving that she was pregnant by outlawed Antonio, I barely felt the gentle vibration of my phone on the bedspread beside me. It was from Marc, and the four short words that punctuated the screen sent a rush of blood straight to my head.

`'Tay, are you gay?'`

It was teetering above freezing outside but I was suddenly hot, so I pushed off the bedspread and began tugging at the collar of my oversized T-shirt, pumping for air. I had known this moment would eventually come but I hadn't expected the question to be posed so bluntly. A roiling wave of frustration mixed with panic washed over me and I felt my eyes well up as I looked down at my phone

`'Hey, Marc. Yeah, I think I might be. Or bi. I dunno. Still not sure. Who told u?'`

No. Stupid, I sound like I'm in *Hollyoaks*.

`'Hey, Marc. Yup, what of it?'`

I could never be that cool.

`'Hi Marc. Yes, I am. Are you?'`

No.

```
'Hey, Marc, I think I might be. I'm not
sure. Who told you? Do you mind?'
```

I needed to know that this didn't mean the end of the friendship, that it wouldn't mean I was no longer a part of his life.
That he would continue to have my back, despite everything
that had happened between us. I pressed send and stared at
the screen, willing him to respond quickly. My heart was
racing so fast that I was sure I could see it pumping beneath
my shirt.

I couldn't bear the waiting, turning my phone over, and
then back again, and then over again. I picked up the book
and tried to focus on the words on the page in front of me.
The Duchess was about to give birth, but even the misery
of her situation wasn't quite enough to distract me from the
uncertainty of my own.

```
1 new message
```

I wished that I had Lauren there to read it out for me.

```
'No, it's OK. I just wish you'd told me
sooner.'
```

I stared at the black pixels swimming in their swampy digital
sea until they became abstracted, meaningless. Just as spoken
phrases lose their connection to reality when they're repeated
over and over again, so too did his message, until it read

precisely how I wanted it to read. With mechanical speed, I typed my response. Ten short words, words which individually held no weight – words which wouldn't amount to anything if you said them in the wrong order or split them into five separate pairs – but together they carried a gravity which the blindness of my feelings made me ignore.

'I think I might be in love with you, Marc.'

I pressed send before I had a chance to think twice about what I was doing. The hopeful part of me – the brave, bold part of me, the part of me that knew we shared a real connection – had real faith that Marc would return the sentiment. But there was another part of me, a barely concealed part, like a poison bulb pushing through the thin membrane of my ego, that knew this most likely wouldn't happen. It was that part that made me turn my phone off after I didn't hear back from him for over half an hour, and it was that part that made me bury it under the bed. Like a bundled pair of white socks.

By the time Dad dropped us off at school the following morning, I had still heard nothing. My stomach had transformed into a tight knot of anxiety. As we exited the car, I told Romy that I would wait and meet Vicky at the church instead of walking with her down to school.

'You OK, Tay?' she asked. Romy knew I usually met my friend down at the other drop-off point, a good 500 metres down the road, because Vicky's parents lived on the other side of Guildford, and that I was therefore probably lying.

'Yeah, I'm fine, Ro, don't worry, you go on.'

'OK,' she said, biting her bottom lip. She walked away, scraping her hair back behind her ears and hiking her skirt up shorter than Mum or Dad would ever let her wear it. Once I was sure that she was gone, I walked behind the church, where the stoner kids would congregate at the end of the day.

The church, which had been built in the seventies and named after one of the earliest twentieth-century popes, backed onto a chain-link fence that protected a glut of rhododendron bushes that belonged to the next-door property. I picked up a few of the loose bits of willow twine that had fallen from the winter-stripped tree above and began plaiting them around the links. As I let the plaits go, the springy twines bouncing back into shape, I took my phone out of my backpack, which was at my feet, and checked it again. The only message I had received was from Lauren.

```
'How are you, Tay? Is everything OK? Call
me x.'
```

I couldn't bring myself to contact her. The last thing I wanted to do was discuss what had happened, even with Lauren. I felt ashamed, humiliated. I checked the time. Enough had passed that registration would be over and that our first classes would just about be starting. I had English that morning and, as Marc was in a lower group, I knew I wouldn't have to face him. I picked up my bag, dusted off the backside of my trousers and plucked one of the willow plaits that had come loose. A good luck talisman.

When I made it inside, I slowed my pace, willing the lessons to have started and no wayward students to be straggling in the halls. Turning the corner past the staff room, I made my way towards the English block. As I did, Marc, Luke, Rich, Atif and Aaron stumbled out from the dining hall into the corridor ahead of me. Marc led the group, pushing one of the double doors open with his left hand, laughing in exactly the same carefree way as he had at the traffic lights over half a decade before. He was simulating an act that involved much jutting of hips, with his right hand in the air, index, and middle fingers aloft.

I froze, knowing it was too late for them not to see me, and as they turned in my direction, the laughing stopped. Marc put his hands in his pockets, looked at me with one eyebrow subtly raised, and turned away, leading the group back in the opposite direction, out towards the playground. The rest of the boys followed suit, the only recognition their silence. As they walked away, Aaron, who was tossing a football back and forth between his hands, turned back and smirked, before running to catch up with the others. 'Anyway, and then I . . . ' Marc's voice, once again raucous, disappeared around the corner and out into the rain-soaked playground.

I took a deep breath and unclenched my fists. Opening my palms, I saw three half-moons the colour of ripe plums with milky edges, embedded just below my heart line and above my head line. I thrust my hands deep into the pockets of my trousers and began walking to my lesson.

'Ah, good of you to make an appearance, Mr van den Broeke,' said Mrs Damson, my English teacher, as I sloped into the room as subtly as I could. 'We were just about to discuss the Duchess of Malfi's apricots, so to speak. I trust you did the reading?'

I waited until I had taken my seat and removed my blazer to answer. The rest of the class turned to look at me. Sat in the front row, Anna mouthed, 'You OK?' which I ignored by looking down at my bag. Chris was sniggering in the opposite corner.

'I did, Miss.' I sounded sullen.

'Well, what did you make of it?' Mrs Dorian did not have much patience for either grumpiness or tardiness.

'I guess it's the moment of her undoing, Miss?'

'I couldn't have put it better myself.'

When I got home that night, I didn't stop in the kitchen to pick up any packets of Mini Cheddars, and I didn't call Lauren to see if she wanted to go and try to get a drink at the local pub. I didn't even plonk myself on the sofa to watch the early evening televisual trifecta of *Neighbours*, *Simpsons* and *Hollyoaks* – the only in-house-ordained mid-week programming schedule on which Romy and I fully agreed. Instead, I went straight up to my room, shut the door, and lay on my bed. I didn't get changed, I didn't take off my shoes, I didn't pull off my tie with my usual garrotting glee. I looked at my phone and then looked at my phone again.

If I listened to our songs, to Harry Nielsen or U2 or Interpol then maybe, just maybe, Marc would pick up on the telekinetic waves and realise that the right thing to do would be to ring me, to respond, to text.

I started typing a message. `Hey, Marc. I'm really sorry for saying that. Can we just be mates again? T.'

I looked at it the words written on the screen and held my breath. Just as I was about to press send, I heard the opening guitar chords of 'Iris' by the Goo Goo Dolls drifting through my earphones. Desperate to avoid the heart-wrenching opening verse, I hastily pulled them from my ears before walking out of my bedroom. With a lump in my throat the size of a large apricot, I was shuddering. I switched on the light of the bathroom and locked the door behind me.

Leaning back against the door, I felt my face begin to crease involuntarily as the apricot rose to meet my epiglottis. In an attempt to steady myself, I put both of my hands on either side of the medicine cabinet and focused on the small brass key positioned in its lock. When Romy and I were little, my parents would hide this key for fear of us gaining access and ingesting too many HalibOrange tablets. It now lived there permanently, more to keep the door from swinging open than anything else.

I looked at myself in the mirror. My shoulders were slumped, my face blotchy, like the surface of a strawberry

Müller Rice. Opening the medicine cabinet, I felt around until I found the bottle of paracetamol, which Mum hid at the back. Mum's biggest fear was that Romy or I would one day accidentally take too many when we had a headache – she often intoned, dramatically, that any more than two would most likely result in liver failure and inevitable death – so she made a point of hiding them as thoroughly as possible, though I could have thought of less obvious places.

Squeezing the sides of the top of the bottle, I turned it clockwise, the contorting plastic pinching at the insides of my fingers. I removed the cap and looked inside. There were at least fifteen pills in the bottle, which, according to my mum's calculations, at least, would be more than enough to do the job. I started shaking the chalky discs into my hand, one by one. My face began to crease up again and I felt the torrid streams of tears carve their way through the crevices, as I counted the pills. Ten, eleven, twelve . . .

'Teo, dinner's ready!' Mum shouted up the stairs.

I heard my sister catapult herself out of her chair in the sitting room and into the kitchen.

'Romy, walk properly, sweedhard,' said Dad tersely.

As if returning to consciousness from a dream, I stuffed the pills back into the bottle as quickly as I had counted them out. I screwed on the lid frenetically and shoved the bottle back into the cabinet with shaking hands. I couldn't quite believe what I had just considered doing, and I wanted to dispose of the evidence as quickly as possible. I turned off the light in the bathroom so that I couldn't look at myself in the mirror and I wiped my cheeks with a towel. As I walked out of the small, stuffy room, I flapped my hands in front of my eyes in a bid to get rid of the blotches.

'Come on, Teo, it's getting cold!' Mum shouted again.

I walked down the stairs slowly, concerned that they would see I'd been crying. When I opened the door into the kitchen, Dad was sat with his back to me and Mum looked up.

'Are you OK, Teo?' asked Mum.

'Yeah, I'm fine, just tired,' I said. 'I fell asleep.'

She didn't look convinced. Romy was pushing a forkful of chicken casserole and mashed potatoes into her mouth and paused the task in hand to look up at me.

'I left the skins on the mashed potatoes, darling, because the skins are the best part for you!' said Mum.

'Not too much, please,' I said. 'I'm not that hungry.'

We ate in silence for a little while until Dad asked, 'So how was school, Dao?'

Looking down at my plate, I tried to focus on the flecks of muddy brown amidst the white clouds of mash. I willed myself not to cry, but a salty drop fell into the tomato sauce of the casserole and my face began to crease once more. The more I resisted, the more it seemed to fold in on itself, like a cardboard box left out in the rain.

'Darling, what is it?' asked Mum. 'What's the matter?'

'Dao, what's wrong?' repeated Dad. 'Tell us.'

'Jan, Romy, maybe you should go into the other room,' said Mum, softly. 'Please . . .'

'But, Mum, I haven't finish—' started Romy.

'Go on, sweetheart,' said Mum.

I kept staring at my plate, willing the border of green porcelain to expand out like the wings of a manta ray and swallow me into a great blue unknown.

Romy shut the door as she and Dad left the room. Their plates remained, piled high with mashed potato and casserole. The fingerprints on Dad's water glass made the steam rising behind it shimmer.

'Teo, what's wrong?' Mum had her hand on the back of my neck and was stroking the bony plateau beneath my right ear with her finger, the cold metal of her wedding ring drumming against my skin. 'You know you can tell me anything sweetheart, don't you?' she said. Her fringe tickled gently against my hand, which was balled up in a fist, shielding the side of my face. I still hadn't looked away from my plate. I dipped my head slightly in assent. I felt like a little boy, unable or unwilling to communicate the fear I was feeling, the intense shock of rejection, which had been reverberating around my body since my encounter with Marc in the morning; the overwhelming sadness that had flooded my brain and was now trickling into my stomach and beyond, down into my legs.

'Teo, darling, look at me,' she said, taking her hands in mine. I let her but I still didn't look up from my plate. 'Darling, whatever it is you will always be my son. My wonderful, thoughtful, intelligent, beautiful boy, and I will always love you.' She paused. I looked up at her slightly. Her face was close to mine and her eyes were wide. She leaned forward and kissed me on the cheek; she smelled of Neutrogena hand cream and bay leaves. Her silver necklace caught the light from the extractor fan, which was still on behind us. 'You can tell me anything. Nothing is too big that we can't overcome it together.'

I nodded, more perceptibly this time. The tears had started falling again and I pushed hard against the heaving in my chest.

'Darling. I think I know what's the matter,' she whispered, pausing. She stroked my cheek with her finger and came closer to my ear. 'Are you gay, Teo?'

The question came as less of a surprise than I thought it might. I suppose I had always assumed that Mum knew. She had seen the porn on the computer, after all. She'd seen me wearing dresses, she'd never questioned me about girlfriends. But somehow, I also thought that was just because girlfriends weren't the kind of thing mums and sons talked about. Mums and sons went to galleries together, they talked about which Shakespeare plays they liked best, they sang James Taylor's 'You've Got a Friend' together when other parents and siblings weren't around, on long car journeys.

'Darling, I love you so much,' said Mum, pulling me into a tight hug. 'And I always will.' I started crying again and pulled back from her again wiping at my eyes.

'Everyone at school knows,' I told her quietly.

'How do they know?' she asked gently.

'Jess Jones told them,' I said. 'And Marc knows too.'

'And how was he about it?'

'I told him—' I paused, wiping my other eye with the heel of my hand '—I told him I loved him.'

'Oh, darling,' she said, pulling me in again. 'The pain you're feeling now won't be there forever. I promise. It'll be gone before you know it.'

I nodded into her shoulder again.

'Please don't tell Dad, Mum. Or the uncles. Or Grandma. Or Romy. Or anyone?'

'I won't, darling. Don't worry.' She paused. 'I tell you what, why don't we get away for a weekend together, just you and me.' She looked at me searchingly. 'Perhaps we could go and visit Louise in Barcelona? You've not been there before, have you? It's surprisingly balmy in February!'

*

In the weeks that followed our trip, the pain I had felt about Marc began to recede, just as Mum had said it would. The bright glimmer of cosmopolitan existence I had been treated to in Barcelona had shed some welcome light on the situation, and I felt buoyed. The taunts had fizzled out at school too, and the wrecking ball I had been so afraid of swung back out of my life as swiftly as it had careened into it, leaving behind considerably less mess than I had originally feared.

My school announced that there would be a mufti day on the Friday before the Easter break, meaning that students would be allowed to wear any clothes they liked, so long as they brought in a cake to sell at the charity bake sale.

Traditionally, mufti day had been my favourite day of the year, an opportunity to wear all the new clothes I'd amassed since the last – my DKNY jumper, my Levi's jeans, my Mostro trainers – but this year, the day felt burdened with an extra weight. I knew that whichever clothes I chose to wear, even if I wore the same T-shirts and jeans as everyone else, they would be judged as signifiers of my freshly realised homosexuality.

'What are you going to wear tomorrow, Vik?' I asked her on the phone the night before.

'Oh, I dunno,' she said, feigning nonchalance. 'Maybe my Miss Sixty bootcut jeans, my Faith boots, you know, the brown leather ones, a pink spaghetti strap top from Jane Norman, and my new boho disc belt from Oasis.' She paused. 'I haven't given it much thought.'

'Ah, OK,' I said.

'What are you going to wear to mufti day, Ro?' I asked my sister later that evening.

'Umm, my new Skechers, you know the pink ones, my purple Miss Selfridge pedal pushers, a pink crop top from Etam and that blue fluffy coat Mum and Dad got me for Christmas,' she said, matter-of-factly. 'Do you think that sounds OK?' she asked, biting her nails.

'It sounds great,' I said, panicking slightly.

I went back into my room and pulled the black Vivienne Westwood T-shirt out from the brown paper bag I had brought it home from Barcelona in. Away from the glamour of the city, I had almost felt scared of the T-shirt and what it meant. I hadn't been able to bring myself to hang it in my wardrobe, let alone wear it, but now, I decided, was the time to be brave. If I was going to be judged for wearing anything, I might as well be judged for wearing something fabulous.

*

The next morning, I woke up early, showered, and attempted to sort out my hair as best I could. I used the nail scissors above the bathroom cabinet to trim the fluffy bits from the edges and I applied a large globule of extra-hold hair gel before combing it forward into a French crop, not unlike Ross's from *Friends*. I used Mum's tweezers to pluck the extra hairs from the middle of my eyebrows and I scrubbed my face extra hard with Clearasil. I went back into my bedroom and pulled on my newer, slimmer vintage Levi's. Surveying the spread of shoes at the bottom of my wardrobe, I noticed that my Gucci loafers didn't look nearly as ragged as I remembered. After a quick brush, I'd managed to get most of the dirt off. Finally, I carefully removed the tag from my new T-shirt before pulling it over my head.

I looked in the mirror and, for the first time in what felt like a very long time, felt a surge of pride in my appearance. I looked somehow older and more erect in my new T-shirt and I felt ready to face whatever the day had to throw at me. No one at school wore Vivienne Westwood, or Gucci. I put on the long black overcoat Mum had bought me in the French Connection sale, which worked well with the T-shirt, and went out to sit in the front seat of her car.

'Why does Teo always get to sit in the front?' moaned Romy as she walked out of the house in her outfit, which made her look a bit like a Bratz doll. 'I never get to sit in the front seat.'

'You look nice, darling,' Mum said to me absent-mindedly, resolutely ignoring my sister as she folded herself into the vehicle.

I requested that she drop us at the front of the school, rather than the church, because I wanted to show Anna and Vicky my outfit before anyone else saw it. The nerves I had mastered in front of the mirror that morning were beginning to flicker in my stomach, and I was eager for the approval of my closest friends. It was a bright April day and the air had a pristine quality, like fresh writing paper. I moved quickly inside and to my form room, being careful to keep my T-shirt wrapped within my coat. Opening the double doors to the main corridor, I was relieved to find it deserted, save for Anna and Vicky, who were chatting in the entranceway to the classroom.

'Let's see it then,' said Vicky, as I walked towards them, sashaying slightly. I opened my coat wide and skipped forward, scuffing the old parquet floor with the black rubber front panel of my loafers as I went.

'Oh my God, it's SO nice,' said Anna, which instantly put me at ease.

'I know, right?!' Laughing, we bustled into the classroom, where I peeled off the coat and threw it over the back of my chair, before excusing myself to go to the loo.

A flotilla of floor-to-ceiling white porcelain urinals which dated back to the fifties lined the wall on one side of the room, and on the other was a row of toilet cubicles shielded by laminate doors the colour of urinal cakes. When I had finished, I went to wash my hands at the large island in the middle of the room. As I turned on the tap, one of the cubicle doors opened and Marc walked slowly out of it. His softly curled hair was slightly longer than usual and he was wearing the same outfit that he'd worn to meet me outside Burger King just one year before, save for the Aviators.

The petals fluttered in my stomach again as my hands began to shake and my heart started to race. Looking determinedly down at the floor, Marc moved quickly to an adjacent sink, where he began washing his hands. I attempted to steady myself, unsure of whether I should say anything or not, and before he had finished, I glanced up, catching his eye for the briefest of moments, before pulling out a series of paper towels from the dispenser and striding purposefully out the door without looking back. I was sure I heard him say, 'Nice T-shirt, Tay', as the door closed behind me with a snap.

My stomach settled and a smile began to spread across my face as I turned into the corridor. I looked down at my T-shirt and saw that a small fleck of tissue paper had attached itself to the centre of the peony, which I removed with the flick of a finger. I brushed down my front, pulled back my shoulders, opened the door to the classroom and walked in feeling like one of the style kings Marc had said we would be – only now I was going solo, and it was absolutely fine with me.

CHAPTER 9

The Pantomime Dress

'Welcome to your Art A level, year twelve,' shouted Miss Jacobs. My teacher's loose black hair was tied back behind her ears; she wore a short turquoise kaftan over a pair of skinny blue jeans and a pair of brown Birkenstocks on her feet. There were only four of us in the class, but that didn't stop her bellowing loudly into the room, straining her voice so it sounded like she had a lump of clay caught at the back of her throat.

'Each term, you will be required to research a specific art movement, to produce a detailed, rigorously documented and referenced sketchbook, and to make a corresponding work, which must be ready before we break up for the holidays. The best of these three artworks will be displayed at our annual end-of-year show.' She paused for emphasis, looking around the room. 'The first artistic movement I want you to investigate is figurative painting.'

My stomach leaped as the words left her mouth. Art had quickly become the most anticipated subject of the four that I'd elected to study for my A levels. In the months since I'd come out to my mum and my closest friends, I had discovered something new and unexpected in the process of making art; something that instilled in me a sense of possibility and optimism which I didn't feel doing anything else. The chance my next brush stroke or pencil line might somehow result in something beautiful or unexpected was nothing short of thrilling, and I had also fallen in love with the sense of pride that came from someone complimenting my work. I wasn't yet ready to offer up the 'news' of my sexuality to the rest of my family, or to boldly confirm the rumours keeping classmates, but my art was something I felt pride in sharing.

Beyond the giddier pleasures of paint, pastel and paper, I also found the process of making art relaxing. It was the one thing that never failed to take my mind away from problems at home or issues with friends. I even used the summer house at the bottom of our garden as a makeshift studio, primarily because my parents were fed up of finding oil paint smeared on the bathroom door, and of the smell of white spirit wafting through the upper floors of the house.

In preparation for the start of a new term, Mum and I had been to see a smattering of big ticket exhibitions. My favourite was of Jenny Saville's enormous paintings at the Saatchi gallery. As I stood in front of the British artist's soaring canvases,

I struggled to conceive how anyone could paint anything so beautiful and yet so ugly at the same time. There was one particular work which stood out from the rest. Titled *Propped*, it had originally been part of Saville's degree show and the painting featured a voluptuous figure seated on a stool at the centre of the frame. The form filled the enormous canvas and the energy exuding from the thick, rich paint strokes, which Saville had worked and reworked into dense, meaty, flesh-like tones, seemed to vibrate from its surface. I came away feeling determined to paint with as much monumental confidence as her one day soon.

As we settled in to start planning our respective projects, Miss Jacobs made her way slowly around the room, taking her time with each student. To help explain what I wanted to do, I sourced several books from her small art 'library', which was really a shelf with around half a dozen titles on it, the majority of which were about the impressionists.

'I want to create a really big painting,' I said, excitedly showing her the books. I couldn't find any of Jenny Saville's work but I showed her a few Francis Bacons and Lucien Freud's famous likeness of Sue Tilley, the benefits supervisor, lying engorged and exposed on the couch of his studio. 'I really want to paint something the way Jenny Saville does,' I said.

'OK,' said Miss Jacobs, who upheld a firm policy of positive reinforcement in her classroom. 'It's very hard to achieve that smeared and visceral painting technique – there's a lot of skill that goes into managing the medium in that way – so I would work on that first. But what do you think you're going to paint? Specifically?' she asked. 'Or I suppose I should be asking, who do you think you're going to paint?'

'I'm not sure yet,' I said, chewing the end of a pencil which I'd found lying loose in the drawer of the workstation. 'I'm not sure.'

I started to spend most of my evenings drawing and painting, and was so absorbed in the company of my pencils and brush that I only occasionally had a night off to go to the rec with Lauren, or out into town with Anna, Vicky and Adam – our friendship quadrangle having been galvanized the previous year when I opened up to them about what had happened with Marc.

Squashing my face up against the glass panes in our kitchen door, I asked Romy to take a photo from which I could replicate the style in which Saville painted her squeezed women, who looked like contorted balls of dough pushed against a photocopier. One of my larger friends at school, Sophie, happily obliged when I asked her to squeeze her bust and stomach against the window of the common room so that I could photograph and draw it. I spent hours painstakingly attempting to replicate Saville's dense brush strokes in the shades of mauve, cornflower, clotted cream, pink and crimson the artist had used to create the bruised hues and cellulite textures that covered her canvases.

Much to the confusion of those who knew about my sexuality, there was something about the female form which particularly fascinated me, and it had played a central role in most of my work over the summer. Perhaps it had something to do with the fact that I could look at it so objectively, unfettered by sexual attraction, or maybe it was because the mounds and curves intrinsic to a female body are simply much more interesting to replicate on paper. Either way, I couldn't get enough of boobs, bums and vulvas, a quirk about which my dad must have, conversely, been thrilled.

With half-term approaching, although my room was a veritable trove of sketches and paintings – collectively demonstrating a satisfying progression in my technique – I'd yet to decide who my subject would be for the end of term piece. It was this I was contemplating one evening as I sat in bed drawing a study of Sue Tilley's stomach with a fine mechanical pencil, when I heard a small knock at my bedroom door.

'Teo?' Romy's voice, quieter than usual, came from the other side. An instinctive feeling of unease ran through me. Romy and I treated each other like cellmates at the best of times, borrowing each other's things without asking, barging in unannounced and making weird noises that no one else understood, attacking each other (and attacking Mum) like a pair of squawking velociraptors, fingers hooked like claws. For my sister to knock was very unusual indeed, and as she opened the door it was clear that she had been crying.

'What's the matter, Ro?' I didn't move from the bed as all I had on was a pair of boxer shorts.

Looking down, she twisted one of her feet on the spot, like she had when she was a little girl. 'Marc and Aaron were kicking footballs at us in the playground today, and they were saying some stuff about you.'

I froze. I'd not told Romy I was gay and I had no intention of revealing it to her anytime soon, which was perhaps naive given that everyone in school already seemed to know about it. 'Oh,' I said. I felt sick. 'What were they saying?'

'Well, Marc was shouting "at least my brother's not gay".' Clearly sensing my discomfort, Romy persevered. 'And a few more of the people in your year told me that you're gay too, Amir said it. And Simon shouted it at me in the playground the other day,' she said quietly. She suddenly looked terribly sad. 'Is it true, Tay?'

A rush of anger ran through me. How dare Marc kick footballs at my little sister? And how dare people I barely know tell her I'm gay before I'd had a chance to? I also felt a flash of anger at Romy for putting me on the spot.

'No, Romy, I'm not!' I shouted at her. 'Now get out, I'm going to bed.'

I threw the pencil down on the duvet as Romy pulled the door closed behind her with a loud sniff. I gathered up my pad and drawing materials and dropped them onto the desk on the other side of the room. Pushing the duvet off, I got up and switched off the overhead light. In the dark, I felt shame wash over me, not only for what Romy was being put through because of me, but also because she had been lumbered with a gay brother who couldn't protect her properly.

After a fitful night I woke up to the realisation that even if I couldn't make it better for Romy at school, I could at least be honest with her. I knocked on her bedroom door and, as I opened it, I felt a swell of pride for how carefully she maintained her small corner of the house. I also felt momentarily guilty for keeping the larger room, but I told myself that I needed the space to paint, which was true.

'Ro,' I said. She was sitting on her bed playing on her phone. Her hair was straight and her backpack was lying neatly on the bed next to her. 'I'm sorry I snapped at you last night,' I said. I took a deep breath. 'You're right, I am gay.' My heart was pounding and my hands were shaking. I didn't want to give her an opportunity to speak out of fear that she might be upset or reject me, so I kept talking. 'I don't really know what it means yet, but it's not a big deal. I haven't had sex or anything. It doesn't mean anything. It's just a word.' I paused, aware that I was rambling. 'It doesn't change who I am,' I said, less frantically. 'I'm still me.'

Crescent pools of tears had collected beneath Romy's eyes. 'I know you are, Teo,' she said, standing up to hug me.

I pulled away slightly and looked at her seriously. 'But you can't tell anyone,' I intoned, gravely. 'Mum knows, but you can't tell Dad, or any of the cousins, or the aunties.'

'I won't,' she said defensively, seeming to confuse the assertiveness in my tone with argumentativeness, 'but they're going to find out soon, Teo. And none of them will care,' she said. 'Even Dad won't care,' she added, with a small smile. It was a point with which I didn't agree.

*

Aside from the moment of tenderness we'd shared on New Year's Eve, my relationship with Dad had become increasingly distant since I'd started sixth form. When it was just the two of us in the car en route to school or town, on occasion we'd resurrect some of our inter-vehicular communication, identifying car brands and discussing our feelings euphemistically. But in general, our interactions had become perfunctory at best, furious at worst.

As much as this shift in our relationship was down to the hormonally-driven challenges faced by all post-pubescent sons and their bewildered fathers, the truth was that Dad and I had struggled to find our footing with one another as I got older and his working life became more stressful. Romy remained the apple of his eye, incapable of wrongdoing while I, more often than not, became the human vector for his ire.

In recent months, despite rarely moving from his study, in which he was prone to brooding, Dad had further developed his uncanny ability to distinguish whatever it was that I was doing in the house and find an argument against it. If I was playing the piano downstairs, I would be shouted at for making too much noise ('Dao, can you stop dat racket, I'm trying to work!') or if I was painting, for leaving barely perceptible marks on the woodwork ('Have some respect for da blahdy house, Dao!'). I'd even incur the same level of irritation if I was simply lying on the sofa watching TV, where I'd be growled at to, 'Stop sitting around and go and do something useful' because 'it's a beautiful blahdy day.' I was 99.9 per cent sure that he would have said it was a beautiful day even if it was raining; it often felt as though I could do little right in his eyes.

Although Dad had always been prone to these fits of temper – particularly in relation to me – a clear turning point in his overall demeanour came after the September 11th attacks in New York, when the airline industry collapsed and he was forced into early retirement. Eventually he took a job flying freight planes with a new airline, which involved him having to live in Hong Kong for a little while. It was a job he hated and, when he was at home, the mood that descended on the house would be as black as runway pitch.

Dad had quickly gone from being the omnipotent patriarch of our household – commanding the skies in a jumbo jet while keeping his family well-fed – to becoming an overworked, under-appreciated paycheck for whom the jet lag was increasingly challenging. As a result, my parents' already fiery relationship intensified, the arguments became more heated, and I'd started getting involved, invariably jumping to the defence of my mum when Dad's level of fury reached explosion point.

I'd become even closer to Mum since coming out to her, and in the same way that she'd protected me by being so unconditionally accepting of my sexuality, I wanted to protect her. The secret we shared must also have made Dad feel even more alienated from the pair of us than perhaps either my mum or I fully realised.

For my seventeenth birthday that year, I invited a handful of friends over for dinner at our house. I had recently discovered a passion for cooking, care of Nigella Lawson's sexually charged television show, and I had planned an elaborate meal of mushroom and truffle soup to start, raspberry and passion fruit syllabub to finish, and pan-fried scallops with bacon and butternut squash puree as the main event.

On the day, I'd gone to the local fishmonger to source the scallops and I'd made a menu on the family computer using Word Art. I was excited to share my (rusty) new cookery skills with my friends, and I had also extended the invitation to Mum, Dad, Romy, and Grandma, whose presence denoted the fact that it was an important event.

Dad had already had a few glasses of wine before dinner rolled around and I could sense that he was in a belligerent mood. He was seated at the head of the table, and he and Mum had shared several barbs before I'd even heated up the soup. By the time I served the scallops, he was smarting for a fight as he refilled his glass.

'Jan, don't you think you've had enough?' said Mum, despite the fact that her own glass had also been drained.

'Oh, shut up, Jane,' he slurred, silencing the rest of the table. 'Don't tell me what to do.'

Grandma looked down at her plate and placed her hand on Mum's arm.

'Don't speak to her like that, Dad,' I said, my voice tremulous with embarrassment. I could feel my hands shaking as I placed the plates down in front of my friends, who were all staring intently at the table. Dad, who I'd served first, was stabbing at the scallops on his own, chasing the white bullets (which were smaller than I had hoped) aggressively around with his fork.

'You can shut up too, you little sod,' he said, suddenly staring at me with his eyes wide. I could see the small burst vessels in the whites surrounding his irises, which were the same grey-blue shade as my own. 'And what's the matter with you?' he continued, his voice dripping with spite. 'Can't you even cook a scallop properly? These things are hard as rocks.'

Dad knew how to wound. I left the room quickly as a hot bubble of mortification pushed up in my chest. Lauren followed me out and into the garden, hugging me from behind, and I could hear my parents screaming at each other, though I couldn't make out the specific sentences. I felt ashamed that the rest of my friends were still sitting at the table enduring it, and I wanted nothing more than for my dad to get up, leave and go on a trip that would take him away – not just for a week, but for a year. Or at least until I'd left home.

*

'I can't tell Dad yet,' I said to Romy, who looked considerably happier than she had the night before, as I made to walk out of her bedroom. 'It's too hard,' I added. My sister, who remained closer to Dad than I was, tried hard to conceal the dismay that had suddenly washed across her face. 'Come on, we're going to be late.' I felt an overwhelming sense of relief that Romy now knew, but also panic that the more people I told, the greater the danger of it spreading to less manageable quarters: keeping a secret in an enormous extended family like mine, where everyone knew everything about each other and gossip was a form of currency, was difficult enough at the best of times.

With the deadline for my painting looming dangerously close, my idea for my final piece was coming together in my head, the smokey edges of its form gradually crystallising into something more firm. I knew I wanted to paint something that challenged not only society's preconceptions of gender and sexual identity, but also the preconceptions held by certain members of my family. In my short time doing my course I'd realised that, beyond simply looking beautiful, art also has the power to confront old ideas and skewer outdated ones. Louise Bourgeois used her sculptures to deal with her trauma of discovering her father had a mistress, while many of Paula Rego's paintings were allegorical protests against the anti-abortion movement. In turn, I wanted my painting to make my dad take me and my creativity seriously. And perhaps to make him take my sexuality seriously, too.

The problem was that I wasn't Rego, Saville or Bourgeois, and I still couldn't quite decide whether my idea was a good one or not. When I mentioned it to Miss Jacobs, her powers of positive affirmation seemed to be working full tilt.

'Well, I think it's interesting,' she said. 'You should certainly continue to consider Jenny Saville and Freud for notes on perspective and style, but Grayson Perry might also be good to look at.'

'I can really visualise it, miss,' I said. 'I guess the one thing I'm worried about ...' I paused. 'I'm a little unsure about how I'm going to get him to pose for it.'

'Artists have painted wild animals, children and stranger subjects than yours for centuries, Teo,' she responded. 'I'm sure you can manage.'

That afternoon, Adam, Anna, Vicky and I were sitting in the common room, sharing a warm cookie from the snack hatch in the canteen. The cookies were the only half edible things you could find there after the rush of lunchtime. The flapjacks tasted like meat.

'Guys,' I said, as I swung my chair around on its metal axis. 'For my big art project I was thinking of doing a painting of my dad in a pantomime dame dress.'

The three of them looked at me blankly.

'I know. It sounds weird. But I thought it could look really cool if I painted it from the perspective of being beneath him, kind of like that Holbein portrait of Henry VIII.'

More blank stares.

'Like he's one of the fighters in WWE.' I nodded along at Adam, who smiled broadly. 'I don't want to make him look stupid.'

'I mean, it would be amazing ...' said Anna.

'Yeah, sounds brill, mate!' said Adam, who had turned his eyelids inside out.

Vicky still looked sceptical. 'But how are you going to get him to wear a dress?' she asked.

'Adam ...' I asked slowly, with a see-saw intonation. 'I spoke to Miss Jacobs, and she said that I might be able to borrow one from the Yvonne Arnaud theatre storeroom.'

'Great!' he said, suddenly looking confused. 'And?'

'Well, I was wondering if you would wear it for me so that I can take photos to use for my painting,' I said quickly.

'Oh yeah, of course, mate!' he said, breezily.

'Oh, great. OK,' I said, raising my eyebrows at Anna and Vicky. 'I promise the the pictures won't go anywhere,' I added, earnestly.

'I don't mind.' He laughed. 'Will be fun!' A great surge of both relief and gratitude washed over me as I jumped up and hugged Adam so hard that I winded him.

*

'If only five-year-old Teo could have seen this place,' I whispered to myself more loudly than I intended to. It was a few weeks later and Adam and I were walking slowly through the corridors of the Yvonne Arnaud Theatre's costume archive in Guildford. I felt like I had been given the keys to my very own sweet shop.

Everywhere I looked there were richly embroidered Shakespearian doublets, manifold furry animal outfits and layers upon layers of gowns. There were voluminous pantomime dame dresses loosely crafted from primary shades of inexpensive satin, densely beaded flapper frocks, cut to finish at the knee, and fur-lined Tudor kirtles, designed expressly to accentuate an ample bust.

Having heard my proclamation, Adam glanced up from the rail he was browsing and half smiled in my direction. Looking back down, he pulled out a cobalt A-line dress, which resembled something that might be worn by a camped-up version of the nanny from *Romeo and Juliet*, and asked, 'Would this do the trick, Teo?'

'Um, no, Ad, I don't think so,' I said, appraising the dress he was holding in his meaty hands, which were the size of hockey blades. 'What do you think of this?' I asked, raising a black floor-length gown that was finished with a lace-up corset and a flash of leopard print down the leg slit. The moment I picked it up, I realised it looked like something Dorian from *Birds of a Feather* might wear, so I put it back on the rail quickly without waiting for his response.

'This looks quite good, mate,' said Adam. He was holding up a giant pink satin pantomime gown with puffball sleeves, which was finished all over with huge white polka dots. It had Dame Widow Twankey written all over it, and he was right. It was perfect. It was imbued with just the right level of camp, a perfect pinch of silliness mixed with a sense of faded glamour, which I knew would make it stand out on the canvas. I wanted Dad to look preposterous, yes, but imperious too, owning the frame like one of Saville's sitters. Because as much as I wanted to challenge Dad, I also wanted him to feel proud of me, and to do that I reasoned that I needed to make him look proud in the painting.

Carefully, Adam changed into the dress, keeping his clothes on, and under my direction posed himself with his legs wide open. I could have kissed him for his lack of inhibition. I instructed him to look down angrily, with his arms set at angles, like one of Rego's women on a mission. Positioning myself low on the floor, I took out my camera and started snapping furiously, barely looking through the view finder as I clicked.

Later that week, after downloading the photos of Adam resplendent in his gaudy pink gown into a file discreetly named 'art' on the family computer, I deleted them from the camera and took it into the living room where Dad was sitting. He was just back from a trip, and he looked tired.

'Dad?' I asked, recycling the up-down intonation I'd used with Adam a few days before. 'I was thinking I might paint you for art. Just a study thing. But I'm trying out flesh tones, and it would be really helpful.'

'Er, um, yes, OK,' said Dad. 'Does it need to be now?'

'Ideally . . .' I said.

I positioned myself on the floor beneath the sofa, in exactly the same way that I had with Adam, and pointed the camera up at Dad, under his chin.

'What da blahhdy hell you doin' down there?' he asked.

'This is just a more interesting angle to paint, Dad. Won't be a minute.'

'OK, OK,' he said. 'Go on then.'

The painting, which was completed in oils and stood at some three metres high, two metres wide, took just under two weeks to finish. I built the canvas from scratch in the school's design technology department, which involved stretching a vast swathe of canvas over a frame constructed from lengths of 2X4 – much to the irritation of our on-the-brink-of retirement DT teacher Mr Timms – onto which I then painted multiple layers of primer to prevent the porous fabric from soaking up the oil in the paint.

Once the canvas was built, I sketched the rough outline of the dress and all its frothiness, before gradually applying patch after patch of paint to the canvas in a bid to create a cohesive whole. Where some painters prefer to apply thin layers over time, allowing each to dry before applying the next coat, my style was to pile on as much paint as possible and work it in with my brushes, fingers and any tools I had to hand, from toothbrushes to butter knives. I loved the richly saturated, totally unexpected colours that could be created by mixing paints directly on the canvas, treating the material, which had the consistency of over-whipped cream, in the same way that a sculptor would treat clay on a block.

The hardest part was linking up Adam's lithe teenage proportions with Dad's sexagenarian ones. The most intricate bit, Dad's head, I left until last, and the final result was nothing if not striking.

'It's definitely got a Rego quality about it,' said Miss Jacobs as she stared up at the magenta-soaked dress dominating canvas. The smudges of pinks, mauves, midnight blues and ochres that constituted the flesh of my dad's face at the top of the frame stared back at her challengingly. 'But it also reminds me a bit of Barry Humphries.' She laughed.

'It looks a bit like that old grumpy one from *Priscilla,*

Queen of the Desert,' piped Jenny, another girl in my class, which would have usually annoyed me, but I thought Terence Stamp's character was very attractive in that film, so I laughed along clubbily.

'Does your dad mind it being shown at the exhibition?' asked Miss Jacobs. 'I think it's got to be this piece that goes in, doesn't it?'

'Well,' I said. 'Dad doesn't actually know that I've painted him in a dress . . . I superimposed his head on.'

'Ah, OK,' said Miss Jacobs, raising one arachnid eyebrow. 'Do you think you ought to tell him?'

The night of the exhibition was cold, so I wore a brown wool blazer which Mum had bought me from Next with my Vivienne Westwood T-shirt tucked into a pair of chinos. I felt nervous, not only about Dad seeing the painting, but I was also worrying, entirely irrationally, that the warmth of the gymnasium, which was where the exhibition was mounted and which was disproportionately superheated in winter, might melt the oil paints and the whole thing would be a sludgy mess on the high-shine parquet floor.

We parked on the playground and followed the light emanating from the gym. As we made our way inside, Mum and Dad picked up their obligatory glasses of warm Chardonnay while Romy and I walked ahead. My painting was mounted at the back of the hall, where the rest of the sixth form art was kept, and I dragged Romy quickly towards it so I could show it to her first.

'OH MY GOD, THAT'S DAD!' she shouted. Everyone around us turned to stare, so I grabbed her by the arm.

'Be quiet, Romy. I want it to be a surprise,' I hissed.

'He's going to be so mad.'

I heard Mum and Dad talking to one of the parents just a few paintings away, so I stood to the side and waited for them to turn the corner. Dad's leg, boat shoe-shod, revealed itself first, and quickly behind him came Mum, who raised her hand to her mouth with a yelp, before turning to me and laughing. Her eyes creased at the edges.

'Teo! That's Dad! In a dress!' she shouted. 'Did you pose for this, Jan?'

'No, I blahhdy did not, Jane!' he snapped, but when he looked back at me, he had a half smile on his face, so I walked over. I was nervous that he might be bluffing, so I took the few steps slowly.

'It's a very good likeness,' he said, pulling me in with one arm. 'Who did you get to wear the dress?' he asked.

'Adam did it,' I said.

'Well, at least I look skinny,' he snorted. I stared at him hard, waiting for an explosion or an angry glance designed only to be noticed by me, but instead Dad continued looking at the picture calmly. He seemed to be more pleased that I'd taken the time and care to paint him at all than he was perturbed by the pantomime confection I'd put him in.

The painting really was something. The giant canvas took up the entirety of the back wall, and the bright swathes of magenta oil paint, which constituted the dress, made it stand out from all the other works around it. I felt briefly sorry for Jenny, whose small but beautiful sculpture of a horse was positioned next to it, but my pride in the piece overshadowed the feeling almost instantly. My sister, who was standing next to me, was looking on aghast, less at the piece and more at how relaxed Dad was being. I felt hopeful about his reaction – an overwhelming sense of relief washed over me. Perhaps he would be ready to accept my news after all.

'Do you think he's OK?' Romy whispered in my ear. 'Is he drunk?'

'If he was drunk, he'd be furious,' I whispered back.

Dad strolled away from the painting, chuckling lightly as he followed Mum towards the upper sixth section of the exhibition, where the extra-polished final year work could be found. Slightly dazed by what had just happened, Romy and I followed them through the hall and out into the cool evening, which felt fecund with renewed possibility.

Many of the meals we went out for together as a family were spent with all of us on tenterhooks, waiting for the imminent explosion, but dinner after the exhibition passed easily in a pepperoni-hued haze of Pizza Express's Finest American Hots for us, a Soho for Mum, and wine for all, even Romy. I had two glasses of Malbec with my meal, and when we got home, announced that I was going to have another.

'Take it easy, Teo,' said Mum. 'You've had a lot already.'

'Oh, leave him alone,' said Dad, who didn't mind us drinking when it suited him. 'I'll have one with you too, Tay.' He paused. 'I've been bloody driving, Jane,' he snapped, as Mum turned to look at him. Romy was biting her lip next to me. Alcohol was the key to the vast majority of arguments in our family, and we both knew that even a little too much could spoil the most pleasant evenings.

I waited in the conservatory while Dad poured two glasses of Campo Viejo for us both, a large one for him, a smaller one for me. Mum was in the kitchen talking to her friend Jill on the phone and Romy had retreated to her room. Perhaps it was the confidence instilled in me by Dad's unexpected response to the painting, or maybe it was the almost-bottle of red wine that I'd drunk, but I decided that this was the moment to tell him my secret. He'd laughed blithely at me depicting him to the world in a dress, after all, so why wouldn't he be able to laugh this off too? I took a deep breath.

'Dad, I've got something to tell you.' He looked up at me from his glass, keeping his chin low so his eyes moved up in their sockets. He looked like a lion.

'Um, well. I don't really know how to say this. It's not a big deal, but, well, I'm gay.' My heart was racing in my chest and I could feel my cheeks beginning to burn.

Dad stayed in his position, analysing me from beneath the hood of his brow.

I took a large gulp of my wine as he took a sip of his and, just like I had with Romy, I started blathering involuntarily. 'I mean, I've known for a while and it doesn't change anything about me. I'm still your son.' I paused, looking at him searchingly.

Finally, Dad looked up at me, square on. 'Dao, you're my

boy.' He paused. 'And I love you.' Another pause. 'But I'm going to need some time with this.' At which point he looked away from me and said, 'Time for a refill', before promptly standing up and leaving the room.

I gulped down the remnants of my wine, put the glass down on the coffee table, and went up to bed. As I placed my head on the pillow, my heart beating fast from the alcohol, I felt stupid that I'd thought the painting could ever encourage Dad to take me seriously – to embrace the big creative, homosexual mess that was his son and ignore all the deeply ingrained prejudices that swirled inside his sixty-five-year-old brain. All those months of work for nothing. I could have just done a self-portrait and saved myself the stress. I felt an overwhelming urge to go back to school and whitewash the imperious face staring down from above the top of the canvas.

I slept fitfully that night. At some point I dreamed that I was performing my very own drag act, wearing nothing but the pink pantomime dress. As I screeched my way through a Diana Ross track to which I couldn't quite remember the words – and in a pitch I could never hope to achieve in real life – Dad looked on from the front row of the theatre in utter dismay.

CHAPTER 10

The Pyjama Bottoms

'Have you listened to Four Tet?' my new friend Jack asked one evening. 'Kieran Hebden's a genius.'

'Um, yeah,' I responded, hoping he wouldn't probe further. For all I knew, he might have been speaking a foreign language.

Jack had a square jaw, a strong nose and blue eyes so crystalline that their brightness belied his general air of sleepiness. As we travelled back to our shared halls of residence, Boddington, after the group induction to the Fine Art programme at Leeds University, he had wasted no time telling me about his favourite filmmakers (Jim Jarmusch and the Coen brothers), the artists whose work he was most into at that moment (Matthew Barney and Gerhard Richter) and, of course, the angular songs by esoteric DJs he had recently downloaded illegally, via LimeWire. And, although I was in awe of Jack's musical tastes and general cultural acumen, I was pleased to have found a friend so quickly, particularly one taking the same course as me.

It was only a couple of weeks earlier that Dad had dropped me off at Boddington for my first day of freshers' week, instructing me softly yet sternly to 'be safe' as he drove away. Dad and I had not really talked about my sexuality since I'd told him I was gay over a year before, but in any moments where we did find ourselves alone together and the conversation moved in an interpersonal direction, he would begin expressing concerns about my general well-being, which I can only assume were connected to his (and, in fairness, the wider middle-class straight public's) fear that as a gay person I might be very likely to catch AIDS.

I also knew that Dad would have probably preferred that I study engineering at Brunel or some other serious university, but all I wanted to go and study was Fine Art. While he might have been disappointed by my decision, he never told me outright, and Miss Jacobs's glee was more than enough to make up for any feelings of guilt I harboured: 'Oh, what I wouldn't give to go back to art school again. You have no idea how lucky you are, Teo,' she'd said after discovering my degree subject of choice.

'I need to get in first, Miss Jacobs,' I had responded, barely concealing a smile.

The most important part of the application process, I learned, would be the construction of a comprehensive portfolio. I loved the way the word 'portfolio' sounded. It made me think of architects with black roll necks and equally inky square spectacles. Of fashion designers, tortured by their genius, stuffing drawings of skeletal women into enormous leather-bound folders, weeping at the brilliance of it all.

The painting of Dad from the first year of my A Levels was too large to include, which I'd been pleased about because I'd struggled to derive much joy or pride from it since the grand unveiling. After that evening the painting had felt like little more than a puerile representation of my desperate need for Dad's approval and I was happy, therefore, to leave it in Surrey with the rest of the relics of my childhood.

Miss Jacobs also suggested that I include two additional oil paintings in the portfolio, one which featured a naked man endowed with an abnormally large penis, stabbing himself in the chest with a sword shaped like a crucifix. The head teacher had vetoed it for inclusion at the end-of-year show, which I had been very satisfied with indeed, given that the idea had been to demonstrate that any expression of my sexuality was curtailed by the Catholic school. Nonetheless, Miss Jacobs felt it demonstrated passion, and that if I explained its meaning to the admissions boards, they would appreciate it even more. The second was a giant painting in the style of Dexter Dalwood, an artist who imagines the interiors of celebrities' houses. Predictably, I chose to imagine the interior of Vivienne Westwood's home, which I furnished with a giant tartan grand piano, a garden swing which – if it hadn't been made from black leather – could have been straight from a Gainsborough painting, and a giant artist's easel full of imagined future creations for a future Westwood fashion line.

To accompany the Dalwood-inspired piece, I'd also produced a papier mâché take on one of the infamous nine-inch platform heels from Westwood's Anglomania collection, which were first shown in 1993 when Naomi Campbell took a tumble wearing a pair on the designer's Fanta-orange runway. But instead of electric-blue mock crocodile skin, I covered mine in dense black velvet and furnished each side with a red velvet tribal inlay, inspired by David Beckham's most recent tattoo. Holed up in my makeshift garden shed studio, I'd started exploring fashion more in my work and I found drawing women's clothes particularly enjoyable, so I'd been excited to share the shoe sculpture with Miss Jacobs.

'Fashion is a hard space,' she had declared. 'It can be very fickle.'

'It's a very competitive field,' agreed Mum, when I asked her about it. 'I'm sure you'd be fantastic, darling,' she mollified, 'but you won't make much money out of it. Unless you're a pattern cutter. You can make lots of money as a pattern cutter.' Cutting patterns didn't sound nearly as exciting as designing clothes, so Fine Art it was.

Thanks to the fact that the government intended to raise the cap on annual tuition fees from £1000 to £3000 the year after I was due to start my course, I wasn't able to do a foundation year prior to my degree. As a consequence I was forced to pick a Fine Art course that would allow me to attend straight from sixth form, which also meant that I had to find a degree that offered as much practical tuition in painting, sculpting and drawing as it did art theory and history. My options were Oxford, Leeds and the Slade in London, and Leeds was the only place I was accepted. Mum and Dad had both originally baulked at the idea of me going so far away to study a subject which, to the former's mind in particular, could just as soon be pursued closer to home. But when eventually they realised that having me further away might make it easier to ignore all the more hedonistic activities I'd be getting up to, they acquiesced.

'Where did you do your foundation year?' Jack had asked me as we sat beside each other at the front of the bus.

'I didn't do one,' I said. 'I came to Leeds straight from school.'

'Oh wow.' He paused, looking surprised. 'I did a foundation year at Wimbledon School of Art,' he said, affording the institution its full name. His voice came from the back of his throat, and I noticed that he had a tendency to use his hands to express himself, which I presumed helped to conceal how shy he was. 'Which school did you go to?' Jack asked casually.

'I went to St Peter's, just a Catholic comp in Guildford,' I said.

'Ah amazing, you must have done pretty well to get here so young,' said Jack kindly, rubbing his nose.

'Where did you go to school?' I asked.

'I was at Tonbridge,' said Jack, waving his hand lightly, as if to bat it away.

'Is that a private school?' I asked.

'Yeah,' said Jack. He looked away from me and out of the window. He seemed a bit embarrassed.

Despite our very different schooling experiences, Jack and I soon become close, travelling to and from lectures together before whiling away the evenings listening to music. I also quickly became taken with his sense of style. The day we met, he was wearing a sun-faded red cap and a blue bomber jacket over a loosely untucked shirt. On his legs were a pair of baggy black tracksuit bottoms, which were ripped at the hems and hung tattily over his trainers.

His was an artfully dishevelled aesthetic – part struggling art student, part off-duty jock – which looked, to me at least, entirely fresh and urbane. It was a look which sat in direct contrast to the perfectly preened European playboy vibe pedalled by Marc, which I think was partly why I was so drawn to it. That, and the fact it was a welcome contrast to the laddish aesthetic I'd cultivated during my sixth form years.

Said aesthetic generally comprised a pair of bootcut Ted Baker jeans – of which I'd accrued multiple pairs while working on the door of the Guildford branch where I was required to chastise customers who left without purchasing with the line, 'What? No bag? Are you mad?' – and fake Ralph Lauren polo shirts. In a thoughtful show of recognition in my interest in fashion, Dad had regularly started to bring these home from his layovers in Hong Kong. While they mistook the fact that I was more into the drama of Vivienne Westwood's orb than I was the prep of RL's polo pony, I wore the shirts regardless, always with the collar popped, teamed with copious amounts of freeze-hold hair gel. More a low-key attempt to fit in with Guildford's prevailing tribe of townies than any kind of assertion of self, the look was easy to achieve and it didn't make me stand out, which suited me perfectly.

The truth was, since that fateful mufti day three years before, when I had felt bold and brave in my peony-clad Vivienne Westwood T-shirt, my confidence had been knocked. The mixed reactions I had received to my coming out had made me second-guess myself. I feared that if I chose to embrace fashion as fully as I wanted to, people might mark me as a specific brand of flamboyant homosexual – a loud, brash, extra camp stereotype into which I wasn't yet ready to be cast. It was easier, therefore, to tread a more mediocre line. I might be gay, but I was still a man: still Teo with a capital T. And I had the townie uniform to prove it.

My other newly found friend, Cara, dressed with a similar sense of studied carelessness to Jack, albeit with considerably more zhuzh.

'That's an amazing name,' I'd said when I'd met her during freshers' week over pints of watered-down Samuel Smith lager. The warm swill of hoppy nectar had coated the walls of my stomach and my social muscles felt lubricated.

'Er, not as amazing as Teo van den Broeke,' she'd said, thrusting her hand onto my arm. A strand of her auburn hair, which was cut short and choppy, fell in front of her eyes from the neck-extending emphasis she'd placed on the last syllable. She was wearing a pair of skinny jeans and a Breton sweater, a bright-green keffiyeh scarf was wrapped languidly around her neck.

'Now, fabulous man,' she had said, both officious and conspiratorial, folding her legs and straightening her back with the dexterity of a secretary bird. 'Tell all. I want to know everything about you.'

A few more pints and a round of DVD shopping later, Cara and I returned to our halls and pitched towards my flat. As we stumbled into the characterless space, both slightly drunk, we made sure to avoid my new flatmates, who consisted of a pair of would-be spinsters called Sally and Claire, a manga porn connoisseur named Mike and a pint-sized fusspot called Michael. Needless to say, we hadn't hit it off. Landing on my single bed I suddenly realised how tired I was from pretending to be more cultured than I actually was during our tour of HMV, and I was pleased to chat to my new pal about the lives we'd left behind.

With no friends from down the road, no school pals to fall in with purely by nature of proximity, no siblings, and (on a particularly positive note in my case) no parents around, we were determined to find our groove in our new surroundings. Although I'd felt nervous about leaving the safe confines of my life in Surrey behind, the truth was that the opportunity to carve my own path felt nothing short of liberating, and my burgeoning connection with Cara allowed me envisage it more clearly. As such, I had an overwhelming urge to tell her about my sexuality.

'I haven't shared this with anyone yet,' I said, 'but I'm gay.'

I paused. 'I don't really know why I haven't told anyone, to be honest.'

Cara looked at me with a hint of surprise before responding. 'It's funny you should say that.' Her face became more serious. 'I've had relationships with girls. And I think I like girls as well as boys.' She raised her eyebrows, turned the sides of her mouth down and gestured with her hands as if she was serving a dish from her chest.

Sharing this part of myself with Cara, and having her share a similar story with me, made the knot that had been tied in my stomach since I had arrived in Leeds begin to loosen. The opportunity to reframe myself as an out-and-proud gay man from the start of this new era suddenly felt within reach, and very refreshing indeed.

In light of the frosty relations between me and my flatmates, it was Cara's house – situated in 'The Annexe', a small semi at the back of Boddington Hall – that quickly became the nerve centre of my fledgling friendship group.

There was Polly, whose icy-blonde hair tumbled loosely on either side of her face, and whose open features were arranged symmetrically around a nose so fine that it looked as though it had been slip cast in bone china. Wild Alice, who seemed perpetually bunged up and spoke primarily with her hands. Izzy, a gentle illustrator who flushed a fetching shade of pink when anyone spoke to her. Binxy, a miniature redhead who didn't live in The Annexe but was a regular visitor, and who looked like a cross between Alex Kingston and Tinkerbell. Katie, a biologist who never had a cross word to say, was perpetually late. Hilarious Bex, a small bottle-blonde who had joined Leeds from Oxfordshire. There was Jack, of course, and finally Fin, who didn't live in our halls, but rather Devonshire – a Hogwarts-style building closer to the town centre, which tended to attract better-heeled students from more expensive schools.

As those early weeks rolled out across the post-industrial landscape of Leeds, I eased into university life, which consisted of the occasional lecture, plenty of hours in the pub, some gentle experimentation with weed and the occasional dinner party if we felt like playing at being grown-ups. But while I was relishing my new-found freedom and revelling in the joy of my newly formed friendships, for the first time in my life, I began to feel like the smallest fish in the sartorial pond; a fully townie-fied style luddite who didn't know his Jack Wills from his Abercrombie & Fitch. The more I surveyed my fellow students, the more I wondered if I was somehow out of step sartorially, a suspicion that would soon be irrefutably confirmed.

A few weeks into our first year, Jack and I were invited to visit an obscure hall on the outskirts of town where Fin's friend Persephone was hosting a dinner in her flat. I had intentionally dressed up for the evening, wanting to make a good impression, and I arrived wearing a pair of my Ted Baker jeans and a grey hoodie, which featured a stylised illustration of Miami Beach on the front, from the same brand. As we walked through the quad and past huddles of students wearing pyjama-style trousers as though they were jeans, invariably teamed with worn-out T-shirts emblazoned with the logos of Thai beer brands, I felt more suburban than ever before.

'Hey, Dao!' shouted Fin, embracing me in a tight hug as he opened the door. I'd been throwing my impersonation of Dad around with reckless abandon and it had gone down a storm, so much so that my friends had started addressing me in the same way that he did. 'This is Chloe,' he said, gesturing at a short girl with a kind face. Her pale skin was peppered with freckles and she had flyaway blonde hair, like wayward candy floss and she instantly put me at ease.

'Hi, my love!' She waved up at me from her position on the floor, where she was rolling a cigarette.

'This is Barnaby,' said Fin.

'Oh, hey, buddy,' drawled a dark-haired man with a face that looked as though it had been hewn from stone, a series of perfectly angled planes, which added up to an inordinately handsome whole. 'Fin tells me you're a gay. You don't look much like a gay,' he said, seriously.

'Um, thanks . . .' I said. Although I was shocked by his comment, I also felt a hint of perverse pride that I'd managed to pass. Because as much as I wanted to be accepted for my sexuality, there was also a part of me that longed to fit in.

'You don't sound much like one either,' he said, giggling into his cigarette. The bubble of pride in my chest grew despite itself.

'And this is Persephone,' said Fin, moving me quickly away from Barnaby. A stout girl with small, straight white teeth and glossy blonde hair stepped out of the kitchen. She was wearing an apron around her front and she had a pair of khaki Thai fisherman trousers – pyjamas, but better travelled – on her lower half. Her flat was much larger than mine, and the communal space was finished with Moroccan rugs, while the sofas were layered with cushions that looked as though they had been taken straight from a market in Fes.

'Hey, buddy,' she intoned in a posh, deep voice from within the kitchen. 'I'll be out in a min, just braising the artichokes.'

'No worries!' I shouted, suddenly nervous. I felt as though I'd walked straight into a scene from *Withnail and I*. Jack, on the other hand, was already reclining on a cushion next to Chloe, the rips in the hems of his hockey trousers, which he'd worn with a hoodie and a denim jacket, were hanging loosely by his hands as he lit a pre-rolled cigarette.

Persephone emerged from the kitchen and, rolling a cigarette with practised dexterity, asked loudly, 'So where did you go to school, Teo?' Everyone in the room stopped talking and I could see Barnaby smiling slyly from the corner of my eye.

'I actually went to a Catholic comprehensive in Guildford,' I said. 'You probably wouldn't know it; it's called St Peters?'

'Oh my goodness!' shouted Persephone, who was blowing out a large plume of smoke in the manner of a battle-worn dragon. 'A real-life peasant in our midst!'

'Perseph!' shouted both Fin and Barnaby in unison, both laughing in what I hoped was shock.

The bottom fell out of my stomach and I looked briefly down at my plate, before lifting my head up and saying,

'That's me: gay and poor!' I forced a laugh. 'Can I have some of that cigarette, please?'

*

The next day I woke up feeling resolved. There was nothing I could do about my schooling, but there was at least something I could about my wardrobe. Lauren and Romy were coming to visit soon, and I wanted them to see that I was thriving, that I was a sophisticated student who'd never be caught in bootcut jeans and who hadn't set foot in a Ted Baker in his life. I wanted them to see me in the same way that I'd seen Jack on the day of our induction. The way I saw my new friends.

As I wiped the sleep and, in turn, the remnants of my hangover from my eyes, I picked up my phone and texted Bex. In the short time that I had known her she had demonstrated the most flair for clothes out of my friends. Like Jack and the Devonshire crowd, she had a knack for the look of studied carelessness but she also had Cara's flair and clearly knew where to shop. It was a look I was desperate to emulate, and copying my new friends seemed like a sensible place to start.

I typed quickly. 'Bex! I need some new clothes. Are you free today? x'

Her response was instant. 'I'm there. Am on way to lectures but I'll meet you at Harvey Nics in half an hour? Shopping! Yay! x'

We spent a good hour wandering the high-shine floors

of the department store, Leeds's smartest, searching the rails for something not only suitable, but also something I could afford. 'How about this, babe?' she asked, holding up a black Ed Hardy T-shirt, which was emblazoned with a rhinestone heart stabbed through with a sword. Bex was wearing a tea-cosy crocheted beanie with a grey Jack Wills hoody, a denim miniskirt and a pair of brand-new Ugg Boots. To my eyes, she looked the picture of understated insouciance, and the fact that she clearly saw me as someone who would wear Ed Hardy cut me to the quick.

'Um, I was thinking of something simpler,' I responded, eager to keep her on side.

'Or what about this?' she asked, holding up a cream cotton bomber jacket emblazoned with the word 'DIESEL' in giant appliqué letters across the front. She looked at me expectantly from beneath the brim of her beanie.

'I probably can't afford that,' I said, trying hard not to screw up my nose in response. 'To be honest, Bex, I was kind of thinking of second-hand or vintage clothes. I don't have much money and, well, between us, I kind of want to go for Jack's look rather than Peter Andre's . . .'

'Oh my God, babe, you should have said! I know loads of great places.'

We spent the subsequent hours trawling the vintage and second-hand shops that peeled off the main drag of Leeds high street. I tried on cable knit cardigans that smelled like pensioners, oversized pleated tweed plus fours complete with moth holes the size of Wagon Wheel biscuits and blousy silk shirts finished with ruffles. There were leather jackets with shoulder pads and sleeves so short they wouldn't fit a toddler, jeans with rises so high they reached my nipples and countless satin *sukajan* bomber jackets. Yet still nothing seemed to work.

'Bex, none of this looks good,' I moaned. 'And I smell like my great-grandma's bathroom.' My head was itchy from trying on the clothes and I felt like a lankier, sweatier version of the titular character in *She's All That*; only in our northern noir remake I was receiving an unsuccessful makeunder, rather than a totally beautifying makeover. By the time I'd pulled off the last army surplus sweater, the surface of which felt like wire wool against my skin, I was more than ready to retreat into the familiar comforts of my Ted Baker basics and bootleg Ralph Lauren polos.

'This calls for Beyond Retro,' Bex intoned as she took in my red face and hedge-backwards hair with a serious look in her catlike eyes. 'Come on,' she said, taking me by the hand. 'It's the best.'

*

To honour the arrival of my best friend and sister, I decided I would throw a party, as much to integrate them into my university world as to show off my new friends and my new look. I had told my flatmates about it well in advance, in the hope that they might vacate; relations had taken a particularly frosty turn since little Michael tried to physically remove a wooden spoon from my hand while I was cooking a ragu, so I didn't hold out much hope. 'No, sorry, I just can't,' he said over my shoulder. I hadn't even realised that he was in the room.

'Can't what?' I asked as he grabbed at the utensil.

'You do not put the onions into the pan at the same time as the celery and carrot.' He tutted. 'They cook slower!'

I grabbed the spoon back from him and slammed the lid on the pan pointedly, as he stalked out of the kitchen.

'Suit yourself,' he cried from the hall. 'It's your funeral!'

On the day, I tidied the communal areas, hoovering aggressively with the old Henry Michael's parents had donated in return for us promising to use it, and I laid out bowls of crisps, like Mum did whenever she hosted events. Romy and Lauren had agreed to get the bus up from the train station. As I waited for their arrival, I poured myself a glass of Campo Viejo and went into my bedroom to get dressed. It was already dark, the streetlights outside casting long shadows across my duvet, and the glowing red digits of the alarm clock next to my bed announced that I had thirty minutes to transform myself into the new, more urbane, fully university-ified version of me.

I switched on the strip light that ran the length of my bedroom ceiling and walked over to my wardrobe. With a deep breath, I pushed the hangers laden with my old polo shirts and jeans to the side, allowing my recent purchases room to breathe. I shrugged off my dressing gown and put on a pair of boxer shorts in preparation for my enrobing. With care, I pulled a pair of wide-leg black jersey tracksuit bottoms from their wire hanger. They were loose around my legs and featured an appliqué letter L, in the style of those found on old variety jackets, on the left thigh. The trousers were frayed at the hems where their previous owner had worn them outside, which was fine with me.

Next, I pulled out an oversized rugby shirt, which had a navy-blue body and a white collar. It was similar to one Jack wore for his hockey meets and the old cotton felt crisp against my skin. Over the top of the shirt, I shimmied on a vintage V-neck sweater in a rich shade of chocolate brown from Marks & Spencer. The old curlicued 'St Michael' label betrayed its age, as did the suede elbow patches, which had been added to cover up years of wear and tear.

The final flourish in my outfit was a heavy knit wool cardigan in a rich shade of raspberry ripple. The garment featured large magenta buttons down the front, which glistened like polished plums, and layered with my jumper it made me look, in Bex's words, 'super chull'. The term chill, I had discovered during my short time at Leeds, was public school speak for 'cool'.

Once dressed, I looked at myself in the small mirror above my sink and applied some of the £1.50 Garnier bronzer, which Bex had recommended and was the colour of Cuprinol fence protector, onto my face. Although I worried slightly that it would make me look like an oversized Oompa Loompa, I trusted my friend, so I rubbed a pea-sized amount, as per the instructions, onto my cheeks with dutiful care. Finally, I scooped a clump of V05 texturising paste into my hair, now longer than it had ever been, and pushed it up into the kind of flyaway style I'd seen other people from Boddington sporting. It was the way Jack wore his.

By the time I'd finished getting ready, the doorbell grizzled loudly throughout the flat. The lack of activity in the other rooms along the corridor suggested that I'd been successful in my plan to alienate my flatmates to the point of departure, so I skipped down the hall, the backs of tracksuit trousers catching under my heels as I went, and buzzed them in.

'Hey, Tay!' shouted Lauren from the base of the stairwell.

'Hi Toushalini!' shouted Ro. Toushy was the nickname which Romy had developed for me in recent years and I, in turn, called her Ratty, the most horrible word I could think of that began with the letter R.

The two girls bustled their way into the flat, their bags dragging against the walls of the hallway leaving inky marks in their wake.

'Ow my gawd, this is so nice!' shouted Lauren, generously. 'I can't believe you live here on your own!' Lauren, being one year younger than me, had yet to start at university, and I felt buoyed by her excitement about my new digs.

'What time is everyone getting here, Tay?' asked Romy. 'Do I have time to get ready?'

'Cara and Jack are coming at six and I think all the rest will follow soon after,' I responded officiously. Standing straight-backed in the doorway, I waited for one of them to comment on my outfit.

'Are you not going to get changed?' Romy asked, suddenly,

looking pointedly at my tracksuit bottoms. 'Also, are you cold? Why are you wearing so many layers?'

'You're as brown as I am, Tay!' Lauren chimed in, her eyes widening as she took in my face for the first time.

'Er, no, this is my outfit,' I said, huffily. 'Everyone wears stuff like this here.' I paused, before adding, petulantly, 'It's chull.'

'Oh, OK,' said Romy, looking unsure as she heaved her bags down the corridor towards my bedroom.

While the two girls were getting ready, I walked back in the direction of the entrance and locked myself in the communal bathroom, the only space in the flat with a floor-to-ceiling mirror. I took myself in slowly, from top to bottom, suddenly unsure about my new look. The clothes I was wearing didn't feel feel as smart or well-cut as the pieces in my former wardrobe, but my new outfit made me feel like I belonged in the brave new quasi-academic world of which I was now a part. I looked more like my new friends than I did my ones at home – and also a little more like I'd just rolled out of bed – but as far as I could tell that seemed to be the point.

As I left the bathroom, I tiptoed down the corridor so that Lauren and Romy wouldn't hear me, the tracksuit bottoms swishing lazily around my legs, and sneaked into the kitchen where I took three long glugs from the half-finished bottle of Campo Viejo on the side. The warm fingers of jammy liquid soothed the knot of anxiety in my stomach, which had become inflamed since Romy and Lauren's arrival, and I walked back towards the bedroom feeling calm as the door buzzer sounded again.

'Oh hey, buddy!' I shouted loudly as Jack came up the stairs. He was wearing a pair of loose jeans with a blue v-neck sweater, not dissimilar to mine, save the colour, over a pale polo shirt. I felt relieved that our outfits were similar but not too alike.

'Hey, mate,' he said huskily, as we embraced in the doorway. If he had noticed my change in appearance, he neglected to say anything. Cara, following closely behind, was unflinchingly herself, wearing a cropped leather jacket with a pair of spray-on denim jeans and a pair of extra pointy winkle-picker lace-ups.

'Hi darling!' she said brightly as she ran up the stairs to meet me.

'Guys, this is Cara ... She's my Leeds wife,' I said, registering how daft it sounded only after I'd said it. I ushered in my new friend to meet Lauren and Romy, who were standing in the doorway craning excitedly behind me, eager to catch a glimpse of my new friends. 'And this is Jack, my great friend who also studies art. He lives just over the road in a different house,' I said.

I was so excited to have the two most important people from my old life in the same room as all of the most important people from my new one. I may have been the only one aware of the special alchemy taking place in the room, and I was revelling in it. Eventually, after more guests had arrived, Romy, who had put away a good half bottle of Ernest & Julio Gallo's Sauvignon Blanc, pulled me aside and asked to speak to me in my bedroom. Everyone seemed to be getting on with each other, so I was reluctant to leave the throng.

'Are you OK, Tay?' she asked seriously.

'Yeah, how come?' I asked. I was more drunk than I wanted to let on, and I was still smarting from her earlier comment.

'No reason, you're just talking differently,' she said.

'No, I'm not,' I responded defensively.

'You are. It's fine obviously, but your clothes are different too.'

'Romy,' I said sternly, with a slight slur, 'I'm exactly the same as I was, I've just got new friends and a new life,' I said a little tersely. There was enough Campo Viejo coursing through my veins at that point to sedate a large cow. 'You'll understand when you go to uni.'

'OK,' she said. Her big eyes looked crestfallen. 'But, just so you know, I liked your old clothes.' She paused. 'Mum and Dad aren't getting on very well at the moment, by the way,' she added, quietly.

'Well, that's hardly a surprise,' I said, still harsh. 'What's happened now?'

'Dad's sad all the time, and Mum keeps saying she's going to leave him.'

'Well, he's horrible to her half the time,' I said, continuing in my spite-spiked furrow, 'he shouldn't really be shocked.'

The memory of the last time I went home for the weekend flicked to the front of my wine-sozzled mind. We had gone down to Brighton for the christening of cousin Daisy's new baby, at a church attended by every member of my extended family. The service was followed by a tea party at my Aunty Catherine's house overlooking the coastal sprawl of the city. Dad had been in a morose mood since we'd got in the car that morning, prompting him to start drinking heavily as soon as we arrived. About two hours into the party, he'd walked into a room to find Mum. She was talking to one of Catherine's male friends who she'd known for many years, who had his hand placed gently on her upper arm as they spoke.

'You don't need to stroke her!' Dad had snarled across the room, the whites of his eyes flaring with familiar incandescence, before adding: 'She's not a dog', to the horror of everyone within earshot.

Mum had stormed wordlessly out of the room past Dad, her face flushed with fury. She had refused to speak to him afterwards. Following a painfully silent car journey, they'd argued well into the night while Romy and I were locked away in our respective bedrooms.

'I can't do this anymore, Jan!' Mum had shouted. 'I can't be with someone who treats me like they hate me!'

'Oh for fuck's sake, Jane, HE WAS HITTING ON YOU.'

'I'm going to go and stay at Mum's for a week or so,' she had said, sounding dejected. 'I need time to think.'

I'd wanted nothing more than to go and console her, but I'd known that placing myself at the white hot centre of my parents' arguments wouldn't be a sensible move, and would instead risk raising my dad's hackles even more. I felt a rush of fury towards him for having pushed Mum so far. I understood why she'd wanted to leave. I would have wanted to if I had been her.

Romy was about to respond to my retort when Lauren came barging into the room.

'Come on, you two!' she shouted. She was dragging Bex, who was still wearing her Jack Wills hoodie and had freshly bleached her hair for the occasion, by the hand. She looked absolutely terrified of the straight-talking demon from Surrey holding her hostage. 'Let's have another drink!' Lauren slurred, before turning to look at Bex as though she'd only just realised she was there. 'You'll have one, won't ya, babe!'

'Um, yeah, sure,' said Bex, looking about as unsure as I'd ever seen her. 'Love the outfit, Tay.' She winked, as she attempted to disentangle the sleeve of her hoodie from Lauren's fist.

Romy stood up and dusted down her front. 'I'm just going to the loo,' she said, looking at the floor.

Watching my sister leave, I regretted the way I'd spoken to her. I knew that the concept of Mum and Dad separating, even if only temporarily, terrified her, as it did me. Not only would their split leave us feeling dislocated from our sense of home, without having Mum on hand to temper Dad, we both knew we would be left to navigate his moods on our own. As much as I knew that Mum deserved to be happier than she was, and that I shouldn't be short with Romy, the shadow of doubt cast by the prospect of their split created weighed heavy on me.

A surge of of anxiety, like cymbals clattering up my spine, through my brain and into my ears, made my hand move involuntarily up to my mouth, and I downed the plastic beaker of red wine that was warming in my hand. I was about to get up and follow my sister out to apologise before I caught myself and turned to Lauren, who I noticed with relief didn't seem to think the changes in me were all that bad, or at least she hadn't said as much. Her half-cut air of unconditional positivity – a kind of booze-induced beatific calm – was an instant salve to the disquiet in my head.

'Lau, have you heard of this DJ Four Tet?' I asked as I took her arm and led her back into the kitchen. 'He's an absolute genius, I swear. You have to listen to him.'

CHAPTER 11

The Flamingo Outfit

'Tay, you are so thin.' Vicky's eyes were wide and she was sitting across from me on my parents' sofa next to Adam and Anna. It was 23 December and they had come over to celebrate both the festive season and Anna's birthday, a tradition we'd honoured since the first year of sixth form. 'I'm so jealous.'

'How's the course going?' asked Anna, who had moved to Exeter to study Drama.

'Um, you know. It is what it is,' I said. 'I don't find the people in my group particularly inspiring.' I paused, laughing lightly. 'And the course leaders don't seem to like painting or drawing, which is a bit tricky.'

'Oh, that's a shame,' replied Anna, turning down the sides

of her mouth in sympathy. 'I thought painting and drawing was what you did on an art degree?'

'Yeah, and you're so good at it, mate,' chimed Adam, kindly.

'What have you been doing with yourself, then?' interrupted Vicky. 'We've hardly heard from you.' She paused. 'Are you seeing anyone?'

'No!' I said, feigning disgust. The truth, which I couldn't face revealing to my friends, was that I would have very much liked to have been seeing someone, but in the year and a bit that I'd been in Leeds, I'd barely kissed a man let alone embarked on a meaningful relationship with one. It might have had something to do with the amount of weed I was smoking – which did very little for my libido – and it might have been due to the fact that the situation with my parents hadn't done much for my faith in romantic relationships, but there was also part of me which knew that my eagerness to fit in with my new group of friends, the vast majority of whom were straight, was providing me with an easy excuse not to engage with the gay world.

Where I was failing miserably to embrace my queerness, however, Cara was thriving. The world and her wives were drawn to my friend like hummingbirds to pomegranate flowers, and she – like many people in the community I was yet to fully immerse myself in – revelled in meeting as many new people as possible. While Cara would reach full plume in the gay bars where we spent most of our weekends, I would calcify, glaring into the middle distance as I stood around downing glasses of wine, desperately trying to drum up the bravery to make eyes at someone – anyone – that I fancied.

Perhaps unsurprisingly, I was thoroughly, truly, utterly appalling at pulling, and the fact that I'd taken the 'studied carelessness' aspect of my new look to 'middle-aged busker' depths can't have helped. I felt comfortable in my new clothes and my new gang, but I did sometimes miss the feeling of clean clothes that held me together rather than draping around me like moth-eaten curtains that smelled of damp.

'You know, darling, it's a lot of money we're spending on that course if you're not enjoying it,' said Mum, who had joined us for a glass of wine and was already slightly squiffy. She'd returned from Grandma's a few weeks before and Dad was out driving Romy to a friend's. 'Are you actually doing any work up there or is it just party, party, party?'

'Of course I'm doing work,' I snapped, taking a gulp of my wine. 'I'm only a third of the way through the second year. I'm still finding my feet,' I said, registering her sceptical look. 'I'll be fine.'

As I took another slug from my glass a familiar sound, like flint meeting flint, reverberated through the house as Dad's key scratched into the lock on our medieval front door. Mum looked intently at her glass and my friends glanced anxiously at me, clearly recalling the way in which he had reacted to my overcooked scallops on my seventeenth birthday, as Dad walked through the door and into the living room and Romy ran up the stairs to her bedroom. He looked tired. The skin around his eyes had a purple quality and his face was grey.

'Hello, girls,' he said lightly, though his tone had a touch of accusation in it.

'Hi Jan,' they said in unison, Anna was smiling manically in his direction as Vicky averted her eyes to me.

'Hi Jane,' said Dad with a sniff.

'Hello Jan,' said Mum dully, keeping her eyes fixed on her glass. She didn't move a muscle as she assiduously avoided his eye. 'There's food in the oven if you want it.'

Dad's chest fell slightly and his face softened for the briefest moment, like the surface of a soufflé being broken by a fork. It hardened quickly again as he stalked out of the room without a word. I glanced at Mum. She looked like she was going to cry.

'You know we love you, don't you, sweetheart?' Mum asked later, when my friends had left and Dad had gone upstairs. Her eyes had softened. 'But it's not really working between your father and me.' She paused, looking up at me to gauge my reaction. 'I'm going to go and live at Mummy's again for a while after Christmas, I think.'

'I know,' I said, with more indifference than I felt. For all the predictability of the situation, and for all the time I'd had to process it, I still couldn't quite compute the fact that my parents might actually be splitting up. The idea was as abstract as Christmas being cancelled or being told I could no longer drink wine to blunt life's edges, which were becoming increasingly sharp. 'Well, you have to do what's right for you,' I said, taking a deep swig from my glass. 'I think I'm going to go to bed.'

*

A few weeks later, the six-hour MegaBus journey back to Leeds felt like a reprieve. Christmas had been a particularly bleak affair that year; instead of the usual mulled wine-fuelled arguments a sense of eerie quiet had settled over the house. The annual Christmas Eve party had been forgone, so instead I went to the pub with Lauren, Mum went to mass and Dad stayed at home watching TV with Romy. On the big day Dad had tried to assist Mum with the mountain of root vegetables as he usually did, but before he could pick up a peeler, she promptly instructed him that she didn't need his help.

'What the blahdy hell is the matter with you, Jane?' shouted Dad as Romy exited the kitchen quickly, nibbling anxiously at a strand of hair that had fallen out of her ponytail.

'Nothing, Jan,' sighed Mum, as I looked down into the bowl of peelings, willing the interaction to end. 'Just go into the other room and keep Mummy company.'

Grandma had been drafted in as a buffer that year and she was sat patiently on the sofa, waiting for dinner to be served.

'She's your blaahdy mutha, Jane, you keep her company,' shout-whispered Dad. He seemed desperate to raise any kind of reaction,

'Thank you, Jan—' Mum sighed again '—I can always rely on you.' She shifted her attention to the task of chopping leeks as Dad retreated from the room, his soufflé pallor returning once more. In all, Christmas had been so miserable that I'd spent most of my time working on essays that were due in the New Year and I couldn't wait to get back to the freedom of the large, seven-bedroom house into which Jack, Fin, Cara,

Polly, Bex, Barnaby and I had moved at the beginning of second year.

Situated on a small road at the heart of Hyde Park Village, Regents Park Terrace was lined with plane trees and terraced houses built in a deep-red brick. Despite being identical to the rest of the buildings that surrounded it, ours looked somehow more careworn than the others. The door, painted a once-glossy blue, would have been a doddle to take off its hinges. The carpets hadn't been replaced in years and the single bathroom at the top of the stairs, which was shared between all seven of us, had a lino-covered floor pitched at such an angle that it was impossible to stand straight on. The boys of the house had quickly learned that it was better for everyone if we sat down to wee rather than stand.

We'd drawn straws to see who would be given which bedroom and I ended up selecting the smallest – a box space that could just about fit a single bed and a wardrobe, positioned at the anterior of the house above the front door. The only positive came in the fact that Cara had picked one of the larger rooms next to mine, and our proximity to one another afforded us excellent easy access when we got ready for our nights out.

My enthusiasm for my room was matched by that for making art, which had dwindled dramatically in recent months. Where applying paint brush to canvas had once served to soothe all woes – to achieve the alchemic effect of taking me out of my life for a brief white spirit-scented moment – my passion had been gradually knocked out of me by the course. On a drizzly winter's day – the specifically northern kind where you can't tell where the clouds end and the rain begins – the atmosphere in our first seminar of the year had set the tone for things to come.

'So I've really been inspired by, like, the takeaway shops of, like, the city.' A small girl stood at the front of the room speaking in a soft, sing-song voice. She had enormous round reading glasses on, which reflected the light in such a way that it wasn't possible to see her eyes, and she placed an upward inflection at the end of each sentence. 'So I've decided to paint, like, a series of floor tiles, selected at random, around the campus with, like, the logos of Chicken Cottage and Lucky's Pizza on them, as, like, a commentary on our consumerist attitudes.'

'Thank you, Tina, that was, err, very enlightening,' said our course leader as he resumed his position at the front of the room. 'I want to remind you all to, like Tina, think beyond the canvas and the kiln this year,' he intoned in a deep melodious voice. He was in his early sixties, he had his ear pierced and he was wearing an oversized blue Parisian chef's smock. 'What is the work for?' he said, placing grave emphasis on the final word. 'Why should it exist? Where does it fit? How can it earn its place?' he boomed. 'These are all questions that must sit at the front of your minds this year,' he said, 'on this course.'

In response to the course leader's brief, I had set about planning a vast series of self-portraits, using straws to blow ink-laced bubbles through stencils. I wasn't sure why I found the technique so appealing, but I loved the sense of delicate contrast it created when layered over the paint.

'Don't you think self-portraiture is a little prosaic?' our blunt-fringed tutor asked as she toured the studio to survey the students' progress. She wore plastic beads the size of a baby's fist strewn around her neck and I didn't much care for her opinion.

'And the "self-as-other" trope has been done to death, don't you agree?'

'And what does it *mean*?' asked Bench, one of the nosier students.

'I like the way it looks, I guess,' I responded, hesitantly. I'd been out to see Fat Freddy's Drop the night before, I hadn't made it to bed until 3 a.m., and I was in no mood for a spot-critique from a fellow student.

'Hmmm,' Bench responded, 'I see', before turning on the heel of her Croc to attend to her own idea, which comprised of spray-painted pig intestines, plaited.

I knew that if I pitched a painting or a drawing or a sculpture that I actually wanted to create, I would be roundly scoffed out of the room. I had a vision of building an alien version of myself fitted with a plaster cast of my head, which clearly wasn't going to be well received, so I had come up with an alternative plan.

*

'Mr van den Broecker, is it?' asked the course leader, mispronouncing my name extravagantly at our seminar the following week.

'It's Broeke, actually,' I said, more quietly than I intended.

He inspected me like a poisonous insect before stating, grandly, 'Please come forward.'

'Good luck, mate,' whispered Jack, tapping me on the arm. His breath was laced with the adult tang of coffee and cigarettes.

'Um, so, well, this year I've decided to try a form of performance sculpture.' I hadn't heard the term before and I felt proud of myself for coining it. 'In many of my painted works over the years, I've focused on the objectification of the body – specifically the female body – and for this project, I thought it would be an interesting commentary to create a giant vulva out of wire and papier mâché.' I paused. 'I will then construct a separate device that will flick a measure of bleach at it every hour until the papier mâché eventually disintegrates and only the wire substructure is left behind.'

The room fell silent. Tina's glowing glowing orbs were focused directly on me, like the eyes of a demon cat, and Bench's mouth had formed into a snarl. Jack had his head in his hands and I could see from the corner of my eye that the course leader was tapping his foot.

'OK, Mr van den Browikah,' he said butchering my name once again, 'but do we not think that that is somewhat misogynistic?' He pushed his glasses up his nose in an obvious signal of distaste. 'You are quite literally disintegrating a vagina.'

'Yes, I have to say, actually,' shouted Bench, shooting her hand in the air, 'I'm deeply offended by this idea, and don't think it should be allowed to continue.' A murmur of agreement or dissent circled the room. I couldn't tell which.

'But, well, um,' I stuttered, 'that's the point. It's a commentary on misogyny.' I could hear the note of pleading in my voice. 'I'm bloody gay!' I wanted to shout. 'How can I possibly be misogynistic? All my friends are women.' Apart from Jack. And Fin, and maybe Barnaby. Oh, and Adam.

'It's not a commentary if it actually is misogynistic,' shouted Bench, who was now standing with her arms folded belligerently against her chest.

'Thank you, Miss, um, Bench,' said the course leader. 'I think it might be back to the drawing board this time, Mr van den Broookah,' he murmured. By that point I didn't have any energy left to correct him.

After the seminar, I railed at Jack as we pushed our way through the drizzle, like a pair of winter soldiers in a blizzard. 'I am so fed up with this course. They say they want you to be creative, and to be free, but it's only on their terms!' I shouted. 'It's ridiculous. What is the point?'

'Your phone's ringing, Teo,' said Jack quietly.

'What?' I snapped.

'Your phone's ringing.'

I looked down at the screen. It read 'Grandma' in small, pixelated letters.

'Oh, it's fine,' I said. 'I'll call her back later.'

'I know what you mean about the course,' he said, 'it's

rubbish.' He paused, rubbing his nose lazily. 'But we've got to play them at their own game. Do what they want, but make it work for you.'

I looked down at the screen again and a message popped up to indicate that I had a new voice message. I imagined Grandma sitting on her gold and blue brocade armchair, fiddling with the silver box chain laced around her neck. I knew she would be calling about Mum and Dad, but I didn't want to engage. The distractions of home no longer felt joyful and comforting, but rather loaded with weight, like a poison ocean pushing down on me from a great distance.

Mum had moved out of our family home almost immediately after I returned to university. She'd done it while Dad was out volunteering as a tutor at a local college. All of his piloting work had stopped when he'd turned sixty-five, which is the cut-off point for people being able to fly commercially, and he had taken the new challenge in his stride. He seemed to enjoy helping the adults in his classes almost as much as he had jetting people around the globe.

'I actually feel like I'm making a difference to these people's lives, Dao,' he'd told me over the phone in a rare upbeat moment. 'It's amazing really.'

I'd been receiving calls from both my parents most days since Mum's departure, the vast majority of which I'd been ignoring. Dad couldn't comprehend why Mum had left ('It's our marriage, Dao; why would she throw thirty years away?'), while Mum wanted reassurance that she'd done the right thing, and I was fed up of taking sides. I wanted them to solve their problems, however they saw fit, without putting me in the middle. As much as I wanted to speak to my grandma, to hear the familiar under-crackle of her voice – as reassuring as a duvet – I also wanted to be left out of it. I knew she would encourage me to make contact with Mum, but I just couldn't face the pressure. I had a life to lead, even if I had no idea which direction I was going in.

I felt a stab of guilt as I stuffed the phone back into my pocket. 'It's definitely making me think twice about what I want to do after uni,' I said to Jack, quietly.

When I got back to my room the rain had begun falling more heavily and the four walls of the tiny space felt oppressive. I switched on the set of fairy lights which I'd draped over my double sash windows before the Christmas break in a bid to banish the misery of the Yorkshire winter, and sat on the edge of the bed looking down at my phone. I paused with my finger over the play button as I worked up the courage to listen to Grandma's voicemail. Taking a deep breath, I picked up the phone and held it to my ear.

'Hello, darling, it's Grandma,' said the voice on the other line, familiar yet distant. 'I hope you're OK. Just calling for a chat so call me back whenever you're free, but I know you're busy so don't worry if you're having too much fun! I love you, Teo. Sending you a big kiss, sweetheart.'

A familiar balloon of sadness expanded in my chest. Grandma's voice, a softer version of my mum's, was like catnip to my tear ducts. I took a series of shuddering breaths. I knew I should call Grandma back, or, even better, Mum, but I couldn't bring myself to do so. In the past I would have picked up my brushes and expressed the emotion through painting, but that outlet had been taken away by my course. The one place that should have been nurturing my creativity was in fact doing entirely the opposite.

Attached to the wall in front of me was a painting I'd made in my first year. On a small A3-sized canvas I'd painstakingly feathered an intricate sfumato oil paint reimagining of a photo I'd found of Mum and Dad in an old album. In the picture, my mum, aged about twenty-five, with hair like Farrah Fawcett, is smiling broadly. Dad is next to her looking like a young Harrison Ford with an equally large grin on his face. They seem happy. I spent hours faithfully reproducing the image at the centre of the canvas, as if, by lovingly reimagining them at their best, it might somehow be manifest in real life.

Sadness turning to anger, I jumped onto my feet and took the few short steps across my room towards the painting, grabbed it off the wall and stuffed it under my bed.

As I headed into my second term, I endeavoured to take Jack's advice and play my course leaders at their own game. My next project would be a series of condoms filled with coloured jelly and toy animals, which I planned to hang as a kind of adults-only mobile. Coitus had been an elusive part of my university experience thus far, which, I reasoned, was down to my lack of security in my own sexuality, which in turn stemmed from an early adolescence spent concealing my identity. Hence, condoms as children's toys. If they wanted conceptual, I would give them conceptual.

I spent much of my first weeks back sat in the corridor between mine and Cara's rooms – my makeshift studio – fiddling with the condoms, quickly discovering that they were frustratingly difficult to work with as they were so slippery. As I sunk into the mouldering carpet, quietly beavering away, I couldn't help but think of how ludicrous it was that I had such an excess supply of condoms in the first place.

'I really think I need a boyfriend.'

My friend looked over at me from her desk, eyeing the brightly coloured latex tubes in my hand with a wry smile on her face. 'Well, we need to start going out more then, don't we?' she said.

In an act of impressive social witchcraft, Cara managed to convince our entire house to join us on our big gay Queens Court (a naff bar that sold cheap jelly shots and played cheesy pop) – Fibre (a *slightly* cooler bar with *slightly* more attractive people and more expensive drinks that we didn't mind paying for because we were drunk on jelly shots) – Mission (a club that played piano house exclusively and smelled suspiciously of cat wee – but who cares when you're drunk on jelly shots?) triumvirate that evening. Most of our friends had returned from equally sleepy breaks with equally dysfunctional families and were itching for as many nights out as possible.

I momentarily considered taking a rare evening off from the lumpy cardigans and vintage cricket sweaters, which had taken over my wardrobe, but instead – lacking inspiration – decided to stick in the studiously careless sartorial trough

I'd been ploughing so thoroughly. Once dressed, I looked in the small mirror embedded in my door and pulled at my pale skin. I did look thin.

'This place is WILD!' Katie shouted into my ear later that evening as she bopped to Herd & Fitz's 'I Just Can't Get Enough' on the expansive dance floor. We'd played a drinking version of Cards Against Humanity before we'd left the house. 'I cannot believe that Barnaby's here too!'

'I know,' I shouted back in her ear between sweet, alcho-pop-soaked breaths. 'Wouldn't surprise me if he manages to pull before me.'

As I surveyed the crowd, I spotted a man who must have been around the same height as me. He had a perfectly round head, like Jack from *The Nightmare Before Christmas*, but he was handsome in a vole-ish kind of way. I didn't have a type as such, but I had noticed that most partners in gay couples tended to look a bit like one another, like owners with their dogs. Equally long of limb as I was, I reasoned that this person might well be a viable option.

He was wearing a white shirt with an enormous collar, his not insubstantial feet had been squeezed into a pair of square-toed Union Jack loafers. As he started walking in my direction, I couldn't help but notice how elegant he looked in contrast to the rest of the Ugg-clad, hoody-sporting students around us – in contrast to me. The lines of his outfit perfectly complimented his physique and I felt a jolt of envy. I couldn't remember the last time I wore my Westwood T-shirt or my

Gucci loafers, which were gathering dust in the back of my wardrobe in Surrey.

'Hullo, I'm Gareth,' he said, in a soft, slightly sibilant Welsh accent. He had long lashes like a giraffe and his eyes were dollish.

'Are you from Wales?' I asked, dumbly. I was mildly shocked to have been approached given my terrible track record of pulling. Cara was waving two big thumbs up and simulating fellatio behind him. 'Nice loafers, by the way.'

'Yeah, Cardiff,' he responded, with a half-smile on his face. 'And thanks.'

'Oh, I'm Teo,' I responded. Trying not to laugh at Cara, who was persisting with her performance in the background.

'Like Theo?' he said.

'No,' I responded. 'Tayo like Mayo.' The phrase had become a linguistic reflex I'd finally decided to embrace because it worked. We stood awkwardly on the edge of the dance floor for a while, attempting to have a conversation over the music. While spraying hot spittle into each other's ears, I learned that Gareth sold sunbed sessions for a living, that he was a regular at Fibre and that he, like me, had a keen interest in fashion. He glanced at me sceptically when I said that Vivienne Westwood was my favourite designer, though he stopped short of saying anything about my intentionally scruffy outfit, a kindness that made the decision to leave the club and head back to mine with him all the easier.

We took a taxi home, each with a portion of cheesy chips in hand. Greasy faced, we fell into my bed like a pair of praying mantises fighting over who would eat the other's head first. To have such close contact with another human male who I actually fancied was thrilling. I realised I couldn't remember the last time I'd kissed a man, and it felt fantastic.

'Are you top or bottom?' he whispered into my ear, the final word sounded even more cartoonish than normal in his sing-song Cymric tones.

'Um,' I replied, 'I don't know? Shall we just kiss for a bit?'

'Oh, OK,' he said, pulling away. He looked at me quizically, the light of the moon outside reflecting in the tight angles of his collar bone. 'Have you slept with a guy before?'

'Yeah, no, I have,' I lied, 'but I just don't like doing it on the first night.'

'That's boring,' said Gareth, flopping into the bed next to me with his arms firmly folded. 'What's the point of being gay if you don't want to have sex?'

If my leggy new paramour had been trying to turn me off, he'd succeeded. One of the reasons I'd been reluctant to properly immerse myself in the gay community, choosing instead to spent time with straight friends, was because of how promiscuously it had been painted in the media. In one fell swoop, Gareth had given me further licence to believe the propaganda. Feeling relieved and a touch vindicated, I switched off the light and lay next to him, trying to sleep. It was lucky we were both so thin, otherwise we may not have been able to fit so easily in the bed.

'What the hell are those?' Gareth said suddenly. I turned to find him staring at the jelly-filled condoms, which I'd left hanging in front of my window. With the moonlight filtering through eerily from behind, they looked like orphaned bubbles from a lava lamp.

'Um, it's my art work,' I said. 'Painting's my thing, really; that's just a stupid experiment.'

'Are those condoms?' he asked.

'Yeah, they are,' I said, buoyed by the fact that he was taking an interest.

'Ironic, that,' he said, as he turned onto his side to face the door.

*

As winter moved into spring, I began to spend more time than usual in the studio. The boyfriend situation hadn't improved since Gareth, so I had plenty of time on my hands, and things at home weren't much better either, which meant I was more motivated to make art than ever before, even if my love affair with painting had come to an ignominious end. I'd stopped speaking to both of my parents unless absolutely necessary. The only person from home that I was in regular contact with was Romy, who was still living in the house with Dad and found his sorrow difficult to manage.

'He just cries all the time, Tay,' she said down the phone one afternoon as I took a break from filling condoms in the studio, her voice cracking down the line. 'I hate seeing him so sad.'

For the first time in my life I didn't resent Romy's closeness to Dad. In fact, I was relieved that she was on hand to bear the brunt of his depression. But it did make me resent him, not only for the fact that he had allowed the situation with Mum to escalate so dramatically, but also because I knew he burdened Romy with more than he would ever burden me. I felt a brotherly urge to protect my sister but I was also unsure of best how to do so without starting World War Three with Dad. I pushed down the frustration and returned my attention to the phone.

'Come up and stay whenever you need to, Ro,' I offered, knowing that her own foundation course would most likely prevent her from doing so.

'Thanks, Tay,' she would say, audibly pulling herself together. Occasionally my sister demonstrated a stoicism I could never hope to replicate, and I found myself in awe of it.

On the regular days that I went into the studio I stopped waiting for Jack to come with me, as he tended to wake up later than I did, and I started experimenting with new techniques. Leaving the condoms in my room, where they belonged, I instead decided to embark on the 'self as alien' project I'd shelved at the beginning of term. I decided that I would make a series of plaster casts of my head and then film them moving around Leeds like extraterrestrials with humanoid agency. The slightly unpleasant casting process involved my head being encased in a thick layer of plaster for an hour and a half while I breathed only through a plastic straw.

'Those are quite frightening,' said Tina, as I pottered in my studio, pointing at the five freshly painted glossy red heads.

'That's kind of the point,' I responded tersely.

'A little B-movie if you ask me,' said Bench, from across the room. The plaiting of the intestines for her own project was throwing up more issues than she had anticipated.

'No one did,' I muttered as my phone vibrated in my hand.

```
'Party at our house this Thursday darling!

Be there or be square. P.S. It's animal-
themed and if you don't dress up you aren't
coming in. Love, Alice x'
```

Feeling like Popeye post-spinach, I was immediately invigorated by the idea of having a new creative challenge to get my teeth stuck into – not to mention one that I didn't have to justify to a room full of self-important students. I was buoyed by the possibility of what I could create. I had begun to tire of the little old lady clothes that had defined my first year at university, which now seemed to represent the slight naivety with which I'd approached my course: the thread and fabric manifestations of my apparently too-twee paintings.

I relished, therefore, the prospect of making a real sartorial statement with colour and fabric and flair. As I started to think of all the weird, wonderful and – most importantly – fun outfits I could create, I was filled with a sense of joy and purpose which I hadn't felt in months. All of a sudden I was once again standing in front of my grandma's dressing-up box, overwhelmed and made new by the potential of all the brilliant fabrics in front of me.

Over the subsequent days, I dedicated as many hours as I could spare to constructing my costume. The planning of the thing was almost as much fun as the making, and the first few sketches I dedicated to paper felt like flexing a muscle which I had almost forgotten I possessed. The swoop of my mechanical pencil against paper in pursuit of the perfect bicep curve or hip jut felt as natural as breathing, and the joy of designing something beautiful but practical – something created to be worn – was intoxicating.

First, I constructed the beak. I spent an entire afternoon teasing layers of chicken wire into the perfect shape, a kind of angular banana with a horn at the crest of the curve. Once the maquette was complete, I draped warm, wet layers of mod-roc – a kind of plaster infused bandage – over the top. When that had dried, I used oil paint to mix rich shades of magenta, candy floss and peach. Starting with lighter colours at the top, I painted the beak in dégradé layers which gradually deepened and darkened into an inky black at the base.

To attach the beak to my face, I decided to use a bright-pink satin belt I'd recently bought from one of Leeds's better vintage shops. I liked it for its high key disco-elegance, but it wouldn't really have complemented my down-and-out busker style. For the webbed feet, I used a pair of sunshine-yellow Marigolds from Poundland, the fingers of which I painted black. The wings were trickier, but I decided to use a cerise feather boa – another vintage shop purchase with tufts of candy-coloured maribou popping all over the place. Strapping it to my arms using lengths of masking tape would do the trick. And finally, I found a bright-pink children's unitard in Primark over which I would shimmy a ballet tutu around my waist.

On the day of the party, before going downstairs to join my housemates, I surveyed myself in the mirror on the back of my door. I looked like an enlarged fruit salad sweet, the campest flamingo that ever existed, and I felt fabulous.

'Tay!' shouted Cara, who had dressed as a macaw, using a vermilion body and a bright-green wig, which made her look a little bit like the Riddler. 'That beak is ridiculous. And amazing!' she added, clutching her chest.

I arched my legs dramatically as I descended the stars, attempting not to slip in my Marigolds, and I felt majestic. It was a feeling I'd not experienced since I strode into school wearing my peony-clad Vivienne Westwood T-shirt. I looked around at my friends and a feeling of warmth suffused through my stomach. I hadn't even had anything to drink.

Jack had dressed as an albatross for the occasion, covering himself in white faux fur and placing a papier mâché skull cap finished with a beak on his head. He squawked his approval in a high-pitched guffaw that sounded like it had escaped from seagull. 'That. Is. Amazing!'

To anyone walking past the house we must have looked like a band of bedraggled rejects from the *Sesame Street* casting couch, but to me we were perfect. Despite the fact that

I woke up the next morning feeling like several flamingo beaks had been forced through my skull, I couldn't help but smile. The night had been gloriously debauched – the best I could remember in a long time. A male stripper in a gorilla suit had arrived, despite the fact that no one owned up to ordering one, and we ended the evening making a documentary about a cast of crazy people who'd accidentally been sent to university instead of an asylum. The cherry on the cake was that I'd managed to keep my costume on all night.

I pushed myself up in the bed and looked at the time; it was 11.45 a.m. I'd slept for longer than I'd intended and my tutorial to discuss my most recent essay was at midday.

'Cara?' I shouted through the wall, rushing to get dressed.

'Yes, darling?' she returned.

'Do you want to meet me at the pub after my tutorial?' Navigating the puddle of magentas and baby pinks pooled around my floor like spilled Pepto Bismol, I pushed hurriedly out of my bedroom door.

'Er, of course!' she shouted back.

It was ten past twelve by the time I arrived and I was both sweating profusely and out of breath. Opening the door to the meeting room, I saw a striking woman with asymmetrical blonde hair sitting on the other side of a broad oak desk, who appeared to be wearing a voluminous grey sack.

'Sit down, Mr van den Broeke,' she said, pronouncing my name with pinpoint accuracy. 'I'm the head of art history and cultural studies and it is I who assess much of the theoretical work.'

'Yes, sorry,' I mumbled. 'So sorry I'm late.'

'No bother.' She paused, making a steeple with her fingers, which were full of exotic-looking rings. 'So, I hear things aren't so hot in the practical department, but I must say that I was very impressed with your most recent essay on "the application of time in the work of the conceptual artists of the twenty-first century"... despite the unnecessarily wordy title,' she added under her breath. 'I've awarded you an eighty-five,' she said, matter-of-factly, 'which is the highest mark I've given to anyone on the module.'

'Oh, wow,' I said, slightly dumbstruck. 'Thank you!'

'I must urge you to consider focusing more on the theoretical and historical aspects for your final year,' she intoned.

'I know. And thank you,' I repeated, 'but I really want to be an artist,' I said, with a hint of stubbornness.

'Yes, well, don't we all, dear?' she said kindly. 'But that doesn't seem to be working now, does it?'

I knew I should have been disappointed to hear her say those words, but in that moment, I was surprised to find her honesty refreshing. Although I hadn't wanted to admit it, I'd long suspected that the life of an artist might not be one for me and the sudden sense of unburdening was enough to counter any feelings of disappointment.

Making my way back through the main space of the building, I heard a familiar voice wailing. 'She gave me a fifty-two!' it cried. 'A sodding fifty-two!'

'It's all right, Bench,' said Tina, holding her friend's hand. 'Think of the intestines! They looked amazing!' she urged.

'Oh, shut up, Tina!' replied Bench. 'Why do bad things always happen to me?'

As I walked down Woodhouse Lane and up towards the pub, I spotted Cara sitting on a bench with a pair of delicious-looking amber cylinders glistening in front of her.

'I got ye a pint, bebe!' she shouted in the West-Country-meets-Yorkshire accent we'd concocted over the course of our friendship. "Coz I know what you like!'

I breathed deeply through my nostrils and broke into a run as I crossed the road to meet her, artfully sidestepping a speeding bus on the way.

'Darling, you look great,' Cara shouted as I pulled up to the bench and kissed her on the cheek. She sounded slightly surprised.

As I looked down at my outfit, I realised that in my haste that morning, instead of my usual tracksuit bottoms, I'd pulled on a pair of my old slim leg jeans. Around my waist, the bright-pink satin belt was glinting softly in the early afternoon sun. 'What, this old thing?' I joked, as I twirled clumsily for her on the pavement.

'Do you fancy going out later?' I asked, taking a deep sip of my pint. 'I'm feeling kind of in the mood . . .'

'Always, bebe!' squawked Cara in response, raising her right hand above her head as she flexed her wrist flamboyantly. 'Always!'

CHAPTER 12

The Blue Suit

'Have you seen that there's a film called *The September Issue* coming out soon, Tay?' Lauren asked, pointing at a small entry at the front of *Time Out* magazine as she fiddled with the G-string of her coral bikini. It was a bright morning in late August and her hair was almost white from a long summer of sun exposure. 'It's about how they make *Vogue*.' She paused, waiting for me to respond. 'Do you want to go and see it together?'

'Sure?' I said, without moving my head, which I'd angled to capture the optimal number of rays on every surface. I'd vaguely vocalised my interest in the creative industries to Lauren, and it was entirely in character for her to be planning my career before thinking about her own.

I had graduated that summer and grudgingly returned to

my parents' house. Mum had moved home after agreeing to give it one last go with Dad, but the prospects didn't look good. Dad, seemingly broken by the previous year's separation, which had lasted for several months longer than he'd expected, was terrified of saying anything that might upset Mum and was, as a consequence, a faded facsimile of his former self. Mum, similarly, was imbued with a new sense of fatalism, and although on the surface she seemed to be willing to give their relationship a go, occasionally holding hands with Dad when they watched TV, or suggesting they attend the cinema together, she also seemed like a woman who had moved on. I knew that I needed to move on too, and that the only option was to get a job and get out of the house as quickly as I possibly could.

As luck would have it I managed to pick up a job selling swimming trunks from a small hut within the Guildford Lido. Each day I would head down to the pool and open the shop before positioning myself in a deckchair far enough away from it so that people wouldn't think I was employed there. I mainly spent my days working on my tan and chatting to my best friend, who would come and sunbathe with me when she wasn't working at the tearoom a few miles down the road.

Returning down the M1 for the very last time with a solid 2:1 had annoyed me more than I had imagined it would, not least because I had spent the vast majority of my (predominantly celibate) final year in the studio, and Jack had done no work until the very last minute and somehow managed to bag a first by building a conceptual fishing boat which took up the entire ground floor of the art block. For my final exhibition, on the other hand, I'd submitted watercolour paintings of the plaster cast alien heads as they travelled around Leeds, but, unfortunately, my rudimentary northern interpretation of ET had not set my course leader's world on fire with quite the same ferocity that I'd hoped.

'I don't think I want to be an artist anymore,' I told Mum at Pizza Express a few weeks after returning to Surrey. The restaurant, as familiar as freshly baked dough balls, was where we met if we wanted to talk on our own because it was difficult to do so at home. Picking at one of the burned edges of a glossy slice of pepperoni, I explained, 'I don't think I have the temerity or the ego, to be honest.' I was sure I saw one of her perfectly plucked eyebrows arch in response.

'Well, what do you think you want to do? The world is your oyster, darling.'

I knew she was trying to be helpful, but the sentiment seemed trite and I couldn't help but feel that my chances were slim – who would want to employ someone with a Fine Art degree who didn't want to be an artist?

'Come on, sweetheart,' she said, taking a large bite of her pizza, 'pull your socks up. You loved English at school.' She said. 'What about becoming a writer? You write beautifully?' She paused, surprising herself with the minor eureka moment. 'Aunty Roz has a friend in publishing. We could ask him for advice?'

'I don't do everything beautifully, Mum,' I responded tersely. I found it difficult not to be short with her since I'd moved back home. I knew it wasn't really her fault and that she'd done the right thing separating from Dad, but I couldn't shift a niggling sense of injustice that she had temporarily shifted the burden of his care onto me and Romy. 'But I did enjoy writing about art at uni,' I conceded. 'Whatever happens, I need to move to London as soon as I can,' I said, intending to bruise.

Mum's eyebrows drooped at the sides and she took my wrist. 'It will be OK, darling,' she said, 'and whatever happens, you will always have a home.' She paused. 'We're both trying our hardest, but I'm not sure how long I can do it for.' Despite the fact that Mum was enacting changes in her life by moving in and out of Grandma's, the truth was that nothing that she did seemed to be soothing her sadness. She looked at me with her eyes swimming, so I pulled my hand away from hers and started tearing at my pizza, shovelling great forkfuls into my mouth as quickly as I could.

*

It wasn't until *The September Issue* was in its final few days of screening that Lauren and I finally made our trip to the Odeon. Lauren, true to dogged form, was determined for us not to miss it and the cinema was empty. We bought a bucket of popcorn, half sweet for me, half salty for her, and as soon as Ladytron's 'Destroy Everything You Touch' thumped its way over scenes of models stalking runways, there was nothing else in the room but me and the screen.

From the improbably glamorous outfits worn not just by the models and celebrities, but by the *Vogue* staffers, photographers and stylists, to the inside perspective it offered on an industry I knew near nothing about, by the end of the film I felt as though a whole new world had opened up to me. The shoots produced by Grace Coddington, *Vogue*'s then Fashion Director, in all their decadent artistry, proved that fashion could be meaningful, while the irrepressible drama exuded by key characters including Yves Saint Laurent's former Creative Director Stefano Pilati, and the late André Leon Talley with his immortal line, 'It's a famine of beauty!' spoke directly to the little boy in me, the same little boy who once revelled in wearing multiple layers of cornflower tulle to a family birthday party.

Within a few short weeks, thanks to my Aunty Rozy's friend Simon, I'd found my stepping-stone into the world of publishing. After a brief and underwhelming stint interning at a countryside-focused magazine, where I was tasked with researching dog friendly hotel breaks by elderly men in full tweed, I managed to negotiate myself an interview at a leading art and design magazine. A shining beacon of fashion, beauty and creativity-soaked hope, I'd cut pictures from its pages for pop art projects at school, and it was situated just a few floors above the countryside title in the same impressively glassy building in London.

Dressing for my first day at the design magazine proved considerably more challenging than landing the gig itself. I had dropped the crusty nana wear of my first and second years over twelve months before, returning to my form-fitting jeans, T-shirts and shirts – a partial result of my transformative turn as a flamingo – but I was still unsure what shape my personal style should take now that I was going it alone in the world. One thing I'd learned from poring over magazines like *Esquire* and *GQ* was that it was important to 'make the most of what I was born with', though I struggled to believe that any clothes could make much good of the birthing hips and shallow shoulders I'd inherited from my mum's side of the family.

Truism lodged firmly in the front of my mind regardless, I chose a bright-pink fitted shirt with a grey pinstripe running through it, open to just below the sternum to show off what *Esquire* would call 'the youthful line of my torso' and my thick matt of chest hair, much like Dad also boasted when he was younger. With it, I wore a pair of slim white jeans that complimented the length of my limbs, if not my pelvic area, and on my feet the white Gucci loafers, as they were still the smartest shoes I owned, despite their catamaran-esque proportions.

On my first day, I emerged from the lift on the seventh floor and was greeted by a small woman wearing a billowing coat-cum-cape. 'I'm here about the internship,' I said.

'Do you have an appointment?' she asked, in a small nasal voice. Wearing a pair of perfectly round black-rimmed spectacles, she had the air of an angry pine martin. I nodded sheepishly.

'Come with me,' she said, raising a single eyebrow. 'You'll

need to see the editor.' She smiled in a manner that was not entirely kind and walked briskly down the grey carpeted corridor and out towards a sea of open-plan desks. People who looked equal parts elegant and bookish were beavering away on Apple Mac computers. All the workstations seemed to be clear of detritus, apart from what looked like a couple of architectural models and a number of artfully positioned coffee table books.

I followed the woman round the corner and past the desks to my right, before eventually reaching a small cubicle.

'This person—' she enunciated the word as though I was poisonous '—says that they have an appointment with you?'

'Who is it?' said a light voice from behind a large, expensive-looking desk chair facing away from us.

'What's your name?' hissed the woman at me. 'Name!'

'Teo,' I said loudly, so that the invisible man could also hear.

'Teo?' questioned the voice. 'I don't know a Teo.'

'I'm looking for an internship,' I said. 'Anything really. I've been stuck downstairs. They want me to write about bed and breakfasts and dogs and horses and I can't bear it. I would love to work here; I'll do anything,' I said, rambling. 'Well, most things. I want to write about art, really. Or fashion, but I did my degree in art so I guess that makes more sense. But I like fashion too, menswear really . . .'

'You want to write about art?' The chair turned to reveal a lean man with a clipped side parting. His nose was delicate and the planes of his cheekbones were high. Wearing a neat blue blazer over a grandad collar shirt in a shade of oatmeal, he had a pair of high-shine chestnut monk strap shoes on his feet. He reminded me of Mr Badger from *Wind in the Willows*. 'Which artists do you like?' he asked with a sly tone in his voice.

'Well, I like Jenny Saville and Francis Bacon and Lucien Freud and Gabriel Orozco and Francis Alÿs, and—'

'All right, all right, a few good names in there.' He paused, before shouting at a scared-looking twenty-something who I assumed was his assistant, 'SIMA! Get this boy an internship on the digital desk, will you?' He shot me a final look, before turning away. 'You start next week.'

I strode out of the small office and back towards the lift with a spring in my step and a feather of excitement fluttering in my stomach. The faces at the desks I walked past were uniformly stoney, each one focusing hard on the screen in front of it, but that didn't stop me smiling broadly as I passed.

My primary role at the magazine turned out to be rewriting press releases about exhibitions and events for the website, which was overseen by a kindly Welsh lord named Ralph. And although I wasn't paid for my work – which meant I would have to continue living at home – I was being sent to enough parties, openings and dinners that I could stay out until the last train, gorging on canapés and free drinks most nights, which suited me fine. My parents moaned about having to pick me up from the station when it was late, but they never complained about my absence from home. In truth, I think that the discomfort that Romy and I emanated whenever we were in the house with them became a mirror for their situation: the difficulty was easier to ignore when we weren't around.

The more publishing people I met on my various jaunts around London, the more embedded in the industry I began to feel. But just as a warm wind of confidence began to blow away the self-doubt I'd had about entering my brave new world, the chill of insecurity quickly returned.

'You might want to wear a shirt that reveals a little less chest,' one of the fashion editors said to me as I left for a shop opening in Mayfair during my first week. 'And do you only own one pair of shoes?' He had short, cropped hair and a Mitteleuropean accent I couldn't quite place.

'Um, no,' I lied. 'I just left most of my clothes at my university flat.'

'Well, you should go and pick them up, honey,' he said. 'And quickly.' The pine marten, wearing an enormous black fur around her shoulders, laughed something into his ear.

The people working at the design magazine may have been judgemental, but they also had both money and style, and it was quickly becoming clear to me that 'what I was born with' wasn't going to cut it at the magazine. All I had in my wardrobe, university busker gear aside, were the few pieces I still had left from my time at Ted Baker, which were also, I reasoned, unlikely to fit the bill.

In order to survive my internship, I realised I would need to develop my own signature look, and I would need to do so as simply and economically as possible. Having once written an essay on the subject, I understood the significance and power that a uniform could wield in the creative professions. Picasso's way with Breton sweaters had always impressed me and Jackson Pollock's overalls seemed, in my own pretentious words, to be 'a direct sartorial expression of the manual nature of his work'. But it was really the artists who stuck to a simple outfit day in, day out, that had always fascinated me most, be it Andy Warhol with his trademark black roll necks, or Gilbert & George with their heavy tweed suits. Suddenly, standing outside the fashion cupboard, I knew what I needed to do.

That Friday, I took the tube up to Oxford Circus with my sights set on the fast fashion mecca of Topman, the only place I knew (beyond the polyester-clad digital rails of ASOS) that sold affordable-yet-stylish men's clothes. Having often been told by Mum that it worked well with our family's colouring, I bought one single-breasted suit in a rich shade of midnight blue with an additional pair of navy-blue trousers, two white T-shirts and two white shirts. I also bought a pair of brown lace-up shoes plus one navy-blue crew neck sweater, which could be worn over the shirts and T-shirts when the weather got cold, but it was really the suit that I was most excited about.

The jacket hugged my shoulders in a way that made me look broader than I was, and it nipped neatly at the waist, accentuating the length of my body without overemphasising my hips. The trousers were lean and rakish, kissing the line of my calves without hugging too close. In it, I felt both held together and ready for whatever the design magazine might throw at me; taking myself in in Topman's unflattering changing room mirrors I thought that I looked the smartest I ever had.

The haul of clothes came to £250 in total. It was the most I had ever spent on anything, but I felt both relieved to have absolved myself of the anxiety of getting dressed each morning, and excited to develop the Teo van den Broeke aesthetic.

The next few weeks at the magazine passed relatively smoothly. I felt more at ease, thanks to my suit, and my shift to a simpler look seemed to have mollified my pickier colleagues, too. The painfully long up-and-down outfit inspections which I had been subjected to on a near daily basis when I first started were replaced with indifference at best and fleeting glances at worst, and if I wasn't setting their worlds ablaze with my outfit choices, then I was at least blending in sufficiently, which was the best I could hope for given my lean fiscal circumstances. One colleague had even mistaken my suit for a Comme des Garçons, and the fact that it looked remotely passable to his exacting eye made me feel very confident indeed.

That I was no longer so cripplingly anxious about how I appeared to my colleagues also meant I was better able to focus my energies on the task at hand: writing. Mountains of writing. I wrote about art exhibitions and book launches and parties, I compiled edits of chairs, and watch guides and pieces about art auctions. The scope was broad and the workload intense, but I found myself revelling in the challenges with increasing gusto as each day passed. Most excitingly, Ralph started asking me to write about fashion, and with every new assignment I felt that fate was anointing me with its elegant hand. I wrote about Vivienne Westwood's son Joe Corré's menswear line, A Child of The Jago, about fanciful fashion exhibitions mounted at Kensington Palace and the most beautifully designed haute couture fashion week invitations. Although I continued writing about art and design, it was really the fashion pieces that gave me the most pleasure. The task of using language to conjure the specific cut of a Savile Row suit or the dramatic spectacle of a fashion show was entirely new and exciting, and I was hungry for practice.

Another great thing about working for a creative company was the fact that I had ample opportunity to meet lots of creative people. And by creative people, I mean gay people.

'You know they're doing some LGBT media mixer at the Green Carnation in Soho?' exclaimed Mark a few months into my internship. He was a pixie-ish twenty-something with an underbite and a penchant for rhinestone T-shirts, whose computer was opposite mine and we'd been flirting over email for weeks, though I wasn't sure I fancied him.

'You should go!' said Sophie. Sophie, another intern on the desk who produced much of the travel content, loved a cause, even if said cause was gay men getting drunk in the same room as one another. 'It'll be good to show your support,' she added, catching my eye and smiling.

'There might be some hot guys there too,' Mark emailed me, with lightning speed. He had positioned a winky face beneath the message.

Mark and I, alongside a few of the more junior members of the commercial department, attended the mixer late the following evening. I wore my new suit for the occasion (which I had specially ironed the night before with the help of a wet towel, under the disapproving eye of Dad) and as a consequence I felt considerably more confident in my mingling abilities than I would have had I not been wearing it. Cara, who was working at a TV development company in Soho, had joined us and we'd been for warm-up pints at another bar first.

'Do you think anyone interesting will be here?' I asked her as we walked up the sticky stairs to the top floor, brushing down my lapels carefully as we entered the bar where the party was already in full swing.

The music in the room was on low and, save for a smatter-ing of coat hanger-hipped media types around the edge of the dance floor, the majority of the attendees were positioned in the middle of the room. A few of the more senior members of the design magazine's team were there, as was the then editor of *Esquire*, Jeremy Langmead.

'Oh my God,' said Mark, too loudly. 'There's Jeremy Langmead!'

'Who's Jeremy Langmead?' asked Cara.

'Yeah, I saw,' I said, looking down, not wanting to draw attention. 'Let's get a drink.' I couldn't quite believe that I was in the same room as Jeremy Langmead, the cream of the men's editors, who oversaw all the editorial content at the magazine I'd been reading since a teenager. The image of the pile of *Esquires* in Marc's room projected into my mind and I knew I should go and speak to him, but I couldn't muster the courage to do so. It would be far too embarrassing if he told me to bugger off in front of my new colleagues, who I'd only just begun to win over.

I felt my phone vibrate in my hand.

> 'Are you home tonight, Teo? Your mother's
> out. It would be good to talk.'

As much as I was concerned about my parents and the estrangement that was unfolding in our family home, Dad and I didn't talk about our feelings that much and the idea that he might be starting to call on me now concocted a queasy feeling at the pit of my stomach. He'd long since accepted that I was gay, but the shame that remained from his initial reticence – like a watermark on wood – meant that I didn't yet feel ready to become an emotional ballast for him.

I shoved the phone back into the breast pocket of my jacket and took a large gulp of my pint. We stood at the bar, unsure of what to do. The group remained engrossed in their conversation, so we carried on ordering drinks until we were eventually kicked out. As we were ushered onto the pavement, I felt angry with myself for not being brave enough to say hello, for having let the opportunity pass me by so recklessly, but the beer in my stomach was helping to soften the edges of my anger, as beer has a tendency to do.

'Well, that was a waste of time,' I slurred. Glancing at my watch, I realised I'd missed my train. I paused, feeling slightly relieved as I didn't really want to go home and face either of my parents, the earlier possibility of Dad's chat hanging heavy in my mind.

'Do you mind if I stay at yours, Cara?' Cara had recently moved into a small flatshare in Brockley, which I took great pleasure in calling 'Broccoli' whenever I had the chance.

'Of course not, Toush. Shall we grab a nightcap?'

*

The next morning, I sat at my desk feeling harassed. Since Dad's initial request to speak he had sent a few more messages and I was working hard to ignore them, given that I was still kicking myself over my inaction the night before. I had been at the design magazine for months and despite having asked the managing editor – a grumpy man with a bald head and a dangerous-looking beer belly – if there was any chance that I might receive proper remuneration for my work anytime soon, the outlook didn't seem positive. I knew that if I ever wanted to progress – to ascend into the hallowed halls of Condé Nast and the humming world of *The September Issue* – I would have to take charge of the situation, so I asked the rest of the Intern Islanders if they happened to know anyone who worked at *Esquire*.

'I did an internship there once,' said Mel on the picture desk. 'Why?'

'I just want to figure out an email,' I said, trying not to catch Mark's eye. 'What was yours?'

Taking a deep breath, I opened a new message and typed:

'Dear Mr Langmead. It was so wonderful to meet you last night at the Green Carnation. I was wondering if you had any availability for internships or junior editorial roles? I think everything you do at *Esquire* is fantastic and I would love to come and work with you if at all possible? My very best, Teo van den Broeke.'

Within half an hour I'd received a response. My heart was racing as I opened it.

'Lovely to hear from you, Teo. I don't remember meeting you but I'd happily meet for a coffee. How about today at 1 p.m.? Does the Nordic Bakery on Golden Square work for you?

*

I arrived at the bakery, which was really a coffee house, fifteen minutes early, having panicked about how long it would take me to get to Soho. I had left the office in a hurry, making the excuse to Ralph that I needed to meet my dad for lunch – a lie that dislodged a globule of guilt from the pit of my stomach. I used the walk from Green Park station to flatten down my hair and prepare my lie for Jeremy about how it was that I thought I had actually met him properly the night before.

'Well, if it wasn't you it was certainly someone who looked like you!' I mouthed repeatedly to myself, as I made my way over Burlington Gardens and crossed the river of Regent Street into Soho.

Unlike the garish cafés that had been popping up across London like brightly coloured toadstools that summer, the Nordic Bakery was set apart in its minimalist design. It stood to reason that the editor of *Esquire* would suggest meeting here. The café served warm cinnamon buns, rolled as tight as new carpets, with coffee poured in dip-glazed mugs without handles.

There was only one customer seated in the café when I arrived, and he was facing away from the entrance towards the back of the shop. I could tell from the perfect angles of his hairline and the immaculate layering of his shirt and expensive-looking worker jacket that it was Jeremy, and decided to take it as a good omen that he was there as early as me. Taking a deep breath, I walked past the counter and over to the man I hoped would one day be my boss.

I thrust my hand into his face just as he was sipping coffee and, panicking, quickly retracted it. 'Um, hello,' I said. I could feel that my face was hot. 'Nice to see you. Again . . . My name's Teo.'

'Ah, Teo,' said Jeremy. His voice was pitched high and had a clipped quality. 'It's nice to meet you. I think for the first time?' he added with a twinkle.

'Thank you for taking the time to see me, I love *Esquire*,' I blurted, quickly weighing up that Jeremy would probably prefer honesty over pretence – the warmth in his manner suggested it. 'I was too nervous to come over and meet you last night, I'm sorry,' I said. 'I think you're fantastic at what you do,' I added, gushing. Part of me was relieved that if he didn't recognise me from the Green Carnation then he wouldn't notice I was wearing the same outfit I had been the night before.

'Why don't you tell me a little more about yourself,' said Jeremy as he pulled gently at his cinnamon bun. I could see that he was eyeing my suit, which I thought, despite being on its second day of wear, still looked relatively crease-free. I felt more relieved than ever, at that point, that I'd made the purchase.

I told Jeremy all about my degree, and my passion for art. I also expressed how much I had loved working on fashion stories for the design magazine, and that it had invigorated my interest in men's clothes and, by extension, my own wardrobe.

Jeremy, who had been eating his bun in small, mouselike mouthfuls as I spoke, eyed my suit again before saying, 'Oh gosh, look at the time. I'm so sorry, Teo, I have another meeting, but it was lovely meeting you.' He seemed earnest, but he also sounded slightly bored. 'I'll need to have a chat with the team about whether there are any ways in which we can work together, but I should warn you that journalism is a tricky business. You mustn't expect to be paid all that much,' he said, as he pulled on the jacket he'd removed while I was speaking.

'I don't care about being paid!' I said dully, as Jeremy stood up to leave. 'I just want to work in magazines!' He stopped then and looked at me with a quizzical half smile on his face, before picking up his coffee mug, draining the dregs and striding out of the café and onto the square beyond.

*

Later that evening I arrived into Cobham station, where Dad was waiting in his car to take me home. 'How was your day, Teo?' he asked as I climbed into the passenger seat. The dejected tone in his voice suggested that he'd just as soon hear about my day as he would stick knives through his hands.

'Um, it was good.' I paused. 'I had a meeting with the editor of *Esquire* and he said he was going to look into whether there might be something for me in the team,' I said, deciding to keep it brief. The truth was I didn't hold out much hope for anything to come from the meeting. Jeremy had been very friendly, but he had also seemed more interested in his baked treat than he had been in my limited editorial experience. I turned to look at Dad, who was staring straight ahead. He hadn't responded to anything I had said, and his eyes were red. 'Are you OK, Dad?'

'Oh yes.' He sounded like he was about to cry. 'I'm fine.'

I looked out at the dark road, unsure of what to do.

'You know, you and Mum haven't seemed happy for a while,' I said tentatively.

'It's not your marriage, Teo,' he spat suddenly. 'You don't know what goes on between two people.' His hair was long, and it didn't look like it had been washed. Although the man sitting next to me was wearing the uniform of the proud Dad I remembered from my childhood, an oversized white Fruit of the Loom T-shirt with a pair of chino shorts and some scruffy-looking boat shoes, the miasma of misery that revolved around him made him almost unrecognisable. I knew Dad was still in there somewhere, but he was difficult to see, like a 747 lost in the ash cloud of a slowly erupting volcano.

'OK,' I said. 'Well, I don't really know what to say.' I looked out of the window to my left.

'No,' said Dad. His gaze re-fixed on the road ahead. 'Neither do I.'

When we got back to the house Mum was out – I knew better than to ask Dad where she was – and it was cold and unlit. I retreated to my bedroom as Dad returned to the living room, where the bum imprint on his favourite armchair looked more entrenched than ever. I felt sorry for him but angry too. If he and Mum were beyond repair, then I couldn't help but feel that he should shoulder a large proportion of the blame for it. His rudeness, his rages, his drinking . . . I knew that he was hurting and that in his own way he was suffering – perhaps more than all of us – but his lack of any sense of responsibility for what had happened incensed me. Rather than enticing me to go downstairs and talk to him, the feeling only firmed my resolve to move to London as soon as possible.

I distracted myself by thinking about the following day's Creative Awards ceremony, hosted by the magazine. Effectively an elongated drinks reception, it was mainly an excuse for lots of attractive people to get paralytically drunk, and I had been tasked with editing the pictures from the red carpet for the website and captioning the winners' names. As the magazine's social event of the year, I knew people would be dressed up, but I would have to wear my blue suit, which was currently lying in a crumpled pile in the corner of the room for the second night in a row. I finally had to admit that, after such constant wear, it was beginning to look a little bedraggled. The knees were baggy, the lapels were lightly splattered with red wine and Heinz tomato soup stains – the two main food groups of any editorial intern worth his unpaid words – and the stitching around the shoulders was beginning to come loose. I felt suddenly embarrassed that I'd worn it to meet Jeremy, but I tried to push the feeling from my mind as I walked across the room towards it. Carefully I picked up the suit, gently unfurled it, and took it into the bathroom where I dabbed at the stains with a sponge until they seemed to come away from the fabric. As quietly I could, so as not to alert Dad, I turned on the shower to full heat and let great plumes of steam fill the small space, hopeful that they would remove the creases from the jacket and the trousers. I needed the suit to look its best; it felt as though it was my one-way ticket into a world I was desperate to be a part of, and out of a house which no longer felt like home.

The next day I returned to London early; everyone at the office was excited for the awards but my brain was consumed with thoughts of Mum and Dad, and my meeting with Jeremy. After a long day of not doing very much work due to my distracted state, Mark, Sophie and I made our way to the event space, which featured a giant version of the magazine's logo, illuminated with enormous bulbs, positioned out the front. I was instantly pulled out of my stupor by the dizzy glamour of the scene, which resembled a Rose Hartman photograph from Studio 54.

As I walked towards the thin girl holding a clipboard, the moment in *The September Issue* where the *Vogue* team strides confidently through crowds to attend a Paris fashion show played through my mind. I looked down at my suit, which seemed even more bedraggled in the bright light of the sign, and I couldn't help but feel a little out of place. The editor's assistant was wearing a giant couture gown crafted from red tulle for the event and the throng of journalists, artists and designers looked impossibly glamorous in their expensive layers of leather, cashmere and velvet. When we entered the packed venue, I took two cocktails from the handsome waiter holding them out on a silver tray, and quickly downed them in an attempt to put myself at ease, before picking up another two and walking out into the crowd with more of a spring in my step.

*

The following morning I woke up feeling like I had been punched in the face repeatedly. I looked around and pushed myself up onto unfamiliar sheets, in a bed which was not mine. The realisation gradually dawned on me, with the same intensity as the headache that was expanding menacingly in my brain, that I had no idea where I was. Light was streaming through the French doors ahead of me, which were slightly ajar, allowing in a soothing autumn breeze.

'Morning, sleepy-head,' said a voice I didn't recognise, with a strong Spanish accent. Looking down at myself, I realised that I was still wearing my suit. I could feel the draught fluttering vigorously around my right leg, and I reached down to discover a giant rip in the trouser. My head was thumping now and my heart was pounding in unison.

As I looked down to inspect my painful leg, I noticed that the tear was across the back, perpendicular to the direction of the seam, which meant there would be no way of repairing it. The cut beneath, which had scabbed over slightly but was still bleeding at the edges, looked like it need stitches.

'How did this happen?' I shouted. 'Where am I? What time is it?'

'Woah woah woah, chico,' said the voice, which was now closer.

I could see through the haze of my gummed-up eyes that the face behind it was handsome. He had a shock of dark hair, his skin was tanned and his eyebrows were bushy like mine.

'You're in Clerkenwell, it's nine a.m., and you're fine.' He paused. 'Apart from your suit. You fell backwards over a railing when you were demonstrating the size of your fashion editor's ego and caught your leg on the spike.' He looked directly into my eyes, which must have been betraying my horror at not remembering anything that happened.

'And don't worry, we didn't do anything.' Another pause. 'Well, not much, at least.'

'Nine a.m.!' I shouted. Jumping out of the bed, I grabbed my phone, which was nearly out of battery, and ran for the door. The flap of fabric was swatting around my leg like a sail, and the cut was painful. 'Sorry, thank you for having me, bye!' I bellowed.

As I rushed down the street, vague shards of memory flicked in front of my eyes. I remembered kissing the Spaniard as we stumbled into his bedroom, I remembered trying to clumsily access his flies, and I vaguely remembered him stopping me. A heady cocktail of both embarrassment and relief shook around my brain, and once I realised that he was right and nothing had, in fact, happened. I felt a pang of regret for not stopping to take his number.

As I rushed to catch the bus, I looked down at my phone and saw that I had four missed calls from Dad. He had tried ringing before I'd woken up, leaving less than a minute between each one. I didn't have the time or battery power to call him back so I stuffed the phone into my pocket and hung onto a rail as the number 40 bus swung south, past Farringdon station and the busy sea of commuters rushing lemming-like towards work.

When I made it to the office, I was fifteen minutes late, and I went up the backstairs in an attempt to sneak in as discreetly as I could.

'What happened to your suit?' asked Sophie, as I sloped in behind her, keeping my head as low as possible.

'And your face?' asked Mark.

'Nothing,' I mumbled, 'it's fine.'

'The fashion editor was looking for you earlier,' said Mark, with a touch of glee. 'He didn't look happy. Apparently one of the award winners was misidentified on the website and he complained personally to the editor this morning. Everyone's furious . . .'

With horror, it dawned on me that I was in the firing line. Powering up my computer in a panic, I immediately spotted an email from the fashion editor, which was cc'd to the entire staff of the magazine.

'WHO captioned the picture of Konstantin Grcic with Marc Newson's name?' The words spat at me out of the screen. 'Heads. Will. Roll.'

My heart shot up into my mouth like a rocket. With my hands shaking, I spotted another email from the editor with the subject line, 'My office. Now.' The staccato in its delivery ricocheted around my skull.

Slowly, I stood up, smoothed out my jacket as best I could, and attempted to conceal the flap of fabric waving around behind my right leg. I considered using the stapler on my desk to hold the disconnected sections together, but imagined that would only make things worse, so I kept my back as straight as possible as I walked out past Intern Island, like a ragged fishing trawler being sent to the scrap yard, and down past the rows of desks leading up to the editor's office.

The room was silent, save for the odd rustle of paper here and clearing of throat there. I swivelled my eyes to my right and saw that everyone was staring in my direction as I continued my slow march towards his lair. The pine marten and the Mitteleuropean were smirking at the entrance to the fashion cupboard. I turned left and walked into the room. Ready to accept my fate.

'Firstly,' said the editor, turning around as I entered, 'what the hell happened to you?' He looked me up and down with a mix of horror and confusion. 'This is exactly what I'm talking about. I don't care how or bloody why the internet thingy occurred,' he shouted, 'but it's about your attitude. You're the last one in at nine, you're the first one out at six. You're the first person in the kitchen when there's a cake! Not impressed, sunshine, not impressed.' He paused, his face had become ruddy from the excursion. 'Get out of my sight,' he said. 'And sort that bloody suit out. You look like you work for sodding *Fisherman's Weekly*!'

I sloped back to my desk as quickly as I could. I lowered myself into my seat carefully, and I stared dead straight at my computer. I was shaking perceptibly, still in shock from the force of the editor's diatribe. Though I tried to tell myself it was fine that I had been going out a lot – that I was young and I was still attempting to expand my network – the truth was that I had been drinking too much during my time at the magazine and he was probably right in his assertion that my focus had been elsewhere. I think I'd known for a while that the magazine was not my natural home – my behaviour over the past few weeks was really a symptom of me having not been all that happy in the job. The fashion pieces I wanted to write were given the meanest spaces on the website, the stories the magazine told tended to be a touch devoid of human interest, and – importantly – there seemed to be no additional money forthcoming. A familiar lump begin to form in my throat and I swallowed hard to keep it at bay. I felt frustrated and lost. I knew I was going to have to sort myself out, to pull my socks up and replace my suit – my poor, beautiful suit – but in that moment I wasn't precisely sure how I was going to go about it. The prospect of getting through the next eight hours seemed challenging enough.

'Are you OK?' mouthed Sophie. I smiled a tight smile her and looked down at my keyboard, not wanting to engage. 'Do you have a spare pair of trousers, Mark?' I emailed, unable to bring myself to ask the question out loud.

'Well, now he emails me,' he responded with lightning speed, before following up. 'Sure, give me a sec.'

I spent the remainder of the day stuck to the seat of my pleather office chair glaring at my computer screen, as much to prove that I could work hard when I wanted to as to avoid any awkward interactions with members of the senior team circling the shallows around Intern Island. Although I was grateful to him for his kindness, the beige chinos which Mark had leant me barely fitted and were stretched like sausage skins across my thighs; I couldn't even risk going to the loo for fear of looking even more ridiculous than I already felt.

I decided I would work an hour overtime, in a limp bid to prove the editor wrong about my punctuality (or lack thereof). The vast open plan space was bare save for his assistant and one of the cleaning ladies when, as I stifled a yawn at 6.44 p.m., an email from Jeremy popped into my inbox. Deciding that its contents couldn't be any worse than the miserable events which had unfolded that day, I opened it quickly, eager to pull the bandage off before too many filaments of hope became attached to it.

'Dear Teo, I'm delighted to ask you to join *Esquire* as contributing editor. This will be on a paid freelance basis. I would like you to run our new best dressed man in Britain project. Sincerely hoping you will join us. Looking forward to hearing from you, Jeremy.'

My heart, which I realised then had been in my mouth for most of the day, seemed to return to my chest and begin beating normally. A broad smile spread across my face, and I felt my earlier embarrassment begin to melt away. I suddenly didn't even care about the rip in my suit, which was folded neatly under my desk. I could buy hundreds more suits! Beautiful Savile Row two-pieces and designer three-pieces, all of them in richer shades of blue than the last – navy, midnight and cobalt, mingling together in a mellow melee of low-key elegance, which I would make my look forever. While I might have been getting a bit ahead of myself financially with this daydream, considering Jeremy's own comments about the salary for the position, I was going to work at *Esquire*. The most stylish men's magazine in the world. And as an editor!

Figuring that 6.47 p.m. was close enough to the full extra

working hour I'd promised myself that I would complete that day, I got up from my desk, picked up my phone, plugged in my headphones and pressed play on Ladytron's 'Destroy Everything You Touch' as I marched out of the office towards the elevator. I wasn't entirely sure where I was going, but I knew I needed to escape the hostile glassy tomb of the magazine's HQ, and I was in the mood to celebrate.

Skipping my way across the high-shine floor of the soaring entrance hall as the chorus of the song kicked in, I felt invincible. I involuntarily strutted in time to the beat as I stomped my way across the street, forcing the oncoming traffic to stop, and over towards the White Hart, the magazine's pub, where I planned on ordering myself a hair-of-the-dog Bloody Mary, my excitement smartly shoving the booze-induced indignity of the night before to the back of my brain.

As I reached the door of the establishment, an invitingly sticky brown slab the colour and texture of treacle, my phone started to ring in my hand. Pausing on the stone step, I pressed the volume button on my headphone wire to answer the call.

'Mum! I've got some news!'

'Darling.' She was sobbing and she could barely speak. I paused and pushed the white plastic bud further into my ear. The late afternoon sun had sliced through the thick layer of cloud and was warming the side of my face. 'I told Dad I was leaving for good, and, and . . .' she continued ' . . . well, he's in hospital.' I could hear her chest shuddering at the effort of crying. 'He's in hospital, Teo; you need to come home.'

The Furry Loafers

Two years later

The fashion cupboard was unusually full for the time of year. *Esquire*'s fashion director Catherine Hayward – the head of the magazine's fashion department and a respected stylist – was uncharacteristically early in the process of planning the big autumn-winter '15 trends story, which set the tone for the rest of the season's style-related content. The thick chrome rails that lined the walls of the cupboard were full to bursting. There were capacious cashmere caban coats finished with laser-cut prints, silky black nylon rain macs, and sumptuous crocodile sweaters in shades of cortado and coco bean. I had entered the cupboard to witness first-hand what Catherine had called in for the shoot, and I wasn't disappointed – the space was full to the brim with treasures, which was no mean feat; as despite the diminutive moniker, the cupboard was bigger than the Camberwell flat that I moved into with my sister a few months after Dad was released from hospital.

Our cohabitation had been motivated by a desire to share the burden of the pain that both of us felt after having witnessed Dad's vulnerable frame lying on a gurney in intensive care, hooked up to a web of tubes and monitors. And though Romy and I soft-footed around each other at first, it quickly became apparent that it would be trickier to live alongside each other as grown-ups than it had been to live together as children. Romy resolutely disliked all of the (few) dates I brought home; and I found her early rises to exercise challenging, but on balance it was more of a comfort than a trial to be within such easy reach of one another.

Once the initial shock of Dad's hospitalisation passed and he'd left intensive care, the incident somehow seemed to have changed my feelings for him; I'd felt a febrile kind of love begin to sprout from the emotional scar tissue left by his actions. Adding the weight of a sentimental proclamation to the already heavy scenario felt somehow reckless – so I didn't tell him at the time – but at that moment something in my conception of him shifted. Perversely, perhaps, I felt as though I was beginning to understand him.

Despite my new-found feelings of empathy for Dad, the first and only time we had met up one-on-one since his time in hospital was for dinner at Bill's in Wimbledon: neutral ground between his new terraced house in Horsham and our

London flat. I tried to broach the subject that he was perhaps in part to blame for Mum choosing to leave him, that it wasn't all her fault, and it hadn't gone down well.

'Teo, I've told you before, you don't know what happens in a marriage,' he'd said, with a flash of old steel. At least the Dad I knew was in there somewhere. 'You only saw one side of what went on between your mother and me.'

'That may be true, Dad, but I heard how you spoke to her. I saw how you'd embarrass her at dinner parties and put her down publicly,' I'd said, shaking as adrenaline rushed through my body. The only times I'd spoken to Dad so frankly was during my childhood when I'd defended Mum, and I'd been worried he would get up and walk out. 'It was horrible, Dad. And you could be awful to me too.' I'd recounted the scallop incident to him for the first time, and his response had been disappointing.

'No,' he'd replied, screwing his nose up incredulously. 'That never happened, Teo,' he'd said, flatly. 'I would never have done that.'

I knew that it was probably too painful for Dad to remember his worst moments. He'd stopped drinking since he and Mum had parted, and there was a new air of clarity about him that had never been there before. It was obvious to me now that Dad had struggled with his own feelings of insecurity and fears of rejection when he was with Mum and that he'd probably used alcohol to mask them, creating a vicious, addictive feedback loop. And, by extension, the fact that I was so close to Mum had also made my relationship with him more challenging. I wanted to be close to this new version of Dad. We just had to figure out our own way of doing so.

And so it was for a lunch with Dad that I was now getting ready. I ran my hand across one particularly tightly packed rail as I strolled the length of the cupboard, stopping occasionally when my fingers landed on something soft: one of that season's cashmere trenches, or a double-faced vicuna cocoon coat. I knew that my suit jacket, which I'd hung in the cupboard earlier so that I wouldn't get it wrinkled before lunch, would be identifiable by its relative roughness, so I continued fondling the fabrics, enjoying the feeling of inordinate expense against my skin.

When I eventually alighted on my inferior garment, pushed down to the end of the rail, I threw it on over my shoulders before surveying myself in the cupboard's enormous floor-to-ceiling mirror. The jacket was part of a Paul Smith suit I'd bought in a sample sale for a bargain, and it had quickly become the mainstay of my working wardrobe. Cut from midnight-blue merino wool, the peak lapels were slightly wider than usual, there was an elegant nip at the waist and the pleated trousers were finished cropped and with a cuff. The suit was an elevated version of the high street two pieces I'd worn to death during my time at the design magazine two years before, and it made me feel urbane and sophisticated whenever I wore it. But, unlike the suits I sported in my former job, with which I was only brave enough to wear white shirts and traditional brown shoes, with this new suit I had begun to take risks, teaming its relative simplicity with wilder pieces like leopard print sweaters and block neon shirts, I would never have dared wear before.

As I straightened the lapel of my jacket and hoiked up the trousers, I looked down at my feet and my stomach gave a small leap. As part of his first collection for Gucci, creative director Alessandro Michele, who looked a bit like a cross between Jesus and Ringo Starr, had reimagined the brand's classic horse-bit loafer as a mule, finished inside with lashings of shearling fur.

Playful and purposely over the top, the moment they walked the runway in Milan, I knew I had to have them. The feeling of longing was one I recognised, having experienced it nearly twenty years earlier witnessing the boy in the white socks on the way to Polesden Lacey, and then later as I perused a sale rail of enormous suede loafers on Sloane Street, desperate to impress the very same boy that I loved. I had watched the fashion show online and placed an order with the shop so that I received them as soon as they came in. They were the most expensive things I'd ever bought, not to mention the most frivolous, and I loved them all the more for it.

Admiring my new shoes in the mirror, I wriggled my toes within their toasty shearling cocoons as if to prove that they actually existed, and that they actually belonged to me. I never thought I would be able to make enough money in magazines to afford my rent, let alone expensive shoes. Miss Jacobs's description of the fashion world as 'fickle' ran through my head, and I was relieved to have proved her wrong, at least temporarily. A point affirmed by the fact that in a few days,

I would be going to the menswear shows in Milan and Paris for the very first time. I intended to wear new shoes for the entirety of the two-week trip.

'I'm just popping out for a meeting,' I shouted across the open-plan space to Sarah, the editor's assistant, who seemed to have a perpetual cold. Locking the cupboard behind me, I threw the key onto my desk. 'I'll be back by three-ish if Alex needs me.'

'Enjoy,' she said with flattened sarcasm. The assistant was required to stay and manage the phones when the editorial team was at lunch, which meant she was never really able to go out for lunch herself. 'Alex said he wanted a chat with you this afternoon, so don't be late.'

Ignoring the snippy tone of her last instruction, I set off down the low-lit corridor towards the lift, my shoes shucking lightly against the carpet as I went. *Esquire*'s offices were situated in a giant, brown-brick seventies building, which looked like a pixelated spool of brown wool, perched on the edge of Soho's Carnaby Street. I took great pleasure in coming into Soho for work each day; a vibrant, thrumming place, which I'd come to associate with boozy nights out spent pinballing between gay bars with Cara, rather than anything remotely related to work.

As I stepped out of the office and onto the street, which was busy with tourists and creatives on their lunch breaks, I breathed in deeply. The sun was high in the sky, which was a New York shade of blue, and bright-white contrails criss-crossed over it in a hazy celestial hatch. I'd planned to catch the tube to meet Dad on the South Bank, but the brilliant London weather had instead inspired me to walk. My new shoes weren't exactly designed for going long distances, but it was too beautiful a day to be stuck underground, and, besides, I wanted to show them off.

Making my way down Broadwick Street, I called Romy. 'Has Mum been ringing you non-stop too?' I asked. 'She called me three times in my meeting this morning.'

'I know, she's just excited,' replied Romy, calmly. 'Have you organised a time to go and see it again?' she asked.

Mum had recently bought a new house. A small semi-detached Victorian red-brick situated on a quiet thoroughfare in the village of Brookwood – a place I had never heard of before Mum discovered it – the house had a snaking wisteria around the lower bay window at the front and it smelled like her already. I'd been to see it with Mum a few months before, but we hadn't stayed long. I found it hard to imagine her living anywhere other than Fetcham, though I didn't tell her that at the time.

'No, I haven't, but I know that I need to.'

The long garden at the rear of the house was filled with enormous hydrangeas, tumbling tea rose bushes, and a story-book apple tree at its centre. At the back ran a long stretch of the Basingstoke Canal, which was lined with towering beech trees and home to a multitude of moorhens, herons and geese.

'It felt real when I saw it for a second time,' said Romy, tentatively. 'I just hope Dad manages to make his place feel as cosy.'

'Hold on, Ro, Mum's on the other line.' I pulled the phone away from my ear. 'Wait one second?'

'Hello, darling!' Mum sounded sprightly. 'How are you today?'

'I'm good, Mum, I'm just walking to lunch. Oh shit,' I said, as I tripped over a loose paving tile. 'How's the move coming along?'

'It's fine!' she said. 'I know you're busy so don't worry.'

'Sorry, Mum, this is the first time I'm doing this trip so I can't let them down.' I paused. 'I'm really excited to be honest.'

'So you should be, darling! I'm so proud of you, you know, Teo. You are an absolute marvel! How did I make such an amazing boy?' she exclaimed happily. I could hear the smile spreading through her voice like good butter on warm bread, before – true to character – she turned briskly to more practical matters. 'Have you packed yet?'

I noticed some crumbs on my shirt, a white collarless cotton number, which I'd put on fresh that morning. While attempting to wipe them off, I very nearly walked head-on into a lamp post. I looked around me to see if anyone had noticed and smiled a tight knowing smile at a couple who had.

'Mum, I'm going to need to call you back. Sorry. Speak later.' I took the phone into one hand and returned to Romy, but the line had gone dead.

Eager to make up time, I trotted quickly down Wardour Street, past discarded polystyrene cups and dehydrated puddles of spilt lager, past the eager patrons of Chinese restaurants pedalling their identical plates of char siu bun and deliciously slippery cheung fun, and out onto the edge of Leicester Square. The afternoon sun was bright, so I placed the phone in between my shoulder and chin and fished around in my brown leather bag for the sunglasses, which I knew wouldn't be in their case. Slowing down at the bottom of the street I redialled Romy's number and tucked the phone into the crook of my neck.

'Sorry, Ro, are you there?'

'Yeah, I'm here,' she said, with a fleeting touch of impatience. 'Are you seeing Dad for lunch today?'

'I'm on my way to meet him now.' I paused. 'I'm a bit anxious, to be honest,' I added, as I cut down the marbled ravine between the National Gallery and the Sainsbury Wing, and out onto the pigeon-peppered tourist Mecca beyond. 'We haven't had much alone time since it all happened,' I said.

'I know. He seems sad, but he's also OK.' Romy paused at the end of the phone. 'Just be patient with him, Tay. See you tonight.'

Crossing the busy roundabout overseen by Napoleon's sleeping lions, I whisked past Waterstones and picked up my phone to check my emails. Alex had started at *Esquire* a year or so prior, when Jeremy left the magazine to join a retail group, and I felt like I still needed to make an impression. His writing was some of the finest I'd read and he was a hard edit, but he was fun and I wanted nothing more than for him to rate me. Just as I was tapping out an email to him, asserting that I would be back at the office no later than three, my phone began vibrating in my hand.

'Hey, Lau,' I said into the brick of plastic next to my face, which was now warm from use. 'I'm just en route to meet Dad.' Lauren had recently graduated with a first from her degree in advertising, and had immediately landed a creative role in one of the most important advertising agencies in the business. Her journey to higher education had been one littered with false starts, including one particularly tricky moment when she got expelled from school for kicking a door off its hinges. The outburst had come during the period that her own parents decided to finally divorce, a shared experience that had made our bond even stronger. I was delighted and relieved that she was doing so well. We'd not missed a moment of contact since the day that she discovered the truth about her awkward friend in his baggy skateboarding jeans.

'Of course, beauty,' she said. 'How are you feeling about it?'

'OK, I guess,' I said. 'I'm going to the shows tomorrow.'

'Whoop whoop! Which city is it first?'

'Milan,' I said. The word felt exotic in my mouth, as hard and seductive as a horse bit. 'And then Paris.'

Every January and June the industry's most important designers decamp to the world's fashion capitals to showcase their seasonal collections. Starting in London, where the edgiest designers show over the course of one weekend, the circus then moves onto Milan, where the big-name commercially driven designers take centre stage. The whole shebang comes to a glamorous close in Paris, where the creatively focused luxury brands tend to have their homes. The run is spread over three consecutive weekends, and each magazine sends at least three members of the editorial team to be present. The primary reason physical attendance is so important, I'd learned, is commercial – big advertising brands liked to have bums on seats – but it's also essential for editors to take in the most important collections first-hand so that they, in turn, can decide what they shoot for the magazine in the corresponding season.

Ever since I'd started at *Esquire*, 'the shows' had been dangled in front of me like Crufts to a baby Bichon Frisé, but I'd never been allowed to attend. This season, however, the senior fashion editor was unable to travel, and I was to represent in his place, alongside Catherine and Alex. We would be driven around in a black Mercedes, we would stay at fabulous hotels and we would have long, wine-soaked dinners with glamorous PR people from all of the world's biggest brands. Most importantly, however, we would be seated at the shows themselves – the high-octane moments when all the fabulous drama of the fashion industry funnelled onto a long white runway, and the world took notice. I soon would be living out my own *September Issue* fantasy, but now that the trip was looming I couldn't help but panic about what else I was going to wear with my new shoes.

'I'm almost at Waterloo, Lau,' I said into the phone. 'I'll call you tomorrow before I go,'

I rushed past the Corinthia at the bottom of Northumberland Place towards the Hungerford Bridge, my shoes clacking behind me like a football rattle in slow motion. I would treat myself to a black cab on the way back, I decided, as much to preserve my loafers for the trip as to ensure that I made it to my meeting on time. Climbing the sandpapery steps of the bridge, I looked over at the towering cumulus clouds building like cotton wool castles behind the Houses of Parliament. I stopped to snap a photo of the scene and sidestepped a young couple taking selfies against the white-metal guard rails, looking a little precarious as they leaned back to achieve the perfect shot. As I trotted down the stairs on the other side of the bridge, my phone vibrated in my hand once again.

`Good luck with your dad, Te. I'll be thinking of you. T x'

I had only been seeing Tom for a few months but already he felt like home. We'd started talking on one of the less salubrious hook-up apps, which up until that point had proven a fertile breeding ground for a handful of toxic, sex-centered relationships rather than anything meaningful. He worked in television, which was close enough to what I did that we shared similar interests, but far enough away that we wouldn't be in competition with each other, and he was unerringly kind. For the first time in a long time, I felt able to fully be myself, and Tom had been instrumental in the shift.

I smiled to myself as I returned my phone to my bag and trotted up the steps into Waterloo station. I suddenly felt more confident about my meeting with Dad. Despite sidestepping the discarded front pages of *Metro*, inky and smudged, I very nearly slipped on the high-shine marble floor at the top of the stairs, which had been worn away by decades of busy footfall. I started walking more slowly towards the clock, which was suspended in the centre of the station.

'Hi Dad,' I said as I reached him. He hadn't seen me coming. I put my arms around his neck and he made a sound that suggested I'd winded him. I could feel that he'd lost weight. He was wearing a slim blazer, cut close in a smart shade of air force blue with a light chalk stripe, and straight-leg jeans in a dark wash with black leather shoes. Under the jacket he wore a pale-blue poplin shirt I'd bought him the Christmas prior. I was surprised to see him in it, as I hadn't thought he'd liked it at the time.

His hair was freshly washed, if a little fluffy, and it looked like it could do with a cut. His sideburns had transformed into wings, which looked as though they belonged to a small bird, and there were snowflakes of loose skin dusting their edges. His eyes behind his glasses, which needed a clean, were rimmed in pink, but less so than they had been when I last saw him.

'Shall we go, Dad?' I said, leading him tentatively by the arm. 'But hold on.' I stopped. 'I don't know how you can see where you're going with those glasses.' Checking first to see that he was comfortable with me doing so, I pulled them off his face gently, breathed onto the lenses, and rubbed them with the lapel of my blazer.

Where once Dad might have flinched at me taking care of him in such a way – too proud to accept an act of grooming from his son – and I might have been too fearful of reproach to even try, this new version of my father seemed to appreciate the intimacy. Dad had point-blank refused to consider the idea of dating anyone new since Mum had left and I sensed that he was missing human touch. The new air of softness suited him. 'That's better,' I said, placing them back on his face. 'Now you can see!' I felt my shoulders relax as he allowed me to link my arm into his.

'Where have you booked, Tay?' he asked, his voice cracking slightly.

'I thought we could go to Bill's in London Bridge,' I said. 'You liked it last time.' I turned my head slightly in his direction. The mention of our previous meeting didn't elicit a response, which was good – I hoped the fact that it seemed to have been forgotten would ease the atmosphere of this interaction.

It took us over half an hour to reach the restaurant because Dad's knee was hurting, and, as we strolled slowly down the South Bank, it struck me that I only had a finite amount of time to spend with him. He was forty-seven when I was born, so had just entered his seventies by the time Mum left. A spool of melancholy unfurled as we slowly made our way up the stairs into the brightly lit restaurant, a sense of relief simultaneously washing over me that we were making an effort with each other now, and that our interactions were no longer wine-soaked. His abstinence might buy us more years – happy ones – than we might never have had when he was still drinking. We were shown to our seats by a young waitress with blue hair who Dad, serving a scoop of his old panache, flirted with gently.

'I'm out for lunch with my son,' he said, puffing out his chest. 'He's a journalist.'

'Oh, very good,' said the waitress indulgently. 'This is your son, eh? I thought you might be brothers.' She smiled. She had a warm-yet-bored look in her eye.

'You're too kind,' said Dad as he settled himself slowly into his seat. We sat in silence for a while as we scoured the menus more intently than necessary, each man silently hoping that the dog-eared piece of A3 card in front of him might provide a script for the conversation that inevitably needed to unfold.

'How are you, Dad?' I asked eventually, as I placed the menu on the table in front of me.

'I'm OK, Tay,' he said. 'You know, ups and downs.'

I put my hand across the table and placed it on his. 'It'll get easier, Dad,' I said, mainly because I didn't really know what else to say. Dad had recovered physically following his time in hospital but mentally he still seemed fragile.

'I know,' he said, pulling at his eye with his hand, which was so like my own, spade-like. 'I don't know how she could have thrown it all away.' There was a sense of anguish on his face, which he was trying hard to mask. I knew he loved Mum and that he missed her terribly, but I still didn't feel able to console him like he needed me to. I wanted to tell him how hard it had been for us when he came back from a trip, grumpy and smarting for a fight. How difficult it had been when he and Mum would scream at each other in front of my friends at my birthday. How scared I had been about telling him about my sexuality, but instead I said, 'I know you do, Dad.'

'You know,' he suddenly said, 'I have never been prouder of anything than I am of you kids. And I am so proud of you.' He paused. 'Your work ethic, everything. I'm so proud.' He started tearing up, and so did I. 'Although, I'm not entirely sure about those blahhdy furry things on your feet!' he said, a flash of the old Dad singeing its welcome way to the surface. 'They look like sad dogs.'

I stretched out my feet into the aisle, nearly tripping up a nearby waiter, laden with plates, and twisted my ankles to show off my new purchases. 'Aren't they fab?' I asked. 'They're shearling-lined, and backless, so you can wear them inside or out.'

'Whatever makes you happy, Dao,' said Dad, smiling. 'Right, I'm starving . . . what shall we order?'

'I don't know why you pretend, Dad,' I said, sighing. 'You know you're going to get the steak and eggs.'

After lunch I walked Dad back to the station, having accepted that I was going to be late returning to work. As we hugged goodbye under the Waterloo station clock, I felt a renewed sense of hope that we might be able to build a new relationship out of the ashes of our former one. I knew it wouldn't be easy, and that I would eventually have to forgive him for everything that had happened when we lived under the same roof, but I also knew that if he had the strength to start a new life and to be a better version of the Dad I loved despite it all, then I had the strength to move on too.

'Let's do this again soon, Teo,' he said with a smile as he pulled out of the embrace and started walking towards his platform. 'Good luck in Milan. And make sure you look after yourself, you hear?'

By the time I made it back to the office, my feet were sweaty in my new shoes, and my watch read 3.35 p.m. I scuttled through the entrance hall of the building, shimmied through the turnstile and slipped into one of the open elevators waiting to deposit the many journalists, publishers, assistants and interns to their respective floors.

I swished past the fashion cupboards where eager interns were now packing trunks full of the suits, trench coats and sumptuous shearling jackets I'd fondled earlier, and I stalked my way across *Esquire*'s open-plan terrain towards Sarah's desk. As I closed in I wondered whether I might have my own corner office one day, just like Alex's.

'Hi AB,' I said, knocking on the door, which was ajar. I was still unsure whether the acronym of his name was allowed, but he was reading the newspaper with his feet on the desk, so I sensed he wasn't in an officious mood.

'Oh, hey, Teo,' he said, returning to a vertical position. 'Nice shoes.' He smiled wryly and raised his eyebrows. 'All sorted for tomorrow?'

'Yeah, I guess so,' I said. I didn't want to reveal how excited I was about the trip so instead I asked, 'And you?'

'Yeah!' he said, shrugging. 'At the very least we'll get a few good negronis out of it.' As if panicking that he needed to say something more boss-like to counter the mention of alcohol, he straightened his back and lifted an envelope from the middle of his desk. Alex had short vulpine hair and a distinctly English face, all soft curves, and his hands were soft. I walked across the room and took the letter from him.

'Do you want me to open it now?' I asked.

'Well, yeah,' he said, 'but I should probably just tell you—' he wiped the back of his palm across his nose '—Teo, I'm pleased to tell you that we're promoting you to style director of *Esquire*.' The news was delivered with characteristic lack of pomp and he seemed relieved to have got the job done. He was holding his breath and his eyebrows were once again raised. He looked as though he wanted me to leave.

'Um, amazing!' I said. I couldn't quite believe it. It sounded like the kind of title people were given in the credits of Bond films, or credits of films which starred Steve McQueen. 'Thanks, Alex. That's, um, great.' I paused. 'What does it mean?'

'Well, you're our most senior style person, I guess.' He sounded a bit exasperated now. 'You look after all things style. Written, rather than pictures,' he said. 'OK?'

'Great!' I attempted to maintain a semblance of surface calm but inside I was jumping. This was the job I'd been waiting for, my very own *September Issue* moment. I would be interviewing designers, reviewing catwalk shows, profiling A-list celebrities . . . a surge of hot potential streamed up from my stomach and I could barely contain it. A brave new life – my new life – was about to begin.

I smiled tightly at Alex, still trying hard not to reveal my glee. As I turned to walk out of the room, a heavy pile of magazines to the left of the door caught my eye. I slowed down to get a closer look at the spines, many of which dated back well before mine, Alex's or even Jeremy's time at the title, and a handful of which had made up a similar pile I remembered from all those years ago, next to the bed in Marc's bedroom, drenched in the sodium light of his Surrey cul-de-sac.

I looked up and caught sight of myself in the mirror that was hanging on the back of Alex's door. I hadn't realised I was smiling. The backs of my fabulously furry loafers clacked triumphantly, like my own personal round of applause, as I turned the corner out of the office and strode towards my desk on the other side of the room. I descended into my chair and flicked on my computer, silently wishing that the boy in the blue princess dress could have seen me then, if only so he could know that everything was going to be OK.

Acknowledgements

There are so many people I want to acknowledge but first and foremost, thanks to you mum and dad for giving birth to me and for allowing all of my stories to happen. I love you. Thank you for always believing in me and encouraging me to be myself no matter what. Mum, you taught me to love books and to love people and I have never felt anything but loved by you. All I want is to make you proud. Dad, thank you for instilling in me your work ethic and your ability to tell a story. You inspire me every day and I'm so impressed by everything you've achieved in the past few years. I'm proud to be your son.

To my sister Romy, I love you and you're my favourite person. Your strength is nothing short of inspiring and you're fantastic. Thank you for allowing me to borrow some of your memories for The Closet. Our lives were shared for so many years, and I appreciate your generosity more than you know. I feel so lucky to know that I'll always have you by my side. To my beautiful niece and goddaughter Gaia and baby Frida, I love you and your dad, Janny (mark II), and I hope you're as proud of me as I am of you. To Lauren, I feel so lucky to have found a friend as dedicated, consistent and inspiring as you so early on in my life. Thank you for being you and for making me believe I had what it took to write a book. You are absolutely amazing. I hit the friend jackpot when I met you, Lauriana! Cara, you are the most vibrant and loyal human I know, you are magic and I adore you. I hope you know that you were my rock at university, and have been since. A singular being, you never apologised for being yourself, and you allowed me to believe that I could do the same. I couldn't have found my voice without you. To Jack, thank you for taking me under your wing at university and for giving me a cultural education. I'm so proud to be wonderful Billy's godfather, and I'm lucky to have you as a friend. Love you mate. Vicky and Anna, you made it ok for me to be me when so many others shunned me. I love you both. With friends like you lot, well, you can write a book! Thank you for being my constants.

To Clen, Bex, Katie, Pol, Iz, Binx, Emma and Ben, you guys are the best. Thank you for supporting me, and for allowing me to include you in my story. To Alex, thank you for loving me, and thank you for being you. To all my friends and family members who didn't feature in this book, I love you, and your omission has zero bearing on that. Just because our stories aren't housed within these pages doesn't mean that they don't mean the world to me. Andy - my bro - Jane, Mia - you Mia! - Brysie, Pheebs, Rudi, Johan, Johanna, Aunty Tessa, Aunty Sarah, Mollie, Sophie, Tom, Robert, Maisie, Jack, Lara, Jamie, Rory Andrew S, Rosa and Jethro. I love you all.

To Tom, thank you for encouraging me to write *The Closet* and for believing in me from the start.

To my Grandpa Bob and to my Grandma Anne. Grandma, your eyes may no longer recognise me, but your encouragement, care and understanding helped shape who I am today. I miss you more than I can express, and I wish you could have read this book. I know you would have been proud of me. I love you.

To those of you whose names have been changed, and specifically to the antagonists in this book, thank you for making me stronger and better. We were all young and I bear no grudges. Without what we went through together, this book would not have been possible. To my agent Ben, thank you for believing in me and for pushing me to get The Closet over the line. To my editors Zoe and latterly Abigail and Louise, you both could take over the world. Thank you for making my words better. To my former magazine editors, Jeremy and Alex (not forgetting Dylan, and now Johnny), you each taught and continue to teach me an incredible amount and I am forever in your debt for affording me a journalistic education.

I have written this book as not only a way of expressing the importance of clothes in our lives - in my life, but also as a dedication to the extraordinary people who have helped shape me. The process of writing it has been exhilarating, cathartic and also challenging. I may have underestimated the gravity of writing truthfully about the people I love - the responsibility of which is greater than I ever realised. I sincerely hope any missteps will be forgiven.

And to Amy, you are the light of our family. Our special, amazing girl. I will always be your werewolf.